KICKSTART MY HEART

KICKSTART MY HEART

A MÖTLEY CRÜE DAY-BY-DAY

MARTIN POPOFF

Backbeat
Books

An Imprint of Hal Leonard Corporation

Published in 2015 by Backbeat Books
An Imprint of Hal Leonard Corporation
7777 West Bluemound Road
Milwaukee, WI 53213

Trade Book Division Editorial Offices
33 Plymouth St., Montclair, NJ 07042

Printed in the United States of America

Book design by Damien Castaneda

Library of Congress Cataloging-in-Publication Data is available upon request.

ISBN 978-1-61713-610-8

www.backbeatbooks.com

Contents

Tommy looks for some love in 1984. © Kevin Estrada

*W*elcome back, folks, and pull up a chair as we enter the wide, wild world of Mötley Crüe, LA's most notorious denizens, bad boys so you don't have to, makers of a gritty, streetwise form of hair metal (wot?) that has sold tens of millions worldwide and caused much drinking and drugging on the side.

But a few things first: as point of process, consider this "introduction" a quick hello from your intrepid author and a place to set the stage for the rock 'n' roll debauchery to come. Oh, indeed, we will learn much about Vince, Mick, Nikki, and Tommy as the pages flame on, but in terms of words direct from your ringmaster, well, I'll be checking in for each of the decades with a treatise on the ten years of the Crüe about to unfold, and then letting the timeline tell the rest.

And hence this is not the place to say too much about the Crüe, but suffice to say, the band has been part of my life for well on more than half of it. I can't say it's all been pretty either, 'cause as Nikki is wont to so honestly attest, the band's third and fourth albums, *Theatre of Pain* and *Girls, Girls, Girls,* marked a degeneration of songwriting quality that this author has never gotten over.

So, in a general sense, loved the band's goofy, charmed debut, but was intimidated, confused, and disturbed by *Shout at the Devil*'s carnal idiocy (but it's far and above my fave); and then kinda checked out for a while, disgusted by how the debauchery impeded the band's ability to deliver what all of us fans not living in Hollyrock desired from the band: actual good records to power up our metal-mad Friday nights with might.

I could spend two pages listing all the bands that were kicking ass all over Mötley once the belching black smoke of *Shout at the Devil* cleared, and like I say, there's been a grudge ever since that decline. More on this in my decade-specific rambles, but to switch into happy glide again (and as a brief survey), it was inspiring to hear the band come back strong with *Dr. Feelgood* (grudge still in place, my brief on this has always been "real stupid people trying real hard").

Mick taking a few cues from Blackie Lawless and the W.A.S.P. man's penchant for microphone decoration. © Greg Olma

The Mad Max look revisited, 2014.
© Kevin Estrada

And then, lo and behold, with *Motley Crue* and *Generation Swine*, me an' my pretty discerning music-fan friends suddenly found ourselves admiring of the band as creative talents, challenging us with extreme productions and arrangements, slowing it down, mixing it up, much thanks to Nikki and Tommy as pushers of envelopes.

But then all the toxicity of the band's bruising private lives . . . I dunno about you, but it wore on me hard. It was depressing. I found it tough looking at the whole inspirational rebel angle to it and found myself checking out again. Not that there was much substance to clutch: we've had two studio records since *Generation Swine*, although both are fun and full of value, especially when received into yer life as the calling cards of old . . . "friends?"

But I'm getting away from myself. We'll talk more as prelude to each of the four decades of the Crüe so far, plus a fifth preliminary chapter of pre-Mötley kiddie Crüe. Instead let's finish up with some musings on method (of mayhem) as far as the structure of the book goes.

What you hold in your hands now is the third volume that myself and the fine folks at Backbeat Books have put together using the "day-by-day" format, the first being *2 Minutes to Midnight: An Iron Maiden Day-by-Day* and the second being *Steal Away The Night: An Ozzy Osbourne Day-by-Day*. The format is essentially composed of three components: 1) diary entries through time charting significant events; 2) quotes from the band and significant satellite speakers designed to elaborate, flesh out, or otherwise bring the story to life with a hint of "oral history" to the proceedings; and 3) lots and lots of tasty photos, not only of the dudes, but of records, promo items, backstage passes, ticket stubs, and my pet favorite, magazine advertisements, which potentially say so much about the way bands are marketed, in my opinion.

The quotes and pretty pictures portion of the story . . . that part of it is explanatory, but there is a point I wanted to make about the diary entries I've carefully chosen to compile for this book. Putting aside the very real dimension that there is a specific word count I had to adhere to concerning our literary Crüe fest, indeed—and back to an earlier point—I found myself down into the dumps at just how much news related to this band is ugly and demoralizing.

Nikki on an even keel in 2009.
© Chris Casella

Mick frying his mane at US Fest, 1983. © Rudy Childs

Vince comes in for a landing. © Kevin Estrada

Dammit, in the telling of the story, as the hours and days and weeks would grind on, reliving the lives of these four drama cases at a safe distance, at times I couldn't place myself far enough away to avoid the contact high. And so a conscious decision had to be made to skip past the graveyards, keep passing those open windows, and stress in the entries as much positive as I could.

Toward that end, I've kept to a minimum discussion and detail of the lawsuits, the punch-ups, the drugs, the drinking, the jail time, the fines, the divorces, the acrimony, the betrayals. To be sure, I'd be remiss if I didn't mention, however briefly, the key events down those dark pathways, because if I didn't, I'd get complaints that I haven't told the story accurately at all, opting for something that was not only too sanitized but worse, too incomplete.

And so, it's interesting, but I think the more perceptive reader of our span of historical turmoil that is the Crüe will indeed begin to notice quite early on that this is a book about the music, and that if and when any of "the dirt" needs mention, the extent of detail is kept low and with minimal follow-up, as we hopefully move quickly to happier trails, namely continual re-engagement with what matters—the songs.

Indeed, those who have been kind enough to partake of any of my other forty-seven books on heavy metal bands and subjects realize that what I like to discuss most is in fact every song, on a chronological album-by-album—even album-as-chapter—basis. First off, that's not the format for these cool day-by-day books, but second, when yer talkin' Mötley, I found myself constantly knocked off the rails into untold personal drama. Bottom line, it took extra effort over and above that of the Maiden or Ozzy books to keep it about the records, but this is what I tried to do. Hope that helps explain both the modus operandi and the tricky tone of what you are about to read. On with the show . . . .

Martin Popoff
martinpopoff.com

KICKSTART MY HEART

CRÜE

The '70s and Times Past

No question, it's hard graft at times to find anything heartening and unsoiled about the sordid story of Mötley Crüe. And the band's mostly awful experiences through childhoods and into the '70s would seem to be no exception. It's relentless, the poop.

And yet there is one interesting and inspiring aspect to the formative years experienced by Vince Neil, Mick Mars, Nikki Sixx, and Tommy Lee, and that is the idea that all four of them came to the band with no musical accomplishments of note. Rather, collapsing into Mötley Crüe for each of these guys, as the '70s became the '80s, represented a degree of desperation for each of them.

Let's lift up the rock and peer under. First off, on the surface, it would seem that if we are to ascribe desperation to Vince's or Tommy's situation, it would be of a lesser sort than that of Mick and Nikki. Essentially, what we will find is that the pathway to Crüe for both of these guys—friends with each other and even roommates of a sort—is quite similar.

Both Tommy and Vince took a pledge of poverty and homelessness by choice, gradually extricating and estranging themselves from family life and educational convention in pursuit of the rock 'n' roll dream—food and accommodation be damned.

Nikki, on the other hand . . . on the surface, it might have seemed he was in the same boat—knocking about Hollywood with goofy-looking glam bands, hiring and firing and getting kicked out, playing house parties and scoring women and drugs instead of pay—but rather, Nikki was pushed into the squalor of Hollywood as much by a horrible broken family life as he was by rock star aspiration. For Nikki, basically unemployable because of the unrealistic and anti-society thoughts in his head, it was construct a job for himself in rock or don't eat.

And then there's Mick, dear old Mick. Older than the rest of the guys by essentially ten years, Mick multiplied that age gap by living too much hardship, wearing much of himself out, throughout those ten years before the Crüe—years when Tommy and Vince were nothing more than happy-go-lucky teenagers on the make (Nikki, not so much). Girlfriends and wives come and gone, kids birthed with no money and no prospects, ridiculous disappointments band after band . . . . Mick's life was a book before Nikki stole his first guitar (thinking it was a bass). But then we get to the end of the '70s, and Mick gets his last chance, throwing in his lot with three guys in roughly the same desperate rock place, and just as dead broke as Mick, but not yet suffocated by disappointment, still spunked and stupidly optimistic about how hard rock is for everybody and not just the most desperate.

Oh sure, read on; the guys liked their rock and there had to be some ambition in there somewhere—that is, ambition beyond the blind ambition of somehow, improbably snorting and guzzling one's way to the top. But the reverberation one gets from the 1970s experienced by these guys is one, again, of different forms and intensities of desperation.

With nowhere to live, rock is survival, and in a quick second breath, rock is chicks and drugs. Rock might also be about acceptance and love. Rock is too fast for art.

MAY 4, 1951 Robert Alan "Mick Mars" Deal—and thus Mötley Crüe—is born, in Huntington, Indiana.

1956 Mick Mars witnesses flashy singing cowboy Skeeter Bond perform and his life as an entertainer unfurls before him. Christmas the following year gifts him a Mickey Mouse guitar and Bob soon learns "My Dog Has Fleas."

DECEMBER 11, 1958 Frank Carlton Serafino Feranna Jr., aka Nikki Sixx, is born in San Jose, California, to a family soon to be broken.

1960 Christmas this year reveals a Stella acoustic (pawn shop) guitar for Mick, courtesy of a cousin. Mick quickly learns "B Flat Blues." Soon the family migrates to California, where Mick's dad works in a cardboard box factory—Fender is a customer.

FEBRUARY 8, 1961 Vince Neil Wharton is born in Hollywood, California, of Mexican descent on his mother's side and Native American on his auto mechanic father's.

Mick, the wise elder of the band.
© Kevin Estrada

Vince still looking boyish in 2004. © Kevin Estrada

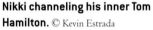

Nikki channeling his inner Tom Hamilton. © Kevin Estrada

AUGUST 18, 1961 Jimmy Dean records a song he wrote with Roy Acuff called "Big Bad John," with the song hitting #1 in *Billboard* by November. Nikki Sixx, as a child, comforted by the sounds coming out of his radio, is captivated by the song, notably the bad-boy mystique of it. As a young boy, he would repeatedly call the local station and request to hear it. Before Nikki's fourth birthday, Nikki's dad abandons him and Nikki's free spirit of a mother.

OCTOBER 3, 1962 Tommy Lee Bass is born, in Athens, Greece. His father is a serviceman and his mother, a Miss Greece contestant in 1957. Meanwhile Mick fashions himself an amp out of a record player and starts learning surf guitar on his St. George Rodeo.

1963 Tommy Lee's family moves to Covina, California, where mom cleans houses and dad works as a superintendent at the LA County Road Department.

DECEMBER 25, 1966 Tommy gets a drum set for Christmas, with a cowbell and a flashing light in the bass drum. By this point, Mick has played in a Beatles cover band called the Jades plus Sounds of Soul, who perform around Orange County.

NOVEMBER 22, 1968 *The Beatles* (aka the White Album) includes one of the first heavy metal songs ever, "Helter Skelter," which Mötley Crüe later covers on their *Shout at the Devil* album.

1971 Mick Mars' first wife Sharon births the couple a son, Les Paul.

1971 Nikki "The Assassin" Sixx becomes an aggressive addition to the school football team; it is said his distinctive non-reflective black eye makeup is an homage to those days. Now living with his grandparents in Jerome, Idaho, in conjunction with football Nikki logs ten to twelve hours a day soaking up the songs coming out of the radio.

APRIL 23, 1971 The Rolling Stones issue *Sticky Fingers*, the album cover of which would be parodied for Mötley's first record ten years later.

NIKKI SIXX:

My dad left when I was three. My Mom wasn't available for me. I had a dysfunctional childhood. You mix that with hormones and teenage angst and you become a runaway. You're running from something that hurts. It gets impacted and infected because when you look back, that doesn't seem like a reason to not feel complete. But if you read any books on child and adolescent psychology, you find those first five to seven years are impactful for the rest of their life. If they don't feel love and they don't feel safe, if they feel things like abandonment, if they feel like a tumbleweed just blowing in the wind, it really affects their life. Then another thing happens, another thing and another, next thing you know, you've got this bucket and barrel and wagon and dump truck full of crap that you're hauling around. And you don't want to feel like that anymore. You've felt like that since you were a very young kid. (*BW&BK*, 2007)

CUM ON FEEL THE NOIZE

SLADE

NEW SINGLE
Cum On Feel The Noize
LATEST ALBUM
Slayed?

The "Shout at the Devil" of a previous generation. Author's Collection

NOVEMBER 1, 1972 UK glamsters Slade issue their penultimate album, *Slayed*. "Mama Weer All Crazee Now" and "Gudbuy T' Jane" get covered famously a decade-plus later within the US hair metal movement. Slade is a major influence on Nikki's future band London, and the band's gimmick of spelling words wrong rubs off on Mötley, who take Mick's suggestion for a band name but bastardize its spelling.

DECEMBER 25, 1972 Tommy gets his first real drum, a snare drum, for Christmas. He works after school to build up a set around it and his father soundproofs the garage so that Tommy can practice. Tommy keeps up his rudiment chops through marching band.

1973 The New York Dolls issue their shocking first album, the cover of which presents the band in garish and oddly tough drag, a touchstone image that would be picked up by Mötley and others (Vince wholeheartedly agrees that the band's initial look was androgynous). A portion of the inspiration for the guys in Nikki's band London with respect to adopting pseudonyms comes from Nikki's admiration for Dolls guitarist Johnny Thunders.

EARLY DAYS MANAGEMENT ASSISTANT ERIC GREIF:

Of course they were into the New York Dolls, and that would've all been Nikki. Nikki was the mastermind of all that was going on, and he was completely in charge of the look and the sound and everything about the band. So he was the one who was influenced by all of that. Tommy, of course, I knew, because he was in my former client's band, my former client being Greg Leon. So they were very much into the hard rock that was prevalent in the '70s. Mick, it would've been the same thing for him, coming from playing in lots and lots of cover bands throughout the Midwest. They were just all influenced by everything from ZZ Top to Zeppelin. But as far as the visual impact of the New York Dolls, and that attitude from New York, I mean, that would've been a big influence on Nikki, as was Sweet. I just think he liked the idea of danger, and the idea that they wanted to be the most dangerous band in the world. But at that point in time things were so at their genesis that I think he just wanted to create a packaged look that would be easy to identify with, and he had that vision from the moment that I ever met him.

PHOTOGRAPHER, IMAGE CONSULTANT, AND CHOREOGRAPHER FOR MÖTLEY CRÜE, BARRY LEVINE:

Nikki really was inspired by the Clash, the Pistols, and the New York Dolls, stuff like that. When you're inspired by bands like that, it leads to imagery and ideas and it just elevated itself. Nikki didn't go, "You know what? I want to look like the New York Dolls." He just loved their music.

AUGUST 1973 Brownsville Station issue their *Yeah!* album, which contains the Michigan band's lone hit, "Smokin' in the Boys Room." Mötley Crüe's cover of the song will be their biggest hit single that is not a band original.

SEPTEMBER 4, 1973 Mick and Sharon have a second child together, Stormy. Meanwhile Mick slowly becomes integrated into a band called Whitehorse, which are said to have considered the name Mötley Croo. By this point, poverty and the stalling of his career have broken Mick's family, and he learns of his chronic disease, Ankylosing Spondylitis (AS).

The Dolls' music and visuals combined for what would have to be the most accurate template for what would become hair metal, stateside or from across the pond. Author's Collection

SEPTEMBER 10, 1973 Proto-power popsters the Raspberries issue their third album, which kicks off with "Tonight," later covered by Mötley Crüe. The band was an influence on Nikki in terms of songwriting, hooks, and melody.

1974 Now living in Seattle with his mother, Nikki haunts the record stores and instrument shops, dreaming about being in a band. His radical rocker-wannabe look at school earns him the nickname Alice Bowie. Also in Seattle, Nikki attends concerts by the likes of Kiss, Mott the Hoople, Queen, Rush, and T Rex. Soon he steals a guitar from a shop when the clerk goes in the back to get him a job application. Needing a bass and not realizing that he had stolen a guitar, he sells the guitar and gets a bass.

MARCH 24, 1974 *The Rocky Horror Show* is staged by the Roxy's Lou Adler, as an LA version of the successful London phenomenon. The nine-month run, as well as the cult success of the subsequent movie, is cited as a key influence on the androgynous fashion sense of the LA hair metal movement.

NIKKI'S LONDON BANDMATE LIZZIE GREY:

When Nikki was still in London and Nigel was gone, and we were going through this horrible period of trying to replace him with people who didn't fit, Nikki even got so desperate he tried to get Brian Connolly, from England, who wasn't in very good health at the time. But he tried to get him out from the UK to join, and I believe he even tried to get Brian Connolly to join Mötley Crüe when they were still looking for a vocalist.

SWEET GUITARIST ANDY SCOTT ON GLAM FASHION:

We had already started to move on, and it was a mixture of metallic leather and jean material, maybe a silk shirt. The whole look had actually changed by then, so really, and truthfully, the look that you think of on bands like Mötley Crüe is definitely from the "Ballroom Blitz" era in Europe.

1975 Capitol issues the highly influential US version of Sweet's *Desolation Boulevard*, which becomes a big inspiration for hard rockers learning their craft in the late '70s, including the members of Mötley Crüe.

ERIC GREIF:

I think Nikki's biggest influence, from what he revealed to me at the time, was the Sweet. He was very much into the whole packaged glam stuff from Britain, from like maybe five, six, seven, eight years earlier. And those were his influences. So I think songs like "Public Enemy #1," that was exactly what they were trying to go for, those big sing-along choruses, that sort of thing, and then the look. The whole hair metal aspect of it sort of evolved from just trying to be outrageous. These are the bands where everybody was dressed with striped clothing, like Eddie Van Halen, with striped guitars, and David Lee Roth clones. But in the forefront of the whole movement was Mötley Crüe, and they were just unstoppable—you could not avoid them at the time.

MARCH 1975 Failing to make the grade for his buddy's band, Nikki spins his wheels looking the glam-punk part and indulging in drugs, booze, burglary, and brawling.

VINCE NEIL:

They were a great show band. I remember seeing them at the Starwood in Hollywood when I was like fifteen years old. But the song just seemed to fit us. And we've usually put a cover tune on our records and we jammed it and it sounded so good.

JUNE 1975 The Tubes issue their self-titled debut album featuring "White Punks on Dope," which Mötley cover on their 2000 album, *New Tattoo*.

JULY 18, 1975 Nikki is caught selling mescaline "chocolates" at the Seattle Center Coliseum before a Rolling Stones concert. Facing a ten-year sentence, he flees back to Jerome, Idaho, to live with his grandparents.

SEPTEMBER 10, 1975 Kiss issue their breakthrough fourth album, *Alive!*, which sets the template for the theatrical presentation of bands like Mötley Crüe and W.A.S.P.

NIKKI SIXX:

I grew up with no father figure at all. And by the time I was seventeen, I was completely out of control. No one ever helped me see what the rights and wrongs in life were about. I was so shattered about things in life. Such as my father abandoning me, that I just thrusted myself into my pain. It's like pouring salt in a wound. (*Late at Night* magazine, 1994)

1976 Nikki receives a lifeline of hope when his uncle Don Zimmerman, high up at Capitol Records (and eventually to be president), encourages him by mailing to Idaho various music magazines and new releases on Capitol. Nikki soon moves to LA, staying temporarily at the Zimmermans', playing one note over and over again on his bass, abusing the family truck, and getting fired from jobs.

PHOTOGRAPHER BARRY LEVINE ON TWO OF HIS CLIENTS, KISS AND MÖTLEY CRÜE:

I don't think Kiss was the inspiration as much as Nikki respected them, and looked up to them. But Nikki wanted his own look. Nikki did get his own look. Again, it's all about . . . you don't get a second chance to make a first impression, that old saying, and it was true with them. I think it was influence in the sense that Kiss was the first real theatrical band. Whether you loved their music, hated their music, irrelevant, they put on one of the greatest theatrical presentations ever. So I think that's where Nikki got his thing. Mötley Crüe actually came to me. A guy named Tom Zutaut, who knew my work and he knew my work with Kiss, and Tom always envisioned Mötley Crüe as a young Kiss. Very theatrical, but more like a punk version of Kiss. Very edgy, very street. As you know, the guys in Kiss are great, but Gene and Paul, they're far from being Mötley Crüe or the Sex Pistols or anything. Very corporate, very great at what they do. They know their business. And I loved . . . all I had to do was look at one picture of them and said I was in. At the time it was pretty cool because I was able to shoot bands that I felt an emotional attachment to—I had to like their music. I wouldn't just shoot a band because somebody was paying me some money. I didn't care any more because I was starting to get bored after so much work. And the Crüe actually revitalized me and made me want to shoot bands more.

In terms of onstage attire, Kiss would represent the most convincing predecessor to Mötley. Not too far off musically, either. Author's Collection

NIKKI SIXX:

I'm like the anti-Led Zeppelin guy. I'm like, oh God! Not another fuckin' Zeppelin song! And actually, I've never really listened that deeply. You know how some people, something just doesn't move them? Aerosmith moved my fucking soul. As a young man, they just freaked me out. And that's when . . . the guys in school that would be like stoned in the corner, Aerosmith was somewhere between those guys and the fact that I was really into Slade, the Sweet, Mott the Hoople, all this British glam rock, Bowie, and then there was early Kiss and Nugent, where you had some of that more meaty American stuff. Aerosmith was kinda between those bands, which I really like. They could really play and they could really sing, but they were really dirty and grimy. And Zeppelin was, to me, kind of like the Grateful Dead, but now I'm starting to kind of appreciate them. But at the same time, as much as I get slagged for that all the time, I'm also the guy that could not stand the fuckin' Beatles. I was like, fuck the Beatles; I was into the Stones. So what's really funny is, I now go, well, the Beatles were really cool. So it's how it strikes you. If every single person on the planet liked the same thing, it would be fucking boring. There's nothing better for me to sit down around a dinner with a bunch of people and argue about music and get my covers pulled, and somebody to go, "You know dude, you haven't listened to John Paul Jones; you don't know what the fuck you're talking about!" "What's he talking about? It's like listening to bass underwater." And they say, "Listen to the song, listen to the bass." And you go, "Whoa, I'm wrong." And then they go, "You know, I never did listen to the Buzzcocks. You're right man, that shit was fuckin' tight."

One of Nikki's favorite records and sometimes cited as his very favorite. Trivia note: *Rocks* was never issued with a white cover. Author's Collection

Nikki's penchant for change and reinvention is somewhat inspired by Bowie. Author's Collection

APRIL 13, 1976 A British war film is issued called *Shout at the Devil*, based on the 1968 novel of the same name.

MAY 3, 1976 Aerosmith issue their seminal *Rocks* album, a record that changes Nikki Sixx's life. The band's "Round and Round" and "Seasons of Wither" are name-checked in "Shout at the Devil." Vince covers "Nobody's Fault" from *Rocks* on his album *Tattoos & Tequila*, and the track is referred to repeatedly in Nikki's book *The Heroin Diaries*.

AUGUST 18, 1976 Mick Mars has a third child, Erik, with former longtime girlfriend Marcia.

1977 Nikki forms his first band, Rex Blade, who look good but play bad.

VINCE NEIL:

We were listening to the Sex Pistols, the Ramones—those were big influences. I used to be in a band called the Wigglers for a short time, and all we did was cover songs of Generation X and all that stuff. A lot of it came up and Nikki was also big into punk.

OCTOBER 27, 1977 The Sex Pistols issue their lone album, *Never Mind the Bollocks, Here's the Sex Pistols*, which includes "Anarchy in the UK," covered by Mötley Crüe on *Decade of Decadence*. Additionally, "No Feelings" is covered by Vince on *Tattoos & Tequila*.

DECEMBER 1977 Mick's band Whitehorse breaks up, with Mick reverting to playing in a Top Forty cover band called Ten-Wheel Drive.

ERIC GRIEF ON THE REVISIONIST HISTORY OF THE PISTOLS BEING AN INFLUENCE ON CRÜE:

Nothing. There's a punk attitude, but I don't think that anybody whatsoever thought, "You know, Sex Pistols was two years previous, and that Johnny Rotten was quite a front man." I don't think that would've ever crossed anybody's mind. Now it's convenient to say that kind of thing if you're in Mötley Crüe, and you can look back and say, "You know, this was three years or four years after *The Great Rock 'n' Roll Swindle*. Man, were we punk!" But at the time, I cannot imagine anyone—and I traveled with Crüe—I can't imagine anyone actually saying that or Nikki saying that we are a natural extension of Sid Vicious or something like that. I don't think that would have contextually been something that they would've said.

ERIC GREIF:

I don't think that they were trying to be anything like Van Halen at all. In fact, if anything, they were trying to be the anti-Van Halen on the scene. Which is why David Lee Roth was so drawn to Crüe at first. He would come to the gigs and sort of stumble into the Mötley Crüe apartment on Clark Street, I think it was. Because they had such an aura around them for what they were doing, because it was so revolutionary for Los Angeles at the time. This was pre-Satan days. So this was before they adopted the whole kitsch, Lucifer angle, purely just to get them noticed and to start some controversy. Before that there was none of that. There was just big hair. What Nikki was trying to do was Dolls. What he was trying to do was have over-exaggerated hair, over-exaggerated looks, and over-exaggerated names—that's what struck me right at the beginning.

One suspects one of Nikki's big regrets is that his band didn't get banned as often as the Pistols did. Author's Collection

FEBRUARY 10, 1978 Van Halen issue their seminal self-titled debut, pretty much single-handedly drawing national attention to LA as a bastion for hard rock. The record eventually goes RIAA-certified diamond, for sales past ten times platinum.

BARRY LEVINE:

I don't know if they were inspired, but they respected Van Halen. They respected their showmanship and I know they respected . . . the individuals respected the drummer and the bass player and Eddie and so on. It's hard to say if they were inspired. I think the older stuff, like I said before—Clash and the Pistols and all that stuff—inspired them more. But respect is there.

BLACKIE LAWLESS:

Sister was . . . I don't know, I'm not going to say we were ahead of our time, but Sister was W.A.S.P. with a different moniker. They were basically the same band, and from a theatrical point of view, Sister was probably more creative. I looked at what was coming before me, obviously Alice Cooper, and my friendship with Ace Frehley. I literally saw Kiss being born, so I knew what was going on with that. To me, I always thought about the approach that we were doing was more of a way of worming itself inside people's heads. Something that was a big influence was *Apocalypse Now* because it'd come out the same year. And I looked at the way Coppola had done that movie; it wasn't so much to me that it was just a war movie, it was the idea that, you know, it goes back to the original book, which was *Heart of Darkness*, which was a journey. The river is a metaphor for the river inside somebody's head, and the further you go down the river, the darker it gets. And I was really intrigued by that concept, of what was happening deep inside someone's head. So I was using a lot of that stuff to create our imagery.

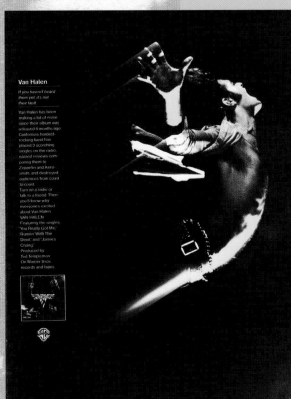

Jim Dandy, David Lee Roth, Vince Neil . . . Bret Michaels.
Author's Collection

EARLY 1978 Nikki meets Lizzie Grey, who is playing with Blackie Lawless in his band Sister. Blackie soon fires Nikki for lack of skills, after the band attempt to record some demos over the course of a couple weeks. Lizzie decides to follow Nikki out of the situation. Things are quite dire for Nikki, who at this point was squatting in the basement of a burnt-out house, his amp in hawk, his only possession a Thunderbird copy bass.

LIZZIE GREY:

Blackie couldn't keep the band together. He was very, very, very picky. And the things he was picky about were things that didn't make sense to a lot of musicians (laughs). I mean, to be perfectly honest, that's how I met Frank Feranna, Nikki Sixx, because I had been playing with Blackie for about a year, and just going through musician after musician trying to find players for Sister. And he considered himself kind of a bass player/guitar player, so he was always picky about it. And he was also attacking the drums too. But we couldn't really keep together a band, and when we pulled Frank into this picture, and we did a little recording down in South Bay, he ended up firing Nikki. And my attraction with Nikki was so profound, that we were both coming from the same place and it just felt right. Which is ironic, because Mötley Crüe ended up stealing all of Blackie Lawless' stage ideas. I mean the thing with the skulls on the stick and all that stuff, the whole look, post-London, when I saw what Mötley Crüe was doing, I thought, that doesn't really go with what they are. They're not really spooky scary, I'm going to be Blackie Lawless-type people. But it worked for them, because it had enough of that shock rock appeal along with the poppy hooks, because Vince Neil's voice was a pop voice, not a metal voice.

LIZZIE GREY ON LOSING THE W.A.S.P. GIG:

When Nikki let Frank go, I said to Frank, "Look, you know what? Blackie's gone through so many musicians. He can't keep the band together. I don't like where this is all going. He seems to have this charisma but it seems almost negative." And a lot of people considered him somewhat of a joke hanging around at the Starwood. And that's when Nikki and I said, "Dude, let's do something fun, which is like New York Dolls, Sweet . . . ." Even Quiet Riot got mentioned as something we wanted to do. So we wanted to do shock rock of the glitter type. So London became kind of the first glam band. As glitter was fading, and the glitter icons like Sweet, Mott the Hoople, and all them were falling apart, out comes London saying let's adopt all this stuff. And so in '78, we started playing shows at the Starwood, and David Forrest just fell in love with us, literally and figuratively (laughs). And he said, "I want to manage your band; you guys are just great." And I think he kind of knew that Quiet Riot, who had been the darlings of the Starwood, were kind of running out of gas, with the guitarist, Randy Rhoads, soon to leave to join Ozzy. So we did the London thing, and the heyday of London was around 1979, when we would play a weekend at the Starwood and it would be just packed, a couple thousand people there. We were the band, and all the Quiet Riot guys hated us because we were kind of taking their space.

MID-1978 Nikki and Lizzie form London, first with Steve Toth on vocals (and later Henri Valentine, then Nigel Benjamin, then Michael White). Dane Rage (today Dane Scarborough, a toy mogul) is the drummer, and John St. John the keyboardist. First rehearsals for the band take place at Selma and Cahuenga, in an upstairs office.

OCTOBER 3, 1978 Vince and his girlfriend Tammi have a son, Neil Jason Wharton. Vince is the only kid at his high school paying child support.

NOVEMBER 1978 Nikki auditions for Quiet Riot. Rudy Sarzo gets the gig. Meanwhile, Nikki is getting evicted for spending the rent money on gig posters, and London are banished from the Rainbow because Nikki keeps smashing the mirror along the staircase at the back of the venue.

DECEMBER 1978 Mick's band Video Nu-R issues what stands as Mick's first recording, a single pairing "Gypsy Woman" with "You Drive Me Crazy." A second single follows in September of '79. Abject poverty contributes to the breakup of Mick and Marcia. Video Nu-R disintegrates and Mick places an ad in the *Recycler* declaring, "Extraterrestrial guitarist available for any other aliens that want to conquer Earth."

DECEMBER 26-27, 1978 Pretty Poison, a local favorite of Vince's, support Quiet Riot at the Starwood. Both bands provide rock 'n' roll inspiration for Vince.

EARLY 1979 Vince Neil plies his trade as front man for Rockandi. "Smokin' in the Boys Room" is part of the band's otherwise Cheap Trick–heavy covers repertoire, which they perform at house parties. Vince is kicked out of high school for lack of attendance but soon enrolls at a different school, Royal Oak, where he befriends drummer for pre-Autograph act US 101, Tom Bass, who in school specializes in music, coed volleyball, and the screen printing of Aerosmith T-shirts. Meanwhile, Mick meets Nikki at the Magnolia Liquor store, where Nikki was working, and they talk music, with Nikki checking out Mick's band Spiders and Cowboys that night.

VINCE NEIL:

This guy with long blond hair asked me if I wanted to sing in his band. And I asked him why, and he said, "Because you've got the longest hair in school." At that time, the places to play were the Top Forty clubs, because that's where the money was. We were doing Aerosmith, Cheap Trick, the Sweet, stuff like that. We weren't doing too badly either. In fact, we sold out the Starwood, which was a big place to play in those days. (*Circus*, 1985)

The heaviest of the UK glam bands, and thus a major inspiration on the American scene of the '80s. Author's Collection

LIZZIE GREY:

That's right about the same time that London started shaking apart, and Nigel wanted Nikki out of London. He wanted to get rid of Nikki and want to get Rudy in the band, and they tried to pitch that to me and I said no way. No way are we getting rid of Nikki. I said Nikki is a star. That guy isn't going anywhere. And so Nigel ultimately ended up leaving the band over that. And so Mötley Crüe came out of the ashes of London, and it was one of those situations where, ironically, Nikki was very good at lifting things that fit. And he put them together in a way that seemed brand new. But I guess we all do that. Unless you grew up in a white room, you have to be influenced by something.

FEBRUARY 28, 1979 Rickie Lee Jones' self-titled debut contains a song called "Danny's All-Star Joint," celebrating a benevolent diner in Hollywood that kept musicians from starving—Nikki and the London guys were appreciative consumers of Cecil's fine cooking. Other bouts of good fortune following Nikki include having a venue burn down with all of London's equipment inside (but in an office, the only room to escape the fire), and a month-long painting job for all the guys . . . in a liquor store, where they would get locked in at night and let out in the morning—a smuggled-in blender helped with margaritas.

APRIL 12, 1979 Influential road warrior film *Mad Max* hits the streets, providing inspiration to Barry Levine and Nikki Sixx for Mötley's most iconic aesthetic.

APRIL 19-21, 1979 Tommy's band with Greg Leon, Suite 19, support Randy Rhoads and Quiet Riot at the Starwood. The band will also play gigs with the likes of UFO and Yesterday & Today (later Y&T), the latter of which will later give Crüe their first support slot and then go on to support Crüe as fortunes reverse. Tommy's family takes in Vince, who is virtually homeless at this point.

MID-1979 London implodes, mostly due to Nikki's inability to get along with the band's latest vocalist, ex-Mott singer Nigel Benjamin, and his huge ego. (A brief period follows where they try to keep the band going with Michael White on vocals.) In an ironic twist, with Randy Rhoads now off to join Ozzy Osbourne's fledgling solo band, Rudy Sarzo had become available, and Nigel insisted he would quit if Nikki wasn't replaced with Rudy. Nikki has estimated that at this point he had half the material written that would emerge on the first Mötley Crüe record.

JULY 27, 1979 AC/DC issue their last album with Bon Scott on vocals, *Highway to Hell*. Nikki later quips that the Beatles' white album, *Shout at the Devil*, and *Highway to Hell* are the greatest records of all time. Other "desert island" favorites of Nikki's include David Bowie's *Young Americans*, Black Sabbath's *Vol. 4*, Queen's *Sheer Heart Attack*, and the Stooges' *Fun House*.

NOVEMBER 1979 Tommy Lee's first professional photo shoot, with Will Boyett taking shots of his band Suite 19 playing live at the Starwood. Boyett then handles photographic duties for Tommy's next band, Dealer. After Dealer, Tommy briefly moves on to Sapphire.

Angus, Malcolm, and Bon had to defend this record's title just like Nikki did with *Shout at the Devil*. Author's Collection

ELEKTRA

2

45 R.P.M.

7-69756

Pub. Warner
Tamerlane
Publishing Corp.
Mötley Crüe
Publishing, BMI
Time: 4:38

PIECE OF YOUR ACTION
(N. Sixx / V. Neil)

MÖTLEY CRÜE
AN RTB (AUDIO-VISUAL) PRODUCTIONS MIX
From Elektra LP 60174
'TOO FAST FOR LOVE'
NEW YORK 10022, 9229 SUNSET BOULEVARD, LOS ANGELES CA. 90069 A DIVISION OF WARNER COMMUNICATIONS INC.

Kevin Estrada Collection

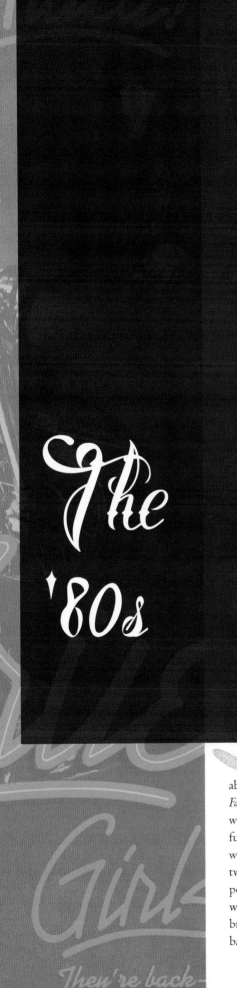

The '80s

Perhaps there's no heavy metal band so much a Sunset strip rock-dawg cliché as the four mutts of Mötley. And once that's said, it's easy to frame Vince, Mick, Nikki, and Tommy as the heavy metal cartoon characters most associated with the '80s, each—bless their hearts—character offering endless hours of fun by proxy, each living lives so fast and flash that, if positives be proffered, they were beloved by millions as inspiration toward . . . I dunno, taking no shit or something like that.

But all through that neon decade, you couldn't miss the Mötley guys, that's for sure. And let's not forget, in 1981, they were in a sense leaders. Loud and large guitar rock had died a death the world over, with the wilting and/or end of (to name a few) Aerosmith, Ted Nugent, Deep Purple, Blue Öyster Cult, Kiss, Uriah Heep, Boston, Rush, Derringer, Starz, Montrose, and Rainbow. One bridge band lit like a comet across the punk and post-punk breach and that was Van Halen. An aberration . . . I don't know where to even put them . . . let's just bow for a moment of silence.

Move into the '80s, and LA had a bunch of baby Van Halens that no one would sign—but then came Mötley, and this is where Nikki, as visionary, was at the leading edge of hard rock, argu-ably for the first and last time. Frankly, *Too Fast for Love* was the first hair metal album, with most similar slabs not coming for fully two more years. But it was a record with a kooky depth. The lead singer had twang, the guitarist, way too much dirty power for the sweet songs written, and then welling up from the rhythm section was a breathing, organic open architecture. This band had more in common with Van Ha-

We are not a glam band, Toronto. Author's Collection

Heavy Metal Day at the US Fest, 1983. © Rudy Childs

len and the Who than pretty lead singers; there was a loose life to the tracks that instantly connected with the LA underground starved for something more electric hot plate than the ridiculous preciousness of skinny tie new wave, which didn't even offer the guitars of punk. And there's nothing more exciting than a buzz band pushed up on top of the police cars by the people, and that's what Mötley were.

The establishment at Elektra had to take notice (you'll see, somewhat against their will), and soon a more dangerous plot would be hatched called *Shout at the Devil*. With that pentagramatic two-tone black cover art, this was like Venom improbably unleashed upon the American masses. And paired with the fake music, the entire package made even the most seasoned metalheads uneasy about society devolving into anarchy. Indeed, the metal churn enclosed was the opposite of introspective; it was rudely and rudimentarily played, but recorded with such sonic force—Tom Werman really is the secret weapon here—that we sophisticated metalheads looked down our nose at these riffs while we were beat upon the head, neck, and chest area with a message that said something like rock is dead, long live rock. *Shout at the Devil* was something like punks making fun of metal and then putting David Lee Roth in as singer, but the dude not getting the joke.

No wonder the toffee-noses at Elektra were embarrassed. The Crüe were horrible and great at the same time. And the last laugh is on the brainiacs: every song on *Shout at the Devil* is great, and every song on this one Crüe album is more measuredly well-written than every Tom Petty song ever.

And what was doubly fun, Crüe were the talk of the town because of this carnal disaster of a kiddie rock record. How dare they rip off Van Halen? How dare they rip off

Not one of
Nikki's finer
sartorial
moments.
© Rudy Childs

The first (in)version of many to come.
© Rich Galbraith

Kiss? But rip they did and then crassly commercialize it like something out of Hollywood. Mötley were the "it" band, young whippersnappers at the *US Festival*, and in the magazines, rubbing shoulders with suddenly old-looking bands who didn't know what hit 'em.

Alas, however, the Herculean booze and drug intake of the band caught up with them and, as Nikki confides—although again, with no reflection or apology, as if it's merely part of a script—that the band sleepwalked through not one but two records. *Theatre of Pain* and *Girls, Girls, Girls* were phoned in, but disturbingly, eaters of rock didn't notice or worse, didn't care. Mötley was massive, through rote power ballad "Home Sweet Home" clunked cover "Smokin' in the Boys Room" and then through the dime store hair metal of "Girls, Girls, Girls" and the much smarter and creative architecture of "Wild Side."

All hands on deck in Toronto. Author's Collection

But were the guys happy? Well, we can't even begin to be able to frame and articulate what goes on in the brains of these guys. As it turns out, Mötley-styled anguish went to all the places visited by the sorry lot of the common lot. Mötley-styled euphoria, on the other hand . . . read their exploits and in any given week, those guys are subsumed by doses of ecstasy it would take the average happy camper two lifetimes to accumulate.

And this would be one of the reasons Mötley had such a grip on the eighth graders and the ladies of the heavy metal '80s. In a sense, we smiled and ate what we were being fed from *Theatre of Pain* and *Girls, Girls, Girls* because the entire package—in a real sense, the record coupled with the concert, but also the lurid news—was a multimedia trip outta here.

Enough grousing, for I myself dug quite a few songs on these records—most notably "City Boy Blues," "Fight for Your Rights," and "Wild Side"—and then was cheering the guys on when they returned with a sparking, dynamic, yet still admirably gritty record called *Dr. Feelgood* to close out the hair metal decade. Mötley found themselves half deaf by the death rattle of drugs and sobered up to a degree, working really hard up in Vancouver, writing at thrice the grunting, dumping brainpower level of the last two records, eventually turning in what became their biggest album of all time.

What's even more fun is that on a vibrant rock 'n' roll level, the old men of the '80s were kicking the asses of Cinderella, Poison, and—worst of the worst—Bon Jovi. Crowing victory, Mötley, raw and proudly lacking of pretense, were proposing to keep the party going for a few more adrenaline-shot nights, and the likes of "Dr. Feelgood," "Kickstart My Heart," and yes, even the maudlin ballad "Don't Go Away Mad (Just Go Away)" had us at yes all over again.

You win some, you break some eggs, you die from drugs and are shocked back to life by more drugs, and then . . . Mötley, endlessly entertaining, had retaken their crown, closing out the '80s with a record that would eventually notch six times platinum. What's more, *Dr. Feelgood* would live on through history as the perfect expression of lessons hard-earned through a decade of '80s metal, straddled to the distorted electric striving of the original bad boy bands from the low '80s, of which Mötley were the first and least rehearsed.

MÖTLEY CRÜE
in
82'
"TOO FAST FOR LOVE"

MÖTLEY CRÜE

Public Enemy #1

Kevin Estrada Collection

Tommy, as yet uncommitted to his superhero character. © Kevin Estrada

Vince from one of the earliest promo shoots.
© Kevin Estrada

Kevin Estrada Collection

1980

JANUARY 1980 UK's Girl issue the first of the their two albums, *Sheer Greed*. The band's glam look, plus their minor hit cover of "Do You Love Me" (according to cowriter of the track with Kiss, Kim Fowley), influence Nikki Sixx in terms of a serviceable glam and metal synthesis.

JANUARY 1, 1980 Bob Deal, now in a band called Vendetta, changes his name to Mick Mars, in part to evade arrest for lack of payment of his growing debts.

MARCH 14, 1980 Def Leppard issue their debut album, *On Through the Night*. Had the band been from LA and not Sheffield, England—and given the future arc of their career—Mötley would have been sharing their status as bridge act between Van Halen and the hair metal explosion commencing in 1983. Similarly, if Dokken's 1981 debut *Breakin' the Chains* had been issued in America at the time it saw release through France's Carrere Records, and not in September of 1983, that band would also be sharing the credit with Crüe.

What have I gotten myself into?
© Kevin Estrada

Nikki knows something we don't.
© Kevin Estrada

Kevin Estrada Collection

AUGUST 14, 1980 Nikki signs a publishing agreement with Kim Fowley, for a song that he had written with Laurie Bell from the Orchids.

KIM FOWLEY:

Nikki Sixx was dating Laurie Bell from Venus and the Razor Blades, who were the baby boy/girl coed metal band of the Runaways. Then she was in a band called the Orchids, an all-girl band, and they didn't sell a lot of records but they were influential. And she knew Laurie McAllister, the last bass player of the Runaways. And they both knew Nikki Sixx, and so Nikki Sixx took the Runaways and Laurie Bell and all this English shit and he called it Mötley Crüe. And his big inspiration was Eric Carmen from the Raspberries, who weren't metal at all. They were pop. And if you look at some of the songs that Nikki Sixx and Mick Mars wrote, they were very reminiscent of Eric Carmen, which is Midwestern pop downwind from metal Detroit. So Nikki Sixx was studying me and studying the Runaways and the Orchids, plus Eric Carmen, and he came up with Mötley.

The big hair really was very much a Mötley innovation.
© Kevin Estrada

NOVEMBER 7, 1980 Frank Feranna legally changes his name to Nikki Sixx, after first being Nikki London and then considering Nikki Nine. Nikki lifts the name from Niki Syxx (aka Jeff Nicholson), bass player boyfriend of a girl he had been hitting on, essentially stealing the musician's identity and his girlfriend at the same time.

LIZZIE GREY:

Well it's funny, I was looking at a Nigel Benjamin interview and he said, "Nikki would do anything to be a rock star." But that was a hard call. I think any of us would've done anything to be a rock star. He was driven like I was driven. We were like Heckle and Jeckle. We lived it. Every day was spent trying to conceive a new better way to market the project. And I hate to use that word marketing, because we were lousy businessmen. We were lovers of rock 'n' roll and the whole stigma of the glitter glam rock star. And as much as Mötley Crüe tried to sell themselves as a heavy, heavy metal band, I just see them as a really strong pop rock band more than anything. Nikki liked punk a little more than I did. But I have to be honest with you, Nikki really wanted it bad. I mean Nikki would put on a record and just lift the bass riffs off of an album, and it used to really irk Nigel Benjamin, who didn't have much respect for Nikki or myself as a musician. One time, Nikki came by and said, "I've got this great song," and he started playing this song. And Nigel just said, "You stole that, mate! You ripped that off of a Cheap Trick album! Why don't you just admit it?" And so Nikki was chagrined a lot by Nigel, and their relationship was very strange. And that project was really a matter of where Nigel had come from this really haughty hoity-toity aristocracy in England, and so he saw us as a bunch of wannabes in LA. But nonetheless he enjoyed the success of all the free gin and tonic he could handle at the Starwood.

1981

1981 Vince enters into his first marriage, with Elizabeth "Beth" W. Lynn.

JANUARY 1981 Nikki, now loose from London, jams with Suite 19's Greg Leon. Leon connects Nikki with Tommy Lee, who considered Nikki halfway to rock star already.

FEBRUARY 1981 Tommy and his bassist friend Joey Vera (later, of Armored Saint) meet Nikki at a Denny's and they transition to Nikki's place to talk music. Tommy moves his drums into Nikki's living room, and shortly thereafter, Nikki fires Greg Leon out of the fledgling band situation.

Kevin Estrada Collection

Truth be told, there really wasn't much Diamond Dave in Vince's stage persona. © Kevin Estrada

One step along
the journey. ©
Kevin Estrada

MÖTLEY CRÜE

Kevin Estrada
Collection

Off to the races!

Kevin Estrada Collection

Tommy Lee, already thinking outside the box. © Kevin Estrada

MICK MARS:

It was like, I found my band (laughs). They were a bit younger than me, of course, but it's weird to me, because I auditioned them. They didn't audition me. I don't know, I knew immediately that this was the people, the right ones, the right choice, for me. (Nikki Sixx: I love that! You auditioned us?! Now I find out after all these years, you bastard.)

Well, I can't help it (laughs). Dude, I went through so many chumpy musicians . . . you know, it's like, you get to a point where you go, I'm not auditioning anymore. I'm going to audition *them* to see if they're good enough. And of course, here's my band.

MARCH 1981 Mick quits Whitehorse in flamboyant fashion, by knocking over his amps at a gig in Yuma, Arizona, after the club owner had warned him to turn the volume down.

EARLY APRIL 1981 Mick Mars dyes his hair black, and places an ad in the *Recycler* looking for a new band, promising to be "a loud, rude, and aggressive guitar player." Nikki Sixx and Tommy Lee, now having lost Greg Leon, respond. Neither of them recall hanging out after meeting at the liquor store back in '79. Mick joins the band and his first duty is to fire the other guitarist, Robin. Nikki, admiring of Mick's dyed black hair, teaches Tommy how to dye his hair to match—the guys didn't consider the color to be jet black but more of a Nice 'n' Easy "blue-black." Tom Bass, or 'T-Bone," is rechristened Tommy Lee. Vince Neil also joins the band in April, after Tommy, Mick, and Nikki see a Rockandi gig and implore him to join forces with them. Vince keeps it to himself that he is fairly intimidated by Nikki, who, through his wild look and reputation with London, was already a local legend, in Vince's estimation (even though somehow Vince never managed to witness London live). But before Vince joins, the band records a four-song demo with previous singer O'Dean, which is played to Vince as additional ammo to get him to join. It was Mick who put his hand up that he didn't think O'Dean was right for the band, citing his Roger Daltrey–type voice, and it was Mick who pushed the hardest for Vince as a potential replacement.

LIZZIE GREY:

Mick Mars I know very little about. I think he was from the Westside, like a beach town, the Huntington Beach area. I think he played in some Top Forty band called Whitehorse or something. I knew very little about him, and he actually had no presence that I ever experienced in the Hollywood rock scene. I think it was more like someone who answered an ad or something (laughs).

VICKY HAMILTON:

I was working at a record store called Licorice Pizza which was on the corner of Sunset and San Vicente, across from the Whisky. The punk stuff was still kind of going strong, but Mötley Crüe then lived on Clark Street, and they came into my record store all the time and I sort of befriended them because Nikki had a German model girlfriend who didn't speak very much English, and I don't know, I just found her very cute, and the two of them together, very cute. And we had a thing called Borrow Book, where we could take out five records at a time and go check them out and bring them back. So he was always like trying to get my records on Borrow Book, but he was never very good at bringing them back (laughs). So I couldn't do that anymore. So I ended up working for Mötley Crüe under their first manager, who was Allan Coffman, who was mostly a real estate guy and didn't really know much about the music business. But I did posters for *Too Fast for Love* when it was on Leathür Records, and put them up in the record stores around town, and actually stapled my fingers to Vince Neil's face at one time, and thought that was very cool. They were very experimental. I can remember Nikki in the backyard lighting his boots on fire and singeing his eyebrows and eyelashes, like trying to figure out that pyrotechnic stuff. At that time, they were listening to Sweet and mostly '70s sort of rock bands. I think that's who really influenced them the most. But they were on a mission. It was all about the band, and it was like the craziest apartment I've ever been in. And my first real brush with fame and fortune as well. You know, I saw somebody go from the gutter to the Forum. I mean, when they played the Forum, I actually cried, because I can remember Nikki telling me about, "Oh, we're going to have these screens in the back and this and that." And when you see that come true, it's just like really overwhelming.

APRIL 8, 1981 Vince, Mick, Nikki, and Tommy sign a ten-year management deal with Allan Coffman, who puts together Coffman & Coffman Productions with his wife Barbara. The name of the band is agreed upon as Mötley Crüe, after Mick dredges the memory of Whitehorse's alternate band name Mötley Croo or Mötley Cru. They also consider Trouble and Suicidal Tendencies, amusingly, soon to be the names of major recording acts. The umlauts in the name are partially inspired by those in the Löwenbräu beer brand they had been drinking at the time, as well as the general military vibe of them.

A rite of passage for any band is its first illustration. Kevin Estrada Collection

BARRY LEVINE:

Struggling? They were all living off the Strip; they had nothing. They were living off women, they were living from hand to mouth. From foot to mouth. They had nothing. But what they did have was dedication. What they did have was that nothing was going to stop them, nothing was going to stop any of them, especially Nikki, from making it. He always believed in himself. And Nikki came from a pretty complex background. He had a lot of things that happened to him when he was growing up. So he made a lot of decisions. He's a pretty strong, adamant guy. Nice guy. Never gave me a problem no matter how screwed up he was at the time; he was just a good guy to work with.

Kevin Estrada Collection

An early promo shot that actually looks more evil than anything the band ever did, save perhaps for the front cover of the second album. © Kevin Estrada

VINCE NEIL:

When we got together, I was a fan of Sweet and Nikki was a fan of the New York Dolls. We were all in these different bands, but we all stood out in each band that we were in because we all looked a little bit crazy. And then when we all got together, everybody thought, wow, how ingenious. But it wasn't—it was just us.

APRIL 24, 1981 Mötley play their first two shows on the same night, at the Starwood, opening for San Francisco's Y&T. They play the Starwood again the next night. Wanting to make an impression, Nikki had at the ready promotional Mötley buttons and T-shirts. In attendance were band managers Allan and Barbara and also Tommy's parents.

BLACKIE LAWLESS:

Nikki and I were very good friends at the time, and with my blessing, I gave them the things that I was using, that I couldn't use anymore. But if I had to pick somebody—and not that he did it with any foreknowledge—but I would've sensed that what we were doing was more akin to Marilyn Manson, because there was a heavy psychological type of warfare that I was using. Mötley, I just saw them as kind of a ballsy Kiss.

MAY 1981 Mötley Crüe rerecord their demo, now with Vince singing. They issue two of the three tracks recorded ("Nobody Knows What It's Like to Be Lonely" is not used) as their first single, "Stick to Your Guns"/"Toast of the Town," which is tossed out to the crowds at shows.

TOMMY LEE:

The formula that we use that worked, I would advise a new band to get some money together and do a single. We used to just chuck 'em out into the audience. Then one kid on the block would have it, and pretty soon he'd play it for his buddies, and word got around and it turned into like a big weed, a street noise that everybody just started rapping about, and pretty soon, we were selling shows out. And we'd only been together for a few months. (*Rock Scene*, 1986)

A gem for the tape traders.
Kevin Estrada Collection

NIKKI ON THE BAND'S VISUAL PRESENTATION:

Our thing was a direct rebellion against what was going on in Los Angeles. The thing is, when this band got together, everybody in the band looked the way they looked. It wasn't like, after we came out, it was, "Let's look like this." It was just four guys that had the same passion and that looked like that. It became something that people talked about more than the music. And we were like, "I've always looked like this; what's the problem? What's the big deal?"

ERIC GREIF:

The very first time I was actually consciously aware of Mötley Crüe was a full-page ad that was taken out by Allan Coffman, their manager—who eventually became my boss—in *BAM* magazine. And they just had the four photos of the guys and their ridiculous names, and it was silly and exaggerated, but at the same time it was . . . I don't know, very charismatic. I mean they looked like a band. They looked like a unit, and I was sitting in a recording class or whatever at the University of Sound Arts, and opened *BAM*, and boom, it hit me. I mean, I just thought wow, this is going to be really big.

NIKKI SIXX:

We made a demo tape and asked record company people to come down and see us play. They'd say, "Oh, you guys look too weird; this is completely out of style. Cut your hair." They would say that we were too hard rock or to pop or . . . they didn't know what we were. We just said to them, "Okay, well, fuck you." We pressed the record ourselves and it started selling—30,000 copies—and that's basically how we got our contracts: by proving to them that we didn't need them. (*Circus*, 1984)

MAY 12, 1981 Mötley play the Whisky A Go Go, for what is essentially their third show ever, at their second location ever.

MID-MAY, 1981 Mötley is videotaped for the first time, at a show in Pasadena.

NIKKI SIXX:

It was Pookie's Sandwich Shop across the street from the Perkins Palace. We loaded in our equipment, and there were twelve people there. Our beer tab was $137. We had to come back to play again for our beer tab. Our dressing room was a closet full of cheese graters, beer kegs, and flour. (*Circus*, 1984)

JUNE 6, 1981 Mötley play the Troubadour for the first time; David Lee Roth introduces the band. Later that month Vince is threatened with firing if he doesn't stop shooting cocaine.

OZZY OSBOURNE GUITARIST JAKE E. LEE:

I saw their show at the Troubadour, because after their first shows, everybody in Hollywood was talking about them. So I said, all right, let's see how good they are, and I thought they were amazing. They were so fucking rock 'n' roll. I loved it—they were just fucking great. And then they showed up at one of our Ratt shows, and we all got along, and we started opening for them on a couple of shows. And the funny thing is, they were awesome in the beginning. They were like the rock 'n' roll band you wanted to be in. Everybody thought, okay, if a band is going to make it out of LA, it'll be Mötley Crüe. And then it didn't happen. Record companies turned them down. They actually started getting . . . well, they started getting a little wasted. They always drank a lot, but it just got kind of sad, maybe a year after I saw them. Initially, they were just fucking awesome, and then I saw them again, and I thought it was really sad because it looked like they'd given up, nobody wanted them, they weren't gonna make it. It became, I don't know, the story of the band that couldn't make it, and they were on their downward spiral. Right after that I joined Ozzy, and then I was out of the loop for a while. And I was kind of surprised when they got signed. It was a very up-and-down thing with them.

Note the naming mix-up.

Kevin Estrada Collection

AUGUST 1981 Mötley record their earliest videos: crude live performance clips, recorded at SIR Studios, for "Public Enemy #1" and "Take Me to the Top."

OCTOBER 3, 1981 David Lee Roth jams onstage with the band at the Troubadour, during a rendition of "Jailhouse Rock."

TOMMY LEE:

I was seventeen years old when I recorded that. That record is just a bunch of like, full-blown adolescent energy and that was a very strange recording process because it was our first time and we didn't know what the fuck we were doing. So that was inexperience, adolescent adrenaline—it was awesome for what it was.

NOVEMBER 1981 Mötley Crüe record, over a four-day period at Hit City West in LA, what will become their incendiary debut album *Too Fast for Love*. The studio's engineer is quickly dismissed, replaced by Michael Wagener of Accept fame. The album is made at a cost of $7,000, and the band essentially run through their ten-song set, sans any covers, which at that point had included the Beatles' "Paperback Writer" and the Raspberries' "Tonight." Now managed by Allan Coffman with further papers having been signed November 9th, Mötley plan to issue the record independently, on Coffman's Leathür Records, distributed by Greenworld, the domain of former Guns N' Roses manager Alan Niven.

NIKKI SIXX ON THE PRODUCTION VALUES OF THE DEBUT:

Punk rock. It took us what? About seven days to record that? We mixed and recorded it in seven days. I think we cut the record live in one day or two days. I mean the whole process was about a week, so there's not a lot of thought that can go into something that quick. I don't think there are a lot of overdubs.

DECEMBER 1981 Mötley Crüe issue their debut record, *Too Fast for Love*, on Leathür Records. Taken by Allan and the band to a few stores to sell, the initial indie pressing of 2,000 copies is also sold at shows. Nikki and ex-Runaways Lita Ford become an item after the two of them meet at the band's record release party at the Troubadour. With the album quickly selling out, a second pressing of 4,000 copies is produced, along with 5,000 cassettes.

MICK MARS ON INITIAL HOPES AND ASPIRATIONS:

I think that pretty much we had every intention of doing what we were doing. All the bells and whistles like stars and gold and platinum albums, all that kind of stuff was like important to us, but we didn't really think about it. We always thought about the music as first and foremost, and whatever came with it, came with it. If you are there and you have a product, people will come.

DECEMBER 25, 1981 A raucous Christmas party and show almost get Vince Neil fired from the band by Nikki, who unsuccessfully courts Ratt's Stephen Pearcy to join the band.

NIKKI SIXX ON THE FIRST BATCH OF SONGS:

Quickly written, under-thought, more about just playing and not the over-examining, which we all tend to do as artists. So in that, what you get is kind of these quirky rhythms where you go to yourself, well, that's a weird change, which later you go, God, I really like that. But we were just kind of doing it. I don't know how long you can hang onto that. It's sort of like hanging onto, you know, losing your virginity. There's the first time, and the next time it's little bit different and then the next thing you know, it's been years. With Mötley, to lose our cherry, was that first record. It was kinda sloppy and punk and very real. And it's hard to go back to that. It's hard even to play some of those songs sometimes because it feels like a different band.

Kevin Estrada Collection

February 1982

An ad more so extolling the charms of Greenworld. Author's Collection

Hard Rock Energy & Heavy Metal Power

Steve Quercio Presents In Concert **MÖTLEY CRÜE**

SANTA MONICA CIVIC
8 P.M. — THURSDAY — APRIL 8, 1982
Tickets available at SANTA MONICA BOX OFFICE
or TICKETRON OUTLETS and CHARGE-LINE (213) 393-9961

For additional information call:
SANTA MONICA BOX OFFICE
(213) 393-9961

Tickets $8.75 in Advance
$9.75 at the Door

Both hard rock energy and heavy metal power. Kevin Estrada Collection

1982

JANUARY 29, 1982 Buoyed by early sales and the landing of a distributor in Greenworld, Mötley press up 20,000 additional copies of their independent debut album. Influential UK music paper *Sounds* hypes the album, but back home, the hype machine is running on its own, with 12,000 copies moving within the first week of taking shipment of the order.

MICK MARS:

The umlauts on the Mötley Crüe . . . European people knew we were from America because the umlauts are in the wrong spot. People in America thought that we were from Europe *because* of the umlauts. So that was kind of cool.

JOURNALIST JOHN KORNARENS:

Mötley Crüe's music is a combination of Van Halen, Cheap Trick, and Sweet, all rolled up into one hairy leather coat. Guitarist Mick Mars plays a nice demonic-sounding guitar, mixing Van Halen–type harmonics with the slightly off-key solos. Vince Neil is a perfect ass-shaker lead singer with a catchy high-pitched voice. Nikki Sixx is the backbone of the band. He writes most of the music and provides strong thumping bass lines that complement Tommy Lee's drumming very nicely. His drumming style is one of the more unique and entertaining in rock today. [*The New Heavy Metal Revue*, 1982]

Vince in 1982, growing into his celebrated persona. © Kevin Estrada

BARRY LEVINE:

Nikki had a lot of ideas. Nikki was an incredible idea man and he needed someone like me to visualize them, help them design it. And I had my ideas, too. The two cool things I liked about Kiss and Mötley Crüe was that they were two bands that kind of left me alone. They just left me alone. They went, "This is the concept we have, and do what you need to do." So Nikki had a lot of faith in me that I believed in his vision and I'd bring that vision to life. It all started with Doc Mc-Ghee, because in a way I was managing them. They had no manager at the time, and besides being their creative consultant, I was managing them and I said this isn't what I want to do. I'm a creative guy and I didn't want to be a manager at the time.

FEBRUARY 11, 1982 Nikki gets in a fight with bikers, who had apparently been assaulting some girls. The incident is immortalized in Mötley song "Knock 'Em Dead Kid."

MARCH 1982 Nikki is evicted from "The Mötley House," after which he moves in with Lita Ford. Vince moves in with his girlfriend, Beth. Tommy, meanwhile, rents a house with his new stripper girlfriend Candice Starrek.

BARRY LEVINE:

They wanted to make a statement. Nikki never felt just the music was enough. Why did they wear what they wore? Why did they act the way they acted? Tommy, you said something wrong to him on the street and he'd want to deck you. These guys were the embodiment of what their music was about, what their lyrics were about. So Nikki always had a vision of being a real, edgy, grounded, theatrical band with no holds barred. You go by the numbers, you know you have lighting, you have effects. What I loved about Nikki is the first effect that I saw him perform just . . . I said that's it, I gotta be part of this. Where Kiss, they're a well-oiled machine, Kiss. They know what's happening from the beginning of the show to the end. But Nikki, the way he showed me the effect and the way he was performing it, I laughed because he almost—well he did—set himself on fire, and almost went a little beyond. What he would do is his roadie would put kerosene on his boots, and he'd light it, and they timed it, and it would go up and he'd just bring his head back. And it was like, yeah, that's a special effect. That's one that puts you in the hospital. So when I saw that I went, yeah, I know what these guys are about. And we worked very closely on creating it.

TOM ZUTAUT:

Mötley Crüe started the glam metal thing. And they looked more like the New York Dolls when I found them. Or Slade or Sweet or any of those glam bands from the '70s. But as far as glam metal goes, I mean, nobody really thought of Sweet or Slade as metal, but when Mötley Crüe and Quiet Riot came out, they were kind of dressing like girls and putting on makeup like the glam bands from the '70s. There were a bunch of bands like Ratt that I would've signed, but Nikki Sixx, you know, Robbin was his roommate and he didn't want me to sign his roommate, so that was kind of the end of that.

APRIL 8, 1982 Mötley sells out the 3,500-capacity Santa Monica Civic. Elektra's Tom Zutaut discovers the band through another sold-out show, the same month, at the Whisky A Go Go. Zutaut puts up with the ridicule of signing Mötley in the middle of new wave–mad LA (Virgin was also in the running), because he'd seen the rabid reaction the band got live that night.

MAY 1982 Saxon issue their landmark *The Eagle Has Landed* live album, which celebrates their success as one of the top "New Wave of British Heavy Metal" bands. Later in the year, Nikki says that Mötley had been offered the support slot on the band's late 1982 UK tour, but the deal with Elektra had been too fresh and thus a UK swing seemed premature.

MAY 20, 1982 The deal to sign with Elektra goes through, after Virgin lobbied hard, presenting to the band a suitcase containing $10,000 as an advance on a proposed $100,000 deal. A forty-one-page, seven-year contract with Elektra is signed, with the band receiving an advance of $28,500. Part of the agreement is a relinquishing of distribution duties from Greenworld to Elektra.

JUNE 3, 1982 A re-polish of *Too Fast for Love*, at the behest of Elektra's Kenny Buttice, is finished up. Vince's vocals were rerecorded and Roy Thomas Baker had been enlisted to remix the album at his Sunset Drive home, amongst much partying.

JUNE 4-JUNE 11, 1982 The band embark on a debacle of a short Canadian trip called the *Crüesing Through Canada* tour, which was designed to create chaos and notoriety for the band well away from their home turf. After brawls, run-ins with police, and trashed hotel rooms, the tour is cut short after a closing two-night stand at the Riviera Rock Room in Edmonton, Alberta, where Allan Coffman and his Canadian associate Eric Greif decide to cut losses and escape. In total, five of the seven dates had been in Edmonton, with one each in Lloydminster, Alberta, and Saskatoon, Saskatchewan. It was the first time the band had played outside of California.

NIKKI SIXX:

What happened in Canada was that we were booked with a promotion company before we signed to Elektra, and they had no idea what we were about. We were booked into discos and gay bars and all other kind of ridiculous things. We come onstage with all this fire and bombs, heavy metal and crashing steel, and it just looked silly. And these cowboys with tattoos of anchors on their arms that said "mom" just didn't know how to relate to it. [*Kerrang!*, 1982]

JULY 1982 With the rest of the band inked, Vince is the last to get a tattoo, of a musical note and snake. Meanwhile a proposed Scandinavian tour fails to finalize.

ERIC GREIF ON WHETHER MÖTLEY IDENTIFIED WITH HEAVY METAL:

It wouldn't make any sense, really, to say that the guys in Mötley Crüe at the time, would have consciously discarded the term or embraced the term. It wouldn't make any sense chronologically, because they just simply saw themselves as being a retooling of things that had been done just several years earlier. And I'm shocked to sit here today and think how close we were to "Fox on the Run" in 1980, you know what I mean? This was only five years earlier. I mean the Bay City Rollers were just as much an influence on Mötley Crüe as heavy metal. The whole idea of mania, the whole idea of look, the whole idea of sing-along choruses. There isn't much of a jump from the writers for Bay City Rollers, and Chinn and Chapman writing for Sweet. So if you take that to the next level, just kind of heavy that up, and listen to Vince's vocals on the first mixes for Leathür Records, before it was cleaned up and redone by Roy Thomas Baker, I mean, that's as '70s glammy as you can get.

AUGUST 16, 1982 "Live Wire" is issued as a first single from *Too Fast for Love*, backed with "Take Me to the Top" and "Merry-Go-Round."

BARRY LEVINE ON MÖTLEY'S LOOK BEFORE HE GOT INVOLVED:

It was pretty basic. Street, torn shit. They still had the hair and all that other stuff, a little bit of glam. When I got a hold of them it was . . . again, Nikki was never in the position . . . if you have champagne taste and a pauper's pocketbook, you don't have shit. You have great ideas but no one's ever going to see them. What I helped with Nikki is I helped bring the money to the situation. I helped sit him down, and then once we had the money we started conceiving these ideas.

Isn't $9.75 at the door kind of pricey for 1982? Kevin Estrada Collection

Generating some excitement right out of the gate. Kevin Estrada Collection

SWEET's ANDY SCOTT:

In '81, certainly very early days, Mötley Crüe had not released their first record even. They had sent me some demos, and Nikki Sixx used to phone me up from LA, and it would be about four or five in the morning, and I knew who it was, a couple of times a week. And we started to get to the point where he would say, "Come over and show us; come over and produce the record." And it was at that time where I was definitely wanting to be a record producer, but it was also at a time where, instead of just getting on the plane like I should have, I was saying, "Look, send me an airline ticket, and tell me where you got me to stay and I'll come over." And in the meantime, about three months later, I had a phone call, and they were going into the studio with Roy Thomas Baker, the guy who produced Queen, to revamp the demos, because obviously, nobody was willing to give them a budget to totally rerecord. And when I thought about that, I went, I'm probably best out of that, because I would've wanted to re-record the lot of it. Anyway, as we now know, even those, like Iron Maiden, when I had Iron Maiden in the studio, their early demos were not good, but it was one of those things, if you don't seize the moment, you sometimes miss it. And that's been twice for me. Because I said, "Well, you need to rerecord all of this." And of course both Iron Maiden's first album and Mötley Crüe's first album are reworkings of demos that were quite successful! So sometimes it's not got anything to do with the quality, it's the moment of the impetus and getting the band out there, yeah?

NIKKI SIXX:

Well, you know, we were very excited. That was very early on in the band's career. During *Too Fast for Love*, we had just kind of thrown it down and did it, and no one was interested. And all of a sudden, it started selling and there was a buzz, and Elektra signed us, and they said, we want you to use Roy Thomas Baker. And we were like, my God, Roy Thomas Baker—Queen, the Cars—this is going to be great. He was a complete disappointment. He just like laid around, hungover all the time. He would come in and say, "Oh, a little bit less reverb, darlings." What the fuck's this wanker, man? This is the guy who did the Queen records. He had, you know, lost his edge. He was fuckin' just a guy who was going through the motions.

AUGUST 20, 1982 *Too Fast for Love* gets major label release through Elektra Records, featuring the additional recording, altered track list (notably the deletion of "Stick to Your Guns"), slightly changed artwork, and the remix by Roy Thomas Baker. Nikki has said that "Stick to Your Guns" was removed to shorten the album so that the bottom end wasn't compromised by the tighter grooves in the vinyl. Alternately on the chopping block was "On with the Show." By this point, the band had moved 35,000 copies as an indie release. The album would enter the *Billboard* charts at #157 and into 1983 stall at #77, but eventually attain platinum certification.

JOURNALIST DAVE DICKSON ON *TOO FAST FOR LOVE*:

The songs are simple in structure, bassist Nikki Sixx, who nabs most of the credits, proving himself an able pop composer. They're fast, catchy numbers that, were Paul McCartney writing HM, he might easily come up with in his sleep. Vince Neil's voice tugs with a casual suggestiveness reminiscent of early David Sylvian. The musicianship too is flashy, and instantly dismissible. Mötley Crüe are not to be taken seriously, but what they offer here is tacky and decidedly pleasing to the ear. Interesting without being fascinating. (*Kerrang!*, 1982)

AUGUST 25, 1982 One of Nikki's idols, Alice Cooper, issues his *Zipper Catches Skin* album. Nikki had met Alice for the first time during the sessions earlier in the month, with both bands recording at Cherokee, the Crüe now working on their second record only a week after the major label issue of their debut.

Nikki looking young
and gothic in 1982.
© Kevin Estrada

NIKKI SIXX

Kevin Estrada Collection

 MÖTLEY

BARRY LEVINE ON WHAT SET MÖTLEY APART FROM OTHER LA BANDS:

Easy. Their attitude. You can talk a good game, but if you don't live it, then it becomes one-dimensional. And I think people could see through that. And I won't mention who the bands were, but there were a few bands who came to see me, one of whom went on to be huge. One I can mention—I don't give a shit—was Poison. I didn't get it. Listen, they're talented guys, but I didn't personally get it. And I just felt it was a bit prefabricated. Where Nikki and Vince and Tommy, they were very real and they were adding a theatrical layer to their honesty. That's what made them. It's funny because I helped get them their West Coast tour with Kiss. And Paul called me up and we talked about this. He goes, "You really sure you want them to tour with us?" and I said absolutely. They've got a great following on the West Coast, and they held their own, big time.

AUGUST 26, 1982 The band put down some demos toward the construction of their second album, including "Red Hot," "Looks that Kill," Knock 'Em Dead Kid" and "Hotter than Hell," the latter of which would be held over to the next album and rechristened "Louder than Hell." As the months progress, Zutaut is concerned that the satanic image Nikki is going for will give Elektra an excuse to ignore the record, just as it did the debut, while showering promotional attention on Australian act Cold Chisel instead. Tom goes over to Nikki's and Lita's apartment to try persuade him to change the title. Meanwhile, three days later, Allan Coffman sells part of his ownership in the band over to a twenty-one-year-old Bill Larson. Despite things not going well with Roy Thomas Baker on the remix of the first album, Nikki nonetheless favors either Baker or Eddie Kramer to work with the band on the sophomore record.

OCTOBER 1982 Mötley are featured in the November issue of soft porn magazine *Oui* through a photo spread; the band fails to get name-checked anywhere on the cover.

Y&T's LEONARD HAZE:

The first gig Mötley Crüe did was with us, at the Starwood, and then we put them on a couple Halloween shows. One, where like the fire marshal was adamant. The grass . . . it was just a really bad fire season—no pyrotechnics. And so they couldn't light this stuff up, right? So Nikki lights himself on fire (laughs), and the fire marshal is telling Nikki, "I'm going to have to fine you." And Nikki's like, "I didn't light nothing on fire. Me—I lit myself on fire! You can't say that's pyrotechnics." The argument was great.

OCTOBER 31, 1982 Mötley play the Concord Pavilion in San Francisco as sandwich act between opener Randy Hansen and headliner Y&T, to a crowd of 9,000. They debut three new compositions, "Looks that Kill," "Shout at the Devil," and "Red Hot." In the middle of the encore's "Knock 'Em Dead, Kid," Vince lights Nikki on fire, prompting a $1,000 fine.

JOURNALIST XAVIER RUSSELL:

Mötley Crüe were totally O.T.T. and delivered perhaps the greatest glam rock show of all time, and that includes Kiss. As far as I was concerned, Mötley Crüe completely blew Y&T offstage; no wonder they wanted to ban the Crüe's special effects (they failed). Tommy Lee has got to be one of the flashiest drummers around, spinning the sticks continuously in his hand, never dropping them, and during "Looks that Kill," Lee hit the snare drum so hard the stick went thirty feet up and he dumbfounded everyone by catching it in the middle of a drum roll. (*Kerrang!*, 1982)

DECEMBER 1982 The band enter the Annex in Northridge for some preliminary recording toward their second album. Not to make the cut are "I Will Survive," "Running Wild in the Night," and "Run for Your Life." All three compositions are quite metallic rockers with meaty riffs and tasteful licks from Tommy. Arguably, the quality of all three tracks is of a level above much of the music that would make the grade for Mötley's third and fourth records, and equal to many of the tracks on *Shout at the Devil*.

THE MOVE PRODUCTION INC. Arcadia, Calif.

Kevin Estrada Collection

Tommy had his own style right from the beginning; in fact, he displayed that signature sound on the first record more than on any that followed. ©
Kevin Estrada

COFFMAN & COFFMAN PRODUCTIONS
156 Mill Street • Grass Valley, CA 95945 • (916) 273-9554

MOTLEY CRUE RIDER-LIGHTING

A. Minimum lighting requirements for Motley Crue will consist of:

1. Overhead downstage and upstage positioning of lighting instruments.

2. Instruments are to be Par 64 100w type with globe configurations of medium focus for washes and very narrow focus for specials.

   Ellipsoidal 6" x 12" or 6" x 16" 1000w.

3) Rigging, cable, dimmer and desk to be used shall be determined by personal preference of lighting director.

4) Minimum power required is 600 amp.

B. Downstage washes are to be, but not limited to:

1) 6 instruments with 821 Roscolene
   6 instruments with 862 Roscolene
   6 instruments with 817 Roscolene
   6 instruments with no color.

C. Downstage specials are to be, but not limited to:

   Stage left: 2 instruments with 840 Roscolene
   Center: 2 instruments with 840 Roscolene
   Stage right: 2 instruments with 840 Roscolene

D. Upstage washes are to be, but not limited to:

   6 instruments with 821 Roscolene
   6 instruments with 861 Roscolene
   6 instruments with 809 Roscolene
   6 instruments with no color.

E. Upstage specials are to be, but not limited to:

   Stage left: 2 instruments with 818 Roscolene
   Center: 2 instruments with 818 Roscolene
   Stage right: 2 instruments with 818 Roscolene
   Drum: 2 instruments with 817 Roscolene
   Drum: 2 instruments with 839 Roscolene
   Drum: 2 instruments with 860 Roscolene
   Drum: 2 instruments with no color

MÖTLEY CRÜE

Coffman & Coffman got serious right away.
Kevin Estrada Collection

PERKINS PALACE-129 N.RAYMOND/PASADENA
KMET/AVALON ATTRACTIONS
PRESENT
A PEOPLE'S CONCERT
MOTLEY CRUE
NO REFUNDS/EXCHANGES
FRI NOV 19 1982 8:00P $5.00

Kevin Estrada Collection

DECEMBER 18, 1982 Allan Coffman is informed on the phone by legal representation that he is no longer the manger of Mötley Crüe. Bill Larson is also cast from the picture. Nikki writes a new song for Allan called "Bastard."

DECEMBER 31, 1982 The band perform a marquee gig at the Santa Monica Civic, inviting potential managers to check them out. At this point, the band had been threatening to throw in the towel. Or at least pretending to—they had even taken out trade ads in advance of the show saying that they were done if they couldn't find a manager. In essence, the gig was framed as sort of last ditch effort. As it turned out, Ronnie James Dio was integral in getting Doug Thaler to the gig. He eventually bites, along with Doc McGhee, both coming all the way from Florida.

The competition heats up. Author's Collection

1983

JANUARY 20, 1983
Def Leppard issue their massive-selling third album *Pyromania*. Quiet Riot issue *Metal Health* two months later, which is lauded as the first heavy metal record to reach #1 in *Billboard*, eventually selling six times platinum in America. The hair metal era is born, and Mötley are well positioned to benefit.

FEBRUARY 1983
After the successful live courtship of the past New Year's Eve, the band join forces with Doug Thaler and Doc McGhee. Doc sufficiently impresses the band after flying them to his Las Vegas headquarters on his private jet.

MARCH 1983
New manager Doug Thaler attends his first Mötley Crüe rehearsal and is dismayed to find each member of the band a good twenty pounds overweight and playing badly. After giving the guys a pep talk and then flying off to New York for ten days, he returns to find the band in fighting form.

MARCH 26-APRIL 3, 1983
The first coup for the band and their new management becomes a string of key dates supporting Kiss. However, the band is tossed from the tour, ostensibly for Nikki and Tommy having sex with Eric Carr's girlfriend behind his drum riser, although it is also rumored that the band had been capably upstaging the headliner.

VINCE NEIL:

Well, the first album, you have to remember, was basically a demo tape. I mean, we re-corded that record in like three days and we ended up pressing independently and sold like 20,000 copies. It was the first time I was ever in a recording studio and nobody was really comfortable in the studio; that was probably the toughest. But that's what really got us our record deal. We weren't even signed when we did that. But when Elektra signed us, they rereleased that. So *Shout at the Devil* was basically really our first album that we actually went in and recorded from scratch with Tom Werman and that's why it sounds so different, because it was really produced, rather than us just kind of throwing down the songs.

APRIL-AUGUST 1983 Mötley Crüe record, at Cherokee Studios, what will become their second album. With Joe Smith gone as the head of Elektra, there is pressure to drop the band from incoming president Bob Krasnow, who considers Mötley an embarrassment to the label's brand.

MICK MARS:

I loved Tom Werman. Working with him was a breeze. He added a few elements to it. I'd go like, "Hey, Tom, what if we try something like this?" When I was in with him by myself or something. And if it worked, great, and if it didn't, that's okay, too. He made the albums sound closer to how we sounded live. It was polished a little bit but not that much. It was still raw and mean and rude and in-your-face.

NIKKI SIXX:

Tom Werman, being a guy who'd done some of our favorite bands, one being Cheap Trick, was brought in, to talk about doing *Shout at the Devil*, and at first I was like, look, I don't really want anybody in there to do it; we can do it ourselves. And Elektra brought us in, and we met with him. He was kind of this square-looking cat, and I was like, what does this guy know? But he did do Cheap Trick, some of the greatest albums—Molly Hatchet, Ted Nugent—and we were like, man, maybe this is what we need, so we went with it. And Tom, in a lot of ways, was the perfect producer because he let us be us, enough to let us make *Shout at the Devil*. He sort of stayed out of the way. He organized the edges, brought them somewhat together. In other words, we never really could have gotten from brain to take to mastering. There were a lot of steps, and he was the guy who did all that. He said look, these guys know what they're doing, just let them do what they're doing. Let me sprinkle a little magic here and there. Geoff Workman, being the engineer, was really the most important part of that whole session, in my opinion.

The impressive lineup for Heavy Metal Day, as presented on the back of the official US Festival shirt. Kevin Estrada Collection

Still using the debut cover shot in 1983. Kevin Estrada Collection

Testing the Satanic waters.

Author's Collection

Nikki rocks US Fest, 1983. © Rudy Childs

BARRY LEVINE:

Sometimes competition lends itself to emulation. Too many bands look the same, too many bands sound the same because there's a style, there's a sound, so everybody jumps on the bandwagon. Nikki didn't care about what anyone else thought. None of the guys in Mötley did—Tommy, none of them. All they cared about was what they felt and what their vision was, and they brought their vision. I think after the *US Festival*, people understood that this is a force to be reckoned with. It elevated them from being a club band or going on tour with whoever, and it really put them in the forefront—it's the *US Festival*. They got national recognition, they got respect from their peers, and they got their record companies to understand what they really had.

MAY 28-30 AND JUNE 4, 1983 The *US Festival* is mounted for the second and last time. A coming out party of sorts for the new American heavy metal—Heavy Metal Day sees an attendance of 375,000—the event particularly catapults Quiet Riot and Mötley Crüe to the next level. Mötley takes the stage at 12:30 p.m., directly after Quiet Riot, who open the day. Vince and Tommy are in fine form but Mick hits some bum notes. Additionally, Nikki and Mick look tentative in very high heels.

Nikki in 1983, showing his dark side.
© Kevin Estrada

Chilling at US Fest. Is that Rob Halford?
© Rudy Childs

MÖTLEY CRÜE

LOOKS THAT KILL

JUNE 1983 Nikki crashes the Porsche he had bought to celebrate the signing of a publishing deal three months earlier. He had been driving naked after misplacing his clothes, having scaled a wall at one of Roy Thomas Baker's infamous jacuzzi parties and driven off, chased at high speed by two girls in a Mustang. He suffers only a dislocated shoulder.

JULY 1983 Pain from Nikki's dislocated shoulder figures into his decision to start smoking, and then shooting, heroin.

US picture sleeve for one of the band's catchiest singles. Author's Collection

NIKKI SIXX ON THE BAND'S NEW SATANIC IMAGE:

I think that was more of the press taking something and running with it, you know? If you forget about the music for a minute, image-wise, by the time *Too Fast for Love* came out, we had already evolved into doing this other thing, getting more macabre and theatrical, and "Shout at the Devil" was just a song, a political song at that. It had nothing to do with Satan; it was about Ronald Reagan, and that got twisted. We were just getting theatrical. It's cool, it was fine with me, it was our *Goats Head Soup*. If you look at the photo session in the first album, the very next version of the record that came out, there was a picture of us with the pentagram in that macabre setting. So that was before *Shout at the Devil* came out. So we were already there.

SEPTEMBER 17, 1983 Mötley play a large package show in San Diego, along with Eddie Money, Uriah Heep, and a fast-breaking Def Leppard. It is a rare live date for the band within a seven-month period dedicated mostly to the recording of the new record, which by this point had been completed.

SEPTEMBER 26, 1983 Mötley Crüe issue their sophomore album, *Shout at the Devil*, which peaks at #17 in *Billboard*, selling 200,000 copies in the first two weeks of release.

BARRY LEVINE ON MÖTLEY'S NEW IMAGE

Nikki had an idea of this post-apocalyptic world. No rules, no nothing. And we actually built this set four months before the video. We built that just for the photo shoot. And we built it in my friend's backyard, piece by piece, and that set was almost a half-block long, a city block long. It was the biggest set I've ever done in my life. As for the credit in the album, I mean honestly, I don't really know about what other bands were, I just know how hard I worked with them and how well I worked with Nikki—but I didn't expect those credits. Those credits were put there by Doc McGhee and Doug Thaler and their partners. And I think those credits went on there to piss off Nikki, too, because they shouldn't have been put on there. The one credit that I loved above all the other credits—I didn't really give a shit about the other credits; I just cared if it was a great package—was "Thank you Barry Levine for not killing us." Because we all worked hard together. That was the best credit.

OCTOBER 29, 1983 Vince and Beth Lynn welcome a daughter, Elizabeth Ashley.

OCTOBER 31, 1983 Mötley appear live on MTV for the first time through live footage from a Halloween-themed show at the Limelight in New York.

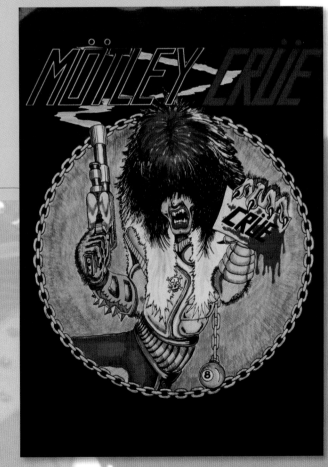

Early flirtation with the idea of a band mascot. Kevin Estrada Collection

An ad that demonstrates how favorable metal was viewed in the heat of **1983.** Author's Collection

Going places with a spiffy tour program, pretty early in the career. Kevin Estrada Collection

NOVEMBER 11–DECEMBER 16, 1983 Promoting *Shout at the Devil*, Mötley embark on a short but intensive western US headline tour, which reveals a *Mad Max*–inspired stage show to match the new "post-glam" look presented in the album graphics. Support comes from Florida's Axe and Australian AC/DC-alikes Heaven.

Nasty . . . plus gratuitous pentagram.
Kevin Estrada Collection

Definitely not *The White Album.* Kevin Estrada Collection

Kevin Estrada Collection

The band's S.I.N. Club gets up and running with some wares to wear.

Kevin Estrada Collection

VINCE NEIL:

We always enjoyed making videos; they were a lot of fun. You can see as time progressed, from our first video to one of our last videos, just the technology advanced so much. There was some really cool stuff that we did. And I think it was great for fans to be able to turn on the TV and actually be able to see your favorite bands, rather than just listen to them and look at the album cover.

NOVEMBER 11, 1983 Mötley's iconic "Looks that Kill" video airs for the first time, commencing the band's long, successful exploitation of the music video format. Vince considers the repetition of chorus lyrics a key success point for Mötley, as evidenced by this song; it's a trait he also recognizes in "Live Wire."

NIKKI SIXX:

We've always been into bands that write songs. We're not into the half-hour solos and the riff, riff, riff style that so many European bands are into. That's pure heavy metal—that's not us. Our biggest influences were bands like Aerosmith and Kiss, where there were some great tunes being played. That's the American tradition. We grew up listening to the radio, and we don't see anything wrong with writing songs that can get played there. The only thing is that we're not willing to sacrifice our ideals just to get that radio airplay. (*Hit Parader,* 1983)

The mayhem, the
majesty, the Mars.
Author's Collection

1984

EARLY JANUARY 1984 With Vince and Tommy coming down from a 1983-ending vacation in the Cayman Islands, the band set up shop at Longview Farm in Brookfield, Massachusetts, to rehearse for the upcoming tour dates supporting Ozzy Osbourne.

VINCE NEIL:

After the last tour, Tommy Lee and I went to the Cayman Islands for a couple of weeks. No TV, just an island. All you can do is snorkel and enjoy the sun. (After a tour) the last thing I want to do is listen to rock 'n' roll for about a week. But then again, you miss it. Tommy and I took a big ghetto blaster and were cranking AC/DC on the beaches. The natives really didn't enjoy that, but we did it anyway and they got used to it. (*Circus*, 1984)

JANUARY 9, 1984 Van Halen reaches new heights, becoming the commanding rock presence of the year with their diamond-selling *1984* album. Shockingly, Vince Neil mentor David Lee Roth would soon be out of the band, replaced by Sammy Hagar for 1986's six times platinum-selling *5150*.

NIKKI SIXX:

The Van Halen thing is ridiculous. Just because we come from LA, there's always been a number of people who've associated us with them. Sure we played some of the same clubs along the way, but we came along six years after they did, so it wasn't like we were exactly following in their footsteps. Just because Vince has blonde hair, people are comparing him to Roth. Shit, when a Van Halen song comes on the radio, it's a race between us all to see who can reach the off switch first. (*Hit Parader*, 1984)

JANUARY 10–MARCH 24, 1984 Mötley embarks on one of two extensive tour campaigns supporting on Ozzy Osbourne's *Bark at the Moon* tour. Ozzy takes a liking to the band and parties with them relentlessly. Decades later, the band frame the first night, in Portland, as their first arena show ever. Decades later, Tommy looks back on the Ozzy tour as the band's first big break.

JAKE E. LEE:

I don't know how much say I had in it, but I do remember we were doing the *Bark at the Moon* tour, and we had options—I say we, like I had any real fucking power in it (laughs). But there were options for opening bands, and Sharon did ask me. And I don't remember the other bands were, but she said, we have this, this, this, and this. And I said, "Mötley Crüe!" And she goes, "Really?" I said, "Yeah, I grew up . . ." Well, I didn't grow up with them, but I said, "I played with them in Hollywood, and they are a band that could be really huge. And they're my friends, so, please let them open." And like I said, I'm not saying that I got them on the tour, but I definitely wanted them on the tour. And it was . . . it was interesting.

A nice black and red ensemble. © Rudy Childs

ERIC GREIF:

I think that *Too Fast for Love* was not going for a heaviness aspect. It was going for a sing-along glam, '70s, Sweet thing. I mean that was the idea. It was changed, I think, by the time that they did *Shout at the Devil*. Everything had changed. The satanic thing was in, the whole movement has gone to a larger extreme. But Mötley predate the big massive MTV 1983 assault of metal on the American public. MTV made it happen. It made the scene. I don't think actually any of that would've happened without MTV. Because what happened was Crüe was exposed immediately, and then there was a flurry of signings. Everybody got a deal after that as a result. Mötley Crüe was signed probably around May of '82. They would've signed their deal with Elektra by the end of May, I'm thinking. So that predates all the deals of what became known as the metal onslaught of the mid-'80s. That predates everyone. After that, all the labels lined up, and up until that time of course, with people like the chairman of Elektra, metal . . . I mean, it was a joke. And the Mötley Crüe signing was not taken very seriously until *Shout at the Devil* broke through. And that wasn't until a year-and-a-half after. And then of course Ratt got their deal, and one by one, labels picked up that something was happening, and the marketing went into full gear, the merchandising, touring, all of that. So by the end of '83 it was mayhem.

JANUARY 12, 1984 *Shout at the Devil* is RIAA certified gold, rapidly on its way to platinum.

TOMMY LEE:

Shout at the Devil is one of my favorite earlier ones. I always think of my favorite albums in terms of the live show. Because live "Shout at the Devil" is so heavy, with the whole place going, "Shout, shout, shout!" [makes the devil horn pumping fist motion]. And you're sitting there, going, "Fuck, this is hands-down the classic." But my least favorite is *Theatre of Pain*, because *Dr. Feelgood* I like too.

I'm rocking. And I'm on a rock. © Rich Galbraith

JANUARY 29, 1984 Mötley are presented with their gold *Shout at the Devil* plaques at the Limelight in New York (Ozzy Osbourne in attendance), in advance of the band's Madison Square Garden gig with Ozzy the following night, at which time they are surprised with platinum plaques.

JANUARY 30, 1984 Mötley play Madison Square Garden for the first time. Before the show, fans hand out flyers to other fans, urging them to call FM stations, who had been ignoring the band's success, to play more Mötley.

PRODUCER TOM WERMAN:

I'm a pop producer. That's why I'm hired—to trying to get the bands on the radio. That's the reason I worked with Ted Nugent, Cheap Trick, Molly Hatchet: to get them on the radio. Mötley Crüe . . . I mean, who ever thought that Mötley Crüe would ever have a hit single? But it happened, and it happened early. When metal wasn't . . . I mean, "Looks that Kill" would have been something different if we hadn't done what we did. There's a lot of stuff that goes down that I get blamed for. But the fact is, I think the primary purpose of my working is to get the band on the radio so that they can get an audience. And then they could do whatever they wanted.

TOMMY LEE:

We owe our success to bad publicity. Kids would read some critic going, they're too loud, they're crude, they've got weird hair, and they'd say, "Hey, this sounds like the band for us." Also we're the best looking band in the world. Us and Twisted Sister are responsible for the popularity of glam rock again. I get a lot of satisfaction out of this, because all the buddies we started out with got short haircuts and skinny ties to jump on *that* bandwagon. We remain true to what we were about and they're stuck in the LA club-go-round. (*Metallion*, 1984)

As practiced by Priest and Kiss before them. © Kevin Estrada

NIKKI SIXX:

She was messing around with Jake and me, so Jake grabs a knife and I cut her shirt open. And she's into it. All of a sudden, this huge guy comes around the corner— it was his girlfriend and he was the bouncer! They threw us out, we got all cut up. These guys with clubs with spikes on them were trying to smash us in the head. (*Circus*, 1984)

FEBRUARY 4, 1984 "Looks that Kill," backed with "Piece of Your Action," is issued as a single. The track's narrative production video becomes a heavy rotation play on MTV, giving huge boost to the band's career. "Looks that Kill" spends ten weeks on the *Billboard* charts, achieving a #54 placement.

FEBRUARY 19, 1984 The band get into an infamous Mardi Gras–fuelled knife fight at a bar called the Dungeon on Bourbon Street in New Orleans. Three nights later, in Lakeland, Florida, Ozzy snorts a line of ants and licks up Nikki's pee.

JAKE E. LEE:

There was a contract that Sharon Osborne gave to everybody, including the road crew for both bands—Mötley Crüe and Ozzy. She gave out contracts that said they would not do drugs, they would not drink, and they would not do anything to degrade the name of Ozzy Osbourne on the tour (laughs). Which was an insane contract to sign. And obviously, the road crew signed it, but I remember Nikki coming up to me and said, "This contract is just weird. Are you signing it?" I said, "No. I'm not signing it." I mean, what are they gonna do, fire me? (laughs). I mean, what could I do to give Ozzy Osbourne a bad reputation? There's absolutely nothing I can do. And I'm not gonna sign a contract that says I won't, because by God, if I could, I will. That would make me even cooler, in a way. But no, Mötley opening for Ozzy was a wild time. There was a lot of shit that happened, but I'm actually very grateful that I was a part of it.

MARCH 24, 1984 Mötley is flour-bombed while they play Portland, Oregon, their last date of the first leg of the Ozzy tour. Not to be outdone, Mötley invade Ozzy's set in monks' garb and flash the band, while Vince delivers Ozzy a drink (actually a cup of flour) dressed in a suit of armor. A week later, *Shout at the Devil* hits its top position on the charts, a #17 placement.

APRIL 4-MAY 15, 1984 Mötley takes a break from the insanity of the Ozzy tour for a short headlining stint, covering the US Midwest. Actually, the break is Ozzy's, who tries to escape with his life by hanging out with Slade for a spell (possibly having something to do with the switch as well is the fact that *Shout at the Devil* had started to outchart and outsell *Bark at the Moon*). Support for Mötley on their headline stint comes from Saxon and Scottish Def Leppard-alikes Heavy Pettin'.

APRIL 30, 1984 "Too Young to Fall in Love," backed with "Take Me to the Top," is issued as a single from *Shout at the Devil*, reaching #90 in *Billboard* and staying there for a mere two weeks. The video's iconic Shanghai storyline was brought to life in a subway tunnel in Manhattan using fifteen actors and at a cost of $75,000.

BARRY LEVINE
ON THE ALBUM'S SATANIC IMAGE:

It's what Nikki wanted. It's all Nikki in the sense of what he wants. He knows what he wants out of life. He knew where his band would be for years from that point. That's how Nikki sees things. That's the problem with most bands. They don't think for the future. They think for the immediate future, and what they can get out of it. He always thought that he would have longevity. He loved *Mad Max*, he loved those films, and he had a lot of influences, too. And he brought them to me and we collaborated. But I mean a lot of his ideas were his ideas. If I were Nikki, when I talk to Nikki again, I'd be proud of my past because maybe sometimes he can't see the forest through the trees. He influenced a lot of other bands, too, that exist today.

MAY 10, 1984 Twisted Sister reach their commercial apex with *Stay Hungry*, issued this day. The record goes on to attain triple platinum status, and the band is constantly linked in conversation with Mötley Crüe as being two of the new breed of hot shock-rock bands on the scene.

An inspiration on the Crüe and Guns N' Roses as well. A career tragically cut short. Author's Collection

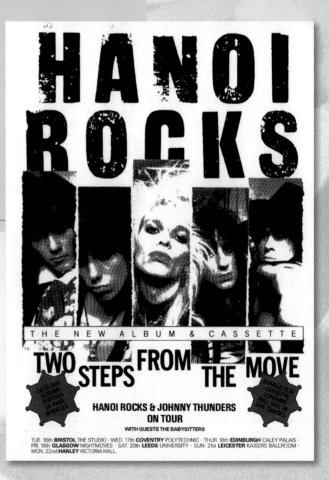

HANOI ROCKS

THE NEW ALBUM & CASSETTE

TWO STEPS FROM THE MOVE

HANOI ROCKS & JOHNNY THUNDERS ON TOUR
WITH GUESTS THE BABYSITTERS

TUE. 16th **BRISTOL** THE STUDIO · WED. 17th **COVENTRY** POLYTECHNIC · THUR. 18th **EDINBURGH** CALEY PALAIS
FRI. 19th **GLASGOW** NIGHTMOVES · SAT. 20th **LEEDS** UNIVERSITY · SUN. 21st **LEICESTER** KAISERS BALLROOM
MON. 22nd **HANLEY** VICTORIA HALL

JUST 10,000 ALBUMS CONTAIN 16 PAGE BOOKLET

DOUBLE PLAY CASSETTE CONTAINS FULL SIDE OF LIVE TRACKS

JAKE E. LEE:

Nikki was the brains. He wrote the lyrics, he wrote the bulk of the songs. And the whole vision was his—the look, the sound, how they were gonna come across. Nikki is a very smart guy, and a very rock 'n' roll guy. I mean, it's not like it was a business thing. But Nikki was the brains. But it was a combination of all of them. I mean, it was just a perfect coming together of those four guys. Mick's rhythm guitars are great, and his tone was great. I think he got a better tone than I ever did. Vince was a great front man, Nikki was always great onstage and Tommy almost single-handedly drew attention to the drummer, which wasn't very common back then.

Tom Wojcik Collection

MAY 16-MAY 28, 1984 Mötley and Ozzy are back together again for a few southern US and festival dates.

MAY 27, 1984 Competitors for Mötley's heavy metal dollar, Scorpions get their moment in the spotlight, issuing *Love at First Sting*, which sells triple platinum. As well, the band's 1979 *Lovedrive* album was a formative favorite of Nikki's and Vince's.

MAY 30, 1984-JUNE 15, 1984 Mötley resume headlining dates, hitting a few eastern US and Canadian cities, supported by Ratt, the new darlings of the LA metal scene, having issued their classic *Out of the Cellar* debut two month earlier. Of note, Tommy appears in two of the band's videos, and Nikki in one.

JULY 1984 The band write and rehearse material for what will become their third album, building upon material conceived on the road with Ozzy.

JAKE E. LEE:

At one point after I quit Ratt—and I knew all those guys—there was talk of me being in Mötley Crüe, either replacing Mick or being a second guitarist. Well, being first guitarist, with Mick being second (laughs). But being an added guitarist. All that fell through, but I thought about it, whoa, what if I was the guitar player for Mötley Crüe? I don't know if it would've been better. Because Mick did exactly what needed to be done in that band. I don't know if Mötley Crüe, with somebody like me, would've been bigger. Maybe they kind of needed a guitar player that was a little less—trying to be politically nice . . . And maybe with me trying to strut my stuff onstage, maybe it would've been too much. I don't know. Me and Nikki were good friends at one time. And I don't want to spell it out specifically, but it's probably more my fault the Nikki's, where our friendship kind of fizzled. But, oddly enough, as our friendship fizzled, me and Mick Mars . . . at first we didn't get along at all (laughs). Because of the thing I was telling you about, where there was talk about me getting in there. And it was not Mick's talk—it was everybody else's. We didn't see eye to eye on a lot of stuff, and we didn't actually like each other. But afterwards we did. But with Nikki, I kinda miss my friendship with him. But that all blew apart because of a woman (laughs).

AUGUST 1984 Hanoi Rocks issue their much-vaunted major label debut *Two Steps from the Move*. The band had been a noted influence on both Mötley Crüe and Guns N' Roses, but their career was cut short by the death of drummer Razzle, killed as a passenger in a car driven by Vince.

LIZZIE GREY:

Everybody who came to see London said, "You guys are so much like Hanoi Rocks! You guys are so much like Hanoi Rocks!" In fact, when Vince got in that horrible accident with Razzle, I know that Nikki was even contemplating getting Michael Monroe to replace who he thought might be going away for a while—Vince Neil. So yeah, they were kind of like doing the same thing we were doing but they were a little more punk rock and raw, while we had a little more mainstream glitter rock going on.

AUGUST 17, 1984 W.A.S.P., quite late to the party given Blackie Lawless' long history on the scene, issue their self-titled debut. Blackie's shock metal band is considered to be a similar but darker version of Mötley Crüe. Pre-W.A.S.P. and post-Sister, Blackie, ironically, had found himself briefly part of a London lineup with Lizzie Grey.

AUGUST 18-SEPTEMBER 7, 1984 Mötley perform short sets, opening on the *Monsters of Rock* tour of Europe, with AC/DC and Van Halen. It is the band's first time outside of North America.

SEPTEMBER 2, 1984 In Nuremburg, Germany, the Mötley boys get Dio keyboardist Claude Schnell in a heap of trouble by throwing the contents of his hotel room out the window, the furniture landing on top of two Mercedes. Returning home for a month, the band begin preliminary recordings of tracks for their third album.

SEPTEMBER 27, 1984 *Too Fast for Love* attains its RIAA gold certification.

OCTOBER 15-NOVEMBER 14, 1984 Mötley support Iron Maiden throughout Europe. Maiden prank the band by handcuffing Vince onstage and singing "Alka Seltzer" into the PA during the band's metalized cover of "Helter Skelter."

NIKKI SIXX ON THE BAND'S IMAGE AT THIS POINT:

People say, "Look at how much they've changed." But it's been a gradual thing. We were always developing. It's just the money helps it change quicker I guess. But we didn't really get more glam. It took us years to perfect this sleazy look! We couldn't afford costumes like these before. Nobody looked like us or dressed like us onstage. But now all these bands are starting to copy us, dressing like us, dyeing their hair black or white, so we have to keep one step ahead of everybody. On the next album we'll probably be even weirder and stranger. (*Creem*, 1985) on drugs when they designed them? "We're on drugs now!"

NOVEMBER 19, 1984 Mötley end their European jaunt with Maiden by headlining a theatre show in England that devolves into debacle of injuries, mishaps, and bad vibes with the demanding British crowd. On a positive note, the demoed but as yet unreleased "Raise Your Hands to Rock" is played for the first time.

MICK MARS:

The old fog machine—this was back when they were dry ice, with water—exploded on Clyde, our drum tech at the time, and he was burnt pretty bad. I thought somebody was cooking hotdogs. Not to be hilarious or funny about it—it wasn't funny—but I was going, "I smell hotdogs." And Tommy said, "Yeah, me too." And it was Clyde. Also Clyde got a dart in the back that went all the way to his scapula, which was hard to pull out.

BLACKIE LAWLESS:

The first album, I guess I would call it beautifully crude, because there is an anger to that record. On the second one, "Wild Child," most of it was written really before W.A.S.P. ever got a record deal. It didn't have the title until the day I actually sang vocals. Because I didn't think "Wild Child" was that great of a title. The song originally, I was going to give to Nikki, to let Mötley Crüe do it, but we knew Vince couldn't sing it, because of the range of it, so I kept it. And good thing for us that we did.

MÖTLEY CRÜE

FTW

SHOUT AT THE DEVIL TOUR '84

SPECIAL GUESTS

From the days of the strictly functional backstage pass.

Kevin Estrada Collection

HANOI ROCKS VOCALIST MICHAEL MONROE:

I stayed behind with Andy McCoy over here for a few days. It didn't really sink in. I just wanted to stay here, and it was hard to believe what happened and I was kind of in a daze. We hung out with Nikki and Tommy and they were really very nice and felt really bad about it, and it was just a really tough time for us. But you know, maybe for three or five days, I flew back, went and saw Razzle's body, and that was the first time I saw the Hollywood sign. I wanted to see it, but I just couldn't believe that he was dead, and for a long time I got chills when I saw the Hollywood sign after that, whenever I came back here. So it was kind of creepy for me. As for whether those guys were influenced by us, you know, I didn't think that. I thought they were very nice, and they were friends. I met them before in London and we hung out at Andy's place one time, and they were always pretty nice and friendly. They were around the same time, so I don't know if they were influenced by us or not.

NOVEMBER 24, 1984 Tommy marries his Canadian stripper girlfriend Candice; amidst much fighting, the marriage ends after three months and he moves on to Tawny Kitaen, later made famous through her association with David Coverdale.

DECEMBER 1, 1984 Nikki goes on a holiday to Martinique with photographer Neil Zlozower and Ratt guitarist Robbin Crosby, who he had been crashing with.

DECEMBER 8, 1984 Finnish glam rock darlings Hanoi Rocks arrive for two high-profile showcase gigs in California, their second visit to the States and first to California, where they had proven to be a huge influence on the nascent hair metal scene. After partying upon arrival with Mötley Crüe in Redondo Beach, Vince and drummer Razzle jump in Vince's Pantera sports car to head off for additional refreshments. Vince loses control of the car, killing Razzle and seriously injuring two occupants of the vehicle that they had hit. Vince is charged with vehicular manslaughter and DUI.

VICKY HAMILTON:

What really surprises me is when anybody does anything on the glam metal thing is how they just leave out Hanoi Rocks, who, in my mind, were probably one of the most important bands in the genre. And here's the story—they were coming over from Sweden to play here, and they had a gig at the Palace, and I worked really, really hard to get Poison on the opening slot of that show. That's when Vince Neil and Razzle . . . when Razzle was killed in that car accident. Hanoi Rocks probably would have been the hugest band of that scene, because nobody was more beautiful than Mike Monroe. And it was like, all of those bands had their records and they were stealing from those records. The accident is very well documented, but they were partying in Newport Beach where Vince lived at the time, and had just gone to go get another case of beer or whatever, and they just shouldn't . . . they were drunk, basically. And I hear that Mike Monroe is here now and writing again. I just feel that Mike Monroe got totally ripped off. It's like, the metal guys and the glam guys were like piranhas. If they saw something cool they stole it from the other band, and some of the bands that should have got the credit for it didn't get it.

NEW ALBUM & TAPE OUT NOW!
THE LAST COMMAND
W.A.S.P.

Long history between Nikki and Blackie, but more importantly, by the mid-'80s, W.A.S.P. had made some headway as a nastier alternative to the Crüe. Author's Collection

1985

JANUARY 9, 1985 *Shout at the Devil* is certified double platinum, as a bearded and distraught Vince is charged in Razzle's death and ordered into thirty days of rehab. Completing the rehab, Vince is convinced that he is a pariah and that his career is effectively finished. There is even talk of Michael Monroe replacing him in Mötley Crüe. Management, however, is supporting him by showering gifts upon him if he can stay sober. Meanwhile Mick is drinking heavily as his relationship with Linda disintegrates.

FEBRUARY 17, 1985 Nikki is intrigued with court jesters and historical theatre styles as he works toward the conceptual feel that will encompass at least the visuals of the band's forthcoming third album. Preliminary recordings are made on a record provisionally entitled *Entertainment or Death*. "Home Sweet Home" is an early work, with Tommy performing the signature keyboard line on a modest Roland keyboard, at the behest of producer Tom Werman, who proposed a switch to the electronic from grand piano. Mick is recorded mostly at Cherokee, where the rest of he work is captured at the Record Plant and, significantly with respect to drums, Pasha, lending the band's forthcoming third record a distinctive sound shared by the likes of W.A.S.P., Quiet Riot, Icon, and Kick Axe. All told, $200,000 is spent on the album, a considerable sum at the time.

VINCE NEIL ON RESTITUTION:

We know PDAP is underfunded and they have a good treatment program. It's like Alcoholics Anonymous for the kids. Our Forum benefit should pay the salaries of five or six counsellors per year. The whole band has come to the realization that the lives to be saved by a program like this are our own audience. That's also why there is the message on the inner sleeve of *Theatre of Pain*. (*Faces*, 1985)

APRIL 23, 1985 Nikki receives an award at Elektra's Mexican branch office for Mötley being the most popular band in Mexico.

MAY 1985 Night Ranger issue their *7 Wishes* album; a track called "Night Machine" features Vince and Tommy on backing vocals.

MAY 23, 1985 Vince and Beth Lynn tie the knot, in LA.

JUNE 17, 1985 As further atonement for his part in Razzle's death, Vince receives a certificate of completion of a training program sponsored by the Palmer Drug Abuse Program.

PRODUCER TOM WERMAN:

Those records were difficult to make, because of their heroin habit. Nikki was very slow, and not a great bass player. He got better as time went on. Tommy was a great drummer. And Mick was a very underrated guitar player. And it took me forever to get the vocals. Vince would try, but he never prepared. You know, he'd get one hour sleep and come in and do his vocals. He would work hard, but he never prepared. And I did quite a bit of work on those records, especially on *Theatre of Pain*, which would have been a disaster because of the drugs.

NIKKI SIXX:

We toured for thirteen months for *Shout at the Devil*. The band has always been extremist, eccentric. We did more drugs, fucked more girls, drank more alcohol, got into more fistfights, blew more bands off the stage and it was full-on all the time. When we got off the road we were millionaires, drug addicts, alcoholics, sex addicts, and fuckin' rock stars. And we made an album that is that. The album is drug-, alcohol-, and pussy-influenced. I mean it's harsh. And I think some of the focus was off because of that. But there are some brilliant moments at the same time—"City Boy Blues" is great. But it was a mess; it was what it was. It was our sort of time. It was like a haze.

JUNE 21, 1985 Mötley Crüe issue their third album, *Theatre of Pain*, which reaches #6 in *Billboard*, after opening its rise at #90. The album is dedicated to deceased Hanoi Rocks drummer Razzle.

VINCE NEIL:

We had the momentum of being on the road for so long, and the success of *Shout at the Devil*. But without that, I don't think it would have done so well. And with MTV being so supportive of "Home Sweet Home" and "Smokin' in the Boys Room."

SPENCER PROFFER:

Mötley Crüe wound up making their record at Pasha. Tommy Lee thought we had a great drum sound and wanted to replicate that, so they came in to Pasha. I didn't produce it, but it was there, and Doc and I became friends back then. We are still friends. He's the best rock manager on the planet, and a great honest guy with a lot of vision. Doc was cheering for me big time. Because he couldn't get Mötley Crüe signed either.

UNSPEAKABLE ACTS.

MÖTLEY CRÜE. THEATRE OF PAIN.

The curtain rises on the 3rd thundering album destined to rip you out of your front row seat. THEATRE OF PAIN, Act I—the showstopper single, "Smokin' In The Boys Room."

Produced by Tom Werman for Julia's Music.
Management: Doc McGhee and Doug Thaler for McGhee Entertainment.

On Elektra Music Cassettes, Records, & Compact Discs.

MÖTLEY CRÜE
THEATRE OF PAIN

Warning: Contains sonic fury. Keep hands and face clear of speakers when playing.
© 1985 Elektra/Asylum Records, A Division of Warner Communications, Inc.

Unspeakable threads, more like.
Author's Collection

Author's Collection

JUNE 24, 1985 A cover of Brownsville Station's "Smokin' in the Boys Room," backed with "Use It or Lose It," is issued as the new album's debut single—almost recorded instead was a remake of "Mississippi Queen." Spending fifteen weeks on the chart, the track peaked at #16; it had done well for the scrappy Detroit rockers that wrote it as well, reaching #3 for them back in 1973. On the US picture sleeve, Nikki is pictured in what looks somewhat like a court jester outfit, underscoring his aesthetic for the album cycle. The song features Willie Nelson's harmonica player Mickey Raphael.

JULY 7-15, 1985 Mötley kick off their *Theatre of Pain* tour with seven dates in Japan, representing the band's first Japanese campaign ever. At this point, Mick switches from Gibson guitars to Kramers, utilizing Kramer Explorers, Barettas, and Pacers. Upon returning, Tommy cooks up a romance with Heather Locklear.

> **VINCE NEIL:** I didn't know how the fans would react to me after the accident. I didn't know if they saw me smiling, if they'd go, "How can that guy be out there smiling after what just happened?" Or if I was onstage, frowning, if they'd say, "Why doesn't this guy try to loosen up?" I didn't know how to react. That was always in the back of my mind until I actually got out onstage. Then it was like, hey man, this is my life, this is my job. (*Circus*, 1986)

JULY 31-DECEMBER 21, 1985 The epic *Theatre of Pain* tour blankets the US and Canada, with support from Y&T, who a short few years ago Mötley used to support.

LEONARD HAZE: You know, they reciprocated more than anybody, I would say, of bands we had given gigs to. When they gave us the *Theatre of Pain* tour, they had people offering them to pay for their tour buses and to pay them to play nightly. Because that was a huge album at the time. And then we won the Cashbox award for the year, of, you know, percentage sold seats, big-ticket award or whatever it was; it was them and us, and we did ninety-two percent business across the country. We started off making not a lot of dough on that tour, hundred bucks a night, and we ended up making like $3,000 a show, because we were good for . . . That was the funny thing about Y&T, is we were good for 2,000 to 5,000 tickets, depending on where we were. In blue states we did better than the red. But, you know, around the edges the country, like the coasts, and parts of the Midwest, we were good for a lot of tickets.

I'd bet that Harvey and Corky have a few good stories to tell. John Chronis Collection

The bill is now flipped, as Y&T are supporting Mötley. Toronto, 1985. Author's Collection

BUFFALO MEMORIAL AUDITORI
CONCERT BOWL · BUFFALO, NEW YORK
HARVEY and CORKY present
MÖTLEY CRÜE
Special Guest
Y & T
Theatre of Pain Tour
No Resale · No Refund · No Exchange

RGHT I
FLOOR
Fri. Oct. 11, 1985-8:00 PM

FRIDAY
OC
1
198
8:00 P

Q107 PRESENTS
A CPI PRODUCTION
MÖTLEY CRÜE
with special guest Y&T
MAPLE LEAF GARDENS 8:30 P.M
TICKETS: $18.50 & s.c.
TONIGHT!
TICKETS AVAILABLE AT THE BOX OFFICE

AUGUST 1, 1985 Lizzie Grey and London finally get a record out. *Non-Stop Rock* is issued by metal-specializing, mid-sized indie Shrapnel Records, after many additional lineup changes throughout the early '80s. At one point the band included among its ranks Izzy Stradlin from Guns N' Roses as well as Cinderella drummer Fred Coury.

AUGUST 2, 1985 Brownsville Station's Cub Koda joins the band onstage in New Haven, Connecticut, for "Smokin' in the Boys Room." Never a dull moment, two days later in Providence, Vince is pulled into the crowd by his scarf and emerges back onstage wearing no pants. He runs offstage and quickly improvises, putting on a pair of Tommy's stage underwear to finish the set.

LEONARD HAZE:

I remember one night, we were sitting in the hotel room, it's like for four, five in the morning. Nikki's like, "I'm hungry. What do ya got?" And I go, "I've got some Cap'n Crunch." And he goes, "Any milk?" "No." He pours Jack Daniel's on the Cap'n Crunch, and he's eating Jack Daniel's and Cap'n Crunch. And he goes, "Come on, try it." "You gotta be kidding me." So he goes, "No, it's pretty good." I took a bite, and I spit it out and he goes, "It really wasn't, but I just had to lie to you anyway" (laughs).

AUGUST 22, 1985 *Theatre of Pain* is certified platinum two months after its release date, achieving the band's highest chart placement yet as well, at #6. Meanwhile, on tour, the band have learned how to mainline Jack Daniel's and gin, while Vince is chastised for any drinking at all, given his legal troubles. To try and maintain a good headspace, Vince is working toward an eventual red belt in Tang Soo Do karate. Proceeds from some Mötley shows are donated to drug abuse causes.

NIKKI SIXX:

Later with Tom Werman, he kinda took on a bit of that Roy Thomas Baker. You know, he all of a sudden started producing all these LA bands and he started becoming quite hot. And we did *Theatre of Pain*, which was really a fucking mess. It's just a pile of rubbish, the whole fucking record, with a few moments of maybe brilliance. And because he was the guy who did *Shout at the Devil*, he didn't really know how to control us, or to do what it is we needed to do to make the follow-up to *Shout at the Devil*.

SEPTEMBER 1, 1985 *Shout at the Devil* and *Theatre of Pain* are each certified two times platinum.

SEPTEMBER 19, 1985 Dee Snider, Frank Zappa, and John Denver testify at the senate hearing concerning the Parents Music Resource Center's campaign against obscenity in rock music. Mötley Crüe are represented in the PRMC's list of "Filthy Fifteen" nasty songs, with *Shout at the Devil*'s "Bastard."

SEPTEMBER 20, 1985 In the car crash incident, Vince is sentenced to thirty days in jail, to be served once the tour is over, plus community service and a large cash settlement.

SEPTEMBER 30, 1985 Signature power ballad "Home Sweet Home" is issued as a single, backed with "Red Hot." The song reaches a mere #89 in *Billboard* (and later, as the rerecorded "Home Sweet Home '91," #37). It is Mötley Crüe's biggest song on which Vince Neil gets a writing credit, his second most notable commercial success being "Wild Side"—Vince is credited on very few high-profile Mötley Crüe tracks. Carrie Underwood scores a hit with the track in 2009. The song bears similarities to "Home Tonight," from Aerosmith's *Rocks* album, a key influence on the band. Despite its poor performance on the charts, over the years "Home Sweet Home" has become one of a handful of the band's most beloved anthems.

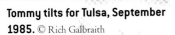

Tommy tilts for Tulsa, September 1985. © Rich Galbraith

VINCE NEIL ON NIKKI WRITING MOST OF THE LYRICS:

Well, I mean Nikki does a great job with them, so I have no aspirations. It doesn't matter to me where they come from as long as they are good. Sure, I would always sit down with Nikki and say that syllable isn't going to work here or the phrasing . . . there's always give or take when you sit down to record it. But the lyrics were always cool, I liked the lyrics. And that's just the way it's always been in the band. He's always been a good lyricist. So why fuck with a good thing?

A&A Welcomes...

MÖTLEY CRÜE

Live In Concert • October 18th at Maple Leaf Gardens

MÖTLEY CRÜE
Theatre Of Pain
cassette or lp

6.97
each

Get details in store for your chance to win a genuine
Nikki Sixx, Hamer Bass Guitar - autographed of course

A&A-sponsored ad for Toronto
show. A&A was one of Canada's
biggest record store chains of
the era. John Chronis Collection

OCTOBER 4, 1985 The band play the Summit in Texas in Houston, which produces some of the video footage used in the "Home Sweet Home" video, with Reunion Arena, Dallas, utilized as well. The video will become one of the band's most popular, spending three months on MTV's daily request chart until the station instigated the "Crüe Rule," limiting requests and subsequent plays.

NOVEMBER 9, 1985 W.A.S.P. issue their second album, *The Last Command*. As mentioned, the album's celebrated opening track "Wild Child" had been offered by Blackie Lawless to Nikki for use in Mötley Crüe. In any event, W.A.S.P. gain notoriety as a darker and more shock-rocking version of Mötley Crüe.

MICK ON GETTING CLASSIFIED AS A HAIR METAL BAND: I think it's part of our growing process. You know, we came out all guns blazing and stuff. It's however people want to categorize or cubbyhole you, or whatever the heck. It doesn't matter. It's all about the music to me. And that's what really put us on the map, as the band, as Mötley Crüe. It's not the makeup and the costuming and stuff that we wore at at the time, it was the music. That's what did it for us.

Tulsa, Oklahoma,
September 29, 1985.
© Rich Galbraith

Y&T'S LEONARD HAZE:

You know, I put live chickens onstage with Mötley Crüe on the last night of that tour, *Theatre of Pain*. But the stories . . . mud wrestling in hotels. Tommy and I took over radio stations, and we'd be playing records like the "fuck you" song by Harry Nilsson, crazy stuff like that. Oh man, Tommy getting married and calling me. He's in Vegas. "Dude, you gotta come and get me." "Why, what's up?" "I just married another stripper, man. You gotta come get me." "What?! You did what?" "Yeah, I got drunk and married a fuckin' stripper, man. Come get me." Him and I used to . . . we had a game called Riot House Horseshoes. And what it was is, we'd get on the balcony of the Hyatt House on Hollywood Boulevard and Sunset, and we'd get a large cheese pizza, and the object of the game was to land pizza pieces on top of police cars. If you landed it on the hood, and stopped the car, that . . . you won, boom, game's over. And it was very dangerous, because now you gotta get out of there, because they're looking for you. And if it lands on the top of the car, chances are it's gonna slide onto the hood when they hit the brakes.

DECEMBER 21, 1985 After the *Theatre of Pain* tour ends, Vince heads to the Cayman Islands, where he runs into Jon Bon Jovi and Pat Travers and jams with them every night at the bar.

DECEMBER 25, 1985 Tommy proposes to Heather.

1986

JANUARY 22-MARCH 3, 1986 The *Theatre of Pain* campaign shifts to Europe, support provided by Cheap Trick.

FEBRUARY 14, 1986 Nikki almost dies, overdosing on heroin in the company of a dealer and Hanoi Rocks' Andy McCoy after a show at the Hammersmith Odeon on London.

MARCH 3, 1986 To close out the European tour, on the last date in France, the band is joined onstage by Ratt's Warren DeMartini and Def Leppard's Phil Collen.

APRIL 1986 Nikki turns his new Sherman Oaks home with girlfriend Nicole into a dark drug den of paranoia. They soon part and he takes up with Prince protégé Vanity.

MAY 10, 1986 Tommy marries Heather in a ceremony involving 500 attendees, including members of Ratt, Autograph, Night Ranger, and Quiet Riot. An epic, violent fight between the happy couple ensues while on honeymoon in the Grand Caymans and the newlyweds are eventually ejected. Meanwhile manager Doc McGhee attempts to detox Nikki on his own over a fraught five-day period, after which Sixx is sent to specialist Bob Timmons, with relapsing soon to follow.

JUNE 13, 1986 Nikki and Gene Simmons contribute musically to the John Stamos film *Never too Young to Die*. Nikki's new girlfriend Vanity is the co-star.

JUNE 15, 1986 Vince begins his thirty days in jail (he would serve eighteen). He is also sentenced to 200 hours of community service and five years' probation for the crash that killed Hanoi Rocks drummer Razzle. He is also ordered to pay $2.6 million in restitution to the gravely injured occupants of the other vehicle involved in the crash. Around the same time, Vince, Beth, and daughter Elizabeth moving in to their new $1.5 million Porter Ranch estate.

JULY 1, 1986 After Vince is released from prison, he and a friend drive around to locate his new house. He has to break into the place to find out that Beth had left him.

JULY 25, 1986 An action film starring Anthony Michael Hall called *Out of Bounds* is released. Although collaboration did not come to fruition, Nikki says that "Nona," a short instrumental dedicated to his recently deceased grandmother, was the product of working on music for this movie. The track appears as a bonus track on the reissue of *Girls, Girls, Girls*.

AUGUST 2, 1986 Cinderella issue their debut *Night Songs* album. The record would notch sales of three times platinum, as would 1988 follow-up *Long Cold Winter*. With Mötley running on fumes, competitors are starting to surface.

AUGUST 18, 1986 Bon Jovi issue their smash hit third album, *Slippery When Wet*, which goes diamond in America for sales of over ten million copies. The bad news for Mötley is that the competition for rock fans' attention is continuing to heat up. The good news is that bands are demonstrating that there's something to be gained by crossing the border into Canada and recording in Vancouver.

TOMMY LEE ON THE BAND'S THIRD ALBUM:

We're going in the same direction as before, but this record's more progressive. It's a really cool style— bluesy rock 'n' roll— it's good, it's hard and dancey at the same time. I'm just freaking out on the album, because the songs are so much better. So is the band. After being on the road for thirteen months you naturally improve. You know what's really insane? We did a ballad on the album, and I play piano on it. For Mötley, that's like, "What?" For us to do something like that is a miracle. (*Hit Parader*, 1985)

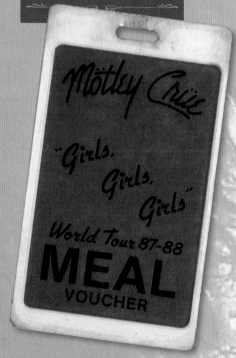

Mötley Crüe "Girls, Girls, Girls" World Tour 87-88 MEAL VOUCHER

Author's Collection

Typical UK ad selling tour dates as well as fancy editions of singles. Author's Collection

Soon this look would be gone, although its replacement wouldn't be much easier on the eyes. © Kevin Estrada

MÖTLEY CRÜE

— THE SINGLE —

SMOKIN' IN THE BOYS ROOM
WITH
HOME SWEET HOME
(Remix)

SPECIAL LIMITED EDITIONS
3-TRACK 12" INCLUDES FREE TOUR POSTER
— ALSO AVAILABLE —
2 INTERLOCKING SHAPED PICTURE DISCS
COLLECT THE SET!

ON TOUR — FEBRUARY

Thursday 6th	MANCHESTER, Apollo
Friday 7th	NEWCASTLE, City Hall
Saturday 8th	EDINBURGH, Playhouse
Sunday 9th	BIRMINGHAM, Odeon
Monday 10th	CARDIFF, St. Davids Hall
Wednesday 12th	NOTTINGHAM, Royal Concert Hall
Thursday 13th	SHEFFIELD, City Hall
Friday 14th	LONDON, Hammersmith Odeon
Saturday 15th	LONDON, Hammersmith Odeon

ALSO AVAILABLE: 'THEATRE OF PAIN' — LP · CASSETTE · CD

TLEY CRÜE ARE: NIKKI SIXX · VINCE NEIL · MICK MARS · TOMMY LEE

DISTRIBUTED BY **wea** RECORDS LTD. Ⓦ A WARNER COMMUNICATIONS CO.

AUGUST 22, 1986 Mötley perform at a celebratory all-star jam at the Roxy, which includes members of Autograph, Dio, Kiss, and King Kobra.

SEPTEMBER 1986 The band sign a new six-album agreement with Elektra.

SEPTEMBER 22, 1986 Alice Cooper, fresh from rehab and armed with a new record called *Constrictor*, returns to attempt a wrestling back of the shock-rock throne he owned in the early '70s, before acceding to Kiss for the back half of that decade.

OCTOBER 1986-MARCH 1987 The band work with returning producer Tom Werman on what will become their fourth album at One to One, Rumbo, and Conway Recording Studios.

OCTOBER 27, 1986 Elektra issues a forty-minute VHS called *Uncensored*, which goes double platinum.

DECEMBER 16, 1986 Guns N' Roses issue a faux-indie live EP called *Live ?!*@ Like a Suicide* and Mötley find themselves up against some stiff local competition in what one might call the "dirty hair metal" category.

DECEMBER 25, 1986 Nikki spends Christmas alone in his Van Nuys mansion in a paranoid drug haze.

CONGRATULATIONS
1985 CIRCUS MAGAZINE
READERS' POLL WINNERS!

MÖTLEY CRÜE
BEST ARTIST!

MÖTLEY CRÜE
BEST Concert

MICK MARS
BEST Guitarist

NIKKI SIXX
BEST Bassist
and
BEST Songwriter

THANKS, FOR USING
ERNIE BALL
THE *PLAYERS'* STRINGS!

Delivered in unmarked brown paper bag. John Chronis Collection

Circus **and its readers were big supporters of the band in the '80s.** Author's Collection

Tommy and a cuddly stuffed friend. © Kevin Estrada

1987

JANUARY 12, 1987
Mötley begin writing and recording the follow-up to *Theatre of Pain*. Nikki loses weight as he tries a methadone program. Through this time, he comes up with "Five Years Dead," based on a 1937 book by Bernard Falk; "Wild Side"; "Dancing on Glass"; "You're All I Need"; and unused tracks "Hollywood Nights" and "Veins."

MARCH 7, 1987 Mixing of the band's fourth record is completed, at LA's Conway Recording Studios.

MARCH 24, 1987 Nikki and Tommy fly to New York to oversee mastering of the new record.

APRIL 1987 Vince marries nineteen-year-old mud wrestler and model Sharise Lee Ann Ruddell, who births him daughter Skylar. Vince had met her mud wrestling at the Tropicana, that night bringing the crew back to his suburban Northridge home to wrestle for himself and his friends at Neil's Naughty Nightie Pool Party.

Blinding, yes, but fortunately this is as glam as Vince would get. © Kevin Estrada

APRIL 7, 1987 Whitesnake issue their smash hit self-titled record, proving that old-timers can also make strides within the "hair metal" scene that was invented in large part through the success of Mötley Crüe in the early '80s.

APRIL 13, 1987 The Wayne Isham video shoot for "Girls, Girls, Girls" taking place at the Seventh Veil devolves into yet another night of drinking. Nikki spends the next few weeks looking into options for cleaning up. Having missed his grandmother's funeral, he even has his grandfather Tom over at the house to try keep an eye on him.

PRODUCER TOM WERMAN, ON HAVING A SOUND:

If there was, I would like to think that it was a fluid, locomotive rhythm. And a prominence of rhythm guitar, doubled rhythm guitar licks, around which the song is based. That's the way I listen to music. The strongest thing to me about rock 'n' roll is the good, elementary, catchy, basic guitar lick, as in "Girls, Girls, Girls." Everyone knows what a hook is, but I prefer to build a song around a real driving guitar hook.

TOMMY LEE:

Myself and Nikki wrote that song. At that time, we were touring so much and I think we must have visited every single strip club on the planet. We were like, you know what? We gotta write about this. We have to write a song about that experience. And the title was like, you're driving down the street and you always see "Girls Girls Girls" in neon lights and it's like OK, let's do it.

MAY 11, 1987 Mötley Crüe release "Girls, Girls, Girls" as the first single from the forthcoming album of the same name, backed with "Sumthin' for Nuthin'." The future stripper anthem peaks at #12 in *Billboard*, sticking to the charts for fifteen weeks. That's producer Tom Werman revving one of the guys' Harleys for the intro to the song.

VINCE NEIL:

Girls, Girls, Girls is probably one of my most favorites, but *Theatre of Pain*, I didn't really like that album that much at all. The songwriting was just terrible except maybe for "Home Sweet Home." But there was just a lot of really great songs on *Girls, Girls, Girls*—"Girls, Girls, Girls" and "Wild Side"—and it sounded a lot better, beefier sounding, with just better-written songs.

NIKKI SIXX:

It's what "Dope Show" is for Marilyn Manson, against *Antichrist Superstar*. You can see the parallel: *Antichrist Superstar/Shout at the Devil*; *Theatre of Pain*, with what Marilyn Manson is doing now. They're doing the same thing. They are rebelling against themselves. I think we were getting so much heat for focusing more on the way we looked. So it was like *Girls, Girls, Girls* we decided, you know what? Let's just go leather and motorcycles, because we were all into that. We were like a gang, and don't forget, there was high drug addiction at that time.

MAY 15, 1987 Mötley Crüe issue their fourth album, *Girls, Girls, Girls*, which debuts at #5 and peaks at #2 in *Billboard*, kept from the top by the concurrent issue of Whitney Houston's smash second album, *Whitney*, which as of this writing is nine times platinum.

Goodnight, LA, 1986. Note that even Tommy made sure to fly the glam freak flag, even if it's only bottoms.
© Kevin Estrada

A fit-looking Mick with
one of his coolest axes.
© David Plastik

Vince in a *Girls, Girls, Girls* mood, May 1987.
© David Plastik

Leather 'n' . . . studs?
© David Plastik

JUNE 19-NOVEMBER 29, 1987 Mötley hit every corner of the US and Canada on the first leg of their *Girls, Girls, Girls* tour, supported by Whitesnake. By now, Mick has introduced Kramer Custom Shop Telecasters to his arsenal. Tommy is fitted inside a drum cage that can spin around and upside down, the whole system costing $80,000. For the first time, the band decided to try their luck with a couple of backup singers, hiring on Donna McDaniel and Emi Canyn. Drugs are rampant during this time, with Mick drinking vodka heavily to dull the pain of his degenerative disease. Mick begins seeing backup singer Emi Canyn, which the band disapproves of, ostracizing him and making him want to quit the band.

TOMMY LEE ON HIS LOVE OF THEATRICS:

I think it came out of boredom. If there isn't too much going on in some part of this song, and all I have to do is hold down the fort, I would just get as fucking showy and as cool to watch as possible. You have to admit, it's no fun to just watch somebody go um, ah, um, ah, um, am (mimes a simple beat). I think the coolest way to do it is to try and make it look easy, and make it look like a big flow. So if you make it look fun, and you're flailing your arms around, and bouncing sticks off the rims, people can dig it. This dude is having fun, you know? He's taking something that is very simple, and just making it more entertaining. I like that, and same with the drum solo. The standard, "OK, here it is," this is usually the part of the show where everybody goes to get a beer. You know, I'm going to keep these motherfuckers in the room, because they've got to check this out, you know? So during the drum solo, I have to do something else that nobody else does. If it's fuckin' spinning around, or if I have to shoot myself out of a cannon, I don't care. These people have to walk out of here going, "I can't believe what I just saw! That dude is insane!"

VINCE NEIL:

Everybody always got along with Tom. He was a cool dude; I liked him. I think he did a great job on *Shout at the Devil*. I don't think he did a good job with *Theatre of Pain*; it was way too slick and it just didn't have the balls to it that the other albums had. Then he turned around and did *Girls, Girls, Girls*, and did a great job with that record. So yeah, it was good working within him. If you notice, we changed every year. We only had a dark image for *Shout at the Devil*—that was it. And then when people started doing that, we completely went the other way with the glam thing with *Theatre of Pain*. If you take those records out and look at them, I'm wearing pink on the back of that. And in a sense, *Theatre of Pain* was a rebellion against *Shout at the Devil*. And then when people started doing that, we went to more of a street look with *Girls, Girls, Girls*. We never, ever stayed the same. We just wanted to stay steps ahead of everybody else.

JULY 11, 1987 Repeating the sales path of its predecessor, *Girls, Girls, Girls* is certified platinum two months after its release, reaching double platinum on September 16th. The album yields three hit singles, with the final one, "You're All I Need" (backed with "Wild Side") being a dark and veiled story of a girlfriend, Nicole, who Nikki believed cheated on him. Jon Bon Jovi called the track the best ballad Mötley had ever written.

NIKKI SIXX ON WATCHING VINCE WORK WITH TOM:

You know, Vince is like heroin chic. Vince can be drunk and rock 'n' roll and looking at his watch because he's got four strippers waiting for him in the parking lot, and pull it off. What those albums would have been if somebody would have said no to me, no to Tommy, no to Vince, and no to Mick, I don't know. We'll never know. But we know what *Dr. Feelgood* is. We know what happened. And *Girls, Girls, Girls*, Tom Werman, by then, was just as fucked up as we were. And that was just a fucking abortion, in my opinion. We really produced that record on our own, because it was more of a lifestyle record. We just kind of brought the lifestyle and put it on tape. At that point, it was time for him to go. I'd heard he had problems of his own, even back to the Ted Nugent days. And you see, we didn't really know about that stuff, and even if we did, it wouldn't matter. You know, what a band like Mötley Crüe is, it's like trying to break a horse. You need to know when to let the horse kick and you need to know when to lay in and not let it get away with bullshit. There were times when we needed for him to have a stronger personality. Much as what Bob Rock had. Bob Rock was able to let us be a band, but at the same time be like, you know what? It's not good enough and we're not going to go home until it's done. That's what we needed after doing *Theatre of Pain* and *Girls, Girls, Girls*.

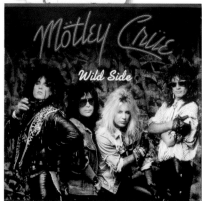

Most fans agree that this was the best song from a record low on batteries. Author's Collection

JULY 18, 1987 The band play Market Square Arena in Indianapolis, which produces the footage used for the "Wild Side" live performance video. The band runs through the song twice, while celebrated director Wayne Isham captures all the angles.

Mick, slightly unclear on the concept. © Kevin Estrada

JULY 21, 1987 Guns N' Roses issue their classic debut record, *Appetite for Destruction*. Mötley Crüe are summarily replaced as the standard-bearers of bad boy rock 'n' roll of an LA disposition.

JULY 22, 1987 *Too Fast for Love* is certified platinum in the US.

AUGUST 10, 1987 "Wild Side" is issued as a single, backed with "Five Years Dead."

TOMMY LEE:

That's another one that Nikki and I wrote. That was my first . . . I sort of brought in my new technology to Mötley Crüe. At that time, in 1984, is when I bought my first Macintosh and I was experimenting with recording direct to disc and using sequencers, so that makes those gun sounds in that track. I sort of brought that in and I was trying to get Mötley Crüe to plunge forward, mine new territory with some sequencers and some electronics. So "Wild Side" was written on a computer. See, a lot of people don't know that about me. They just think that, I don't know, the songs just appear or something. And I've been writing music for a long time. You know, I got really frustrated at one point. As a songwriter, if every time I felt the urge to write a song, I have to call three other band members and say "Come over, I want to write this song," that's when I started going, "I've got to learn guitar." Because I can't always have Mick Mars here, or bass, because Nikki isn't always around. And I fuckin' better learn how to sing, because I hear melodies. So I just started doing everything myself, recording it, engineering it, fucking producing it, playing all the instruments, and I would walk out of there with done songs—a whole fucking band. It was just that frustration of not having access to it which made me say, "Okay, I have to learn this stuff."

Kevin Estrada Collection

AUGUST 25, 1987 Vince's clothes and wallet containing $5,000 are stolen before the show in Rochester, New York. Having a bad day, he smashes a jar of mustard against the wall and seriously injures his hand, requiring eight hours of surgery and the wearing of a large cast for a month.

OCTOBER 1987 Aerosmith issue "Dude (Looks like a Lady)" as the second single from their comeback *Permanent Vacation* record. Steven wrote the lyric about Vince, after once at a bar, having to do a double take at this girl picking up girls.

OCTOBER 1, 1987 A substantial earthquake hits LA, but Nikki escapes his house naked with his crack pipe, having to smash a window to get back in after locking his keys inside.

OCTOBER 19, 1987 "You're All I Need" (backed with "All in the Name of . . .") is issued as the third single from *Girls, Girls, Girls*.

OCTOBER 27, 1987 As Whitesnake prepares to leave the Mötley tour, to be replaced by Guns N' Roses, David Coverdale joins the band in Montreal for their rendition of "Jailhouse Rock."

OCTOBER 31, 1987 The band and Wayne Isham shoot a dark, *Taxi Driver*–influenced video for "You're All I Need." Elektra instructs them to lighten it up by adding some band footage, but MTV still bans the video.

NOVEMBER 3, 1987 Guns N' Roses support Mötley Crüe for the first time. On tour, Vince coaches Axl on vocal technique.

DECEMBER 13-18, 1987 The band play five dates in Japan, including three at the Budokan, after a couple days of press and a close call for Vince when he offends four Japanese gangsters by overturning their table because he thought they were making fun of him.

DECEMBER 19, 1987 Back from terrorizing Japan with brawls, blood, arrests, public urination, and much vandalism, the band part. Mick and Emi continue their courtship, Tommy and Heather go home to their new $3M mansion, Vince reconnects with Sharise, and Nikki plans a solo vacation to the southeast. Japanese promoter Mr. Udo says that he will go with Nikki to keep watch, and Doc McGhee does the right thing and goes along, more to protect Mr. Udo than his own charge.

DECEMBER 22, 1987 Back in LA, Nikki, Slash, and Steven Adler party at the Cathouse, with Nikki and Slash both overdosing on heroin. Slash is soon revived but Nikki has turned blue and remains unconscious. Nothing works, but paramedics soon arrive and give him a shot of adrenalin. This is Nikki's famous out-of-body experience, where he claims to have been dead for several minutes. The paramedics wheel Nikki out with the sheet over his face and words spreads quickly that Nikki is gone. In the ambulance, a double shot of adrenaline is applied and Nikki jerks back down into his body and comes to. Two fans holding a vigil for Nikki on the curb wind up driving him home, as the three of them listen to news of his death on the radio. He arrives home at 5:45 a.m., shoots up again, and promptly passes out.

DECEMBER 24, 1987 Fed up, Doc McGhee cancels the upcoming European tour at great expense and tells the band he is quitting them unless they all go into rehab. Even Tommy and Heather had just had a huge dustup, which Tommy blames on his own drinking, as he does most of his fights with romantic partners throughout the years.

John Chronis Collection

NIKKI SIXX:
I don't know if I believe in life after death so much as I believe that there is something out there. Before that I was a non-committal person to religion, although I was a bit spiritual. My eyes opened after the OD. It's hard to explain the experience. (*USA Today*, 2001)

One of the more well-designed and balanced ads ever for a Mötley record. Author's Collection

DECEMBER 25, 1987 Nikki's estranged father dies of a heart attack while in the shower, but Nikki won't find out about it for a decade.

1988

JANUARY 1988 The entire band enter a rehab facility in Tucson, Arizona, scotching a proposed European tour. Also this month, Vince completes his 200 hours of community service arising from the DUI auto crash that killed Hanoi Rocks drummer Razzle and caused other serious injuries.

TOMMY LEE ON CANCELLING THE EUROPEAN TOUR:

We had ten days off in six months; that's not very regular, is it? It's the travelling that really beats you up, not the playing. That's the fucking easy part. It was a last-minute decision; we were planning to come. At the last minute, we just decided not to because if we'd gone we'd not have done as good shows as we were capable, so we said, fuck, we'll cancel there and work on some new material. But we'll start in Europe next year so nobody feels cheated out of the tour. Why go and do some half-assed shows? [*Metal Hammer*, 1988]

Vince at NAMM, 1988. © David Plastik

Tagline ties in nicely with the Mötley record currently flying off the shelves. Author's Collection

FEBRUARY 2, 1988 Lita Ford issues the platinum-selling *Lita*, which includes "Falling in and Out of Love," a cowrite from December 1986 with her old boyfriend Nikki Sixx.

APRIL 1988 Vince, in and out of rehab through the early months of '88, marries Sharise Ruddell, who is encouraged to quit mud wrestling. Three months later, rumors fly that the two had been arguing a lot and have now separated.

MAY 3, 1988 Poison issue their second album, *Open Up and Say . . . Ahh!* which goes five times platinum. Poison are considered the new kids on the hair metal block, overshadowing Mötley, who were a spent force in 1988. Vince's new wife Sharise can be seen posing with Bret Michaels in one of the photos on the inner sleeve to the record. Meanwhile, as discussed, there was also stiff competition from Bon Jovi, with 1986's *Slippery When Wet* (currently twelve times platinum), and Whitesnake, with their 1987 self-titled (currently at eight times platinum). Closest to home, however, will be Guns N' Roses, who soon take over Mötley's mantle as the bad boys of Hollyrock.

SEPTEMBER 1988 Nikki enters a fragile mental state, having kicked heroin, and finding Prozac to level himself out.

NIKKI SIXX: I've had friends over the years say, "I've always wanted to try heroin" and I say "Don't! Don't!" And they ask why? It will be the worst and best journey of your life. It is so enticing. It takes you away from whatever it is you're trying to get away from. I look at it as the greatest painkiller in the world—and why would you need a painkiller? Obviously you're in some form of pain. This to me is an important issue. Addiction is a global epidemic. Drug addiction and alcoholism is rampant. Am I on a soapbox? Am I a preacher? Am I a bumper sticker that says "Don't do drugs?" No. I am telling you my experience. There's a big difference in partying, spring break, having a good time, and being an addict. I'm not telling people don't do whatever you want to do. I'm just saying my experience on heroin ended on a downward spiral into depression and death. (*BW&BK*, 2007)

Vince and Sharise, 1988. © David Plastik

OCTOBER 22, 1988 Nikki and Mick conduct a productive writing session at Mick's house, coming up with "Don't Go Away Mad (Just Go Away)," "Rattlesnake Shake," and a Christmas tune all in one day.

VINCE NEIL:

I bottomed out near the beginning of *Theatre of Pain*, end of *Shout*. And Nikki was the end of the Theatre. No, it was the middle of *Girls*—we had just finished the US tour, and we had to cancel the other part.

NOVEMBER 23, 1988 Elektra issues the Japan-only *Raw Tracks* EP, featuring alternative versions of six Crüe classics. Otherwise, it's a quiet year for Crüe, who play no dates in 1988.

NIKKI SIXX:

We all bottomed out at different times. Tommy is right about the same time, near the end of *Girls*. Mick was the same thing. That's when we all kind of decided to re-evaluate what the band was all about musically and emotionally. We'd been strung out and fucked up for ten years. Hard. Not kidding. It's like there's kidding—there's like Poison? Like kidding, like, "Hey let's go have a party." And then there's like puking up bad smack at a $500-a-night a hotel room in New York City ten minutes before you have to go onstage. Even when we were doing our first session, during "Live Wire," Vince was shooting cocaine (Vince: Because I had a rich girl friend who was a drug dealer). Lovey! She's dead, you know? She got stabbed sixty times in a drug deal. Dead.

Nikki, looking much too healthy, given what we know about his 1988. © David Plastik

DECEMBER 1988 Safety in Numbers, the Mötley Crüe fan club (aka S.I.N. Club), closes up shop.

Tommy looking sideways for some time off. © David Plastik

1989

1989 Billy Idol guitarist Steve Stevens issues *Atomic Playboys*, on Warner. Stevens' next significant gig would be with Vince Neil's solo band. Here, Stevens covers Sweet's "Action," and on Vince's album, the two would address that band's "Set Me Free," with Vince yet again covering Sweet with *Tattoos & Tequila*'s inclusion of "A.C.D.C."

EARLY 1989 Mick and Emi move house. Meanwhile, Tommy and Nikki team up as the Terror Twins, a production company, which results in a flood of demo tapes from bands. Nikki, now sober, is set up on a blind date with Brandi Brandt, Playboy Playmate for October 1987.

FEBRUARY 1989 The band convene at Little Mountain in Vancouver, British Columbia, to begin work on the follow-up to *Girls, Girls, Girls*. What they soon find out is how hard celebrated producer Bob Rock is about to drive them; of note, angering Mick with the precision that Rock demands with respect to the doubling of the guitar tracks. Given a fragile but workable sobriety, the band blow off steam by jogging and working with their personal weight trainer. They proceed to come up with so much material that the band consider issuing two separate single albums, given that their contract forbids a double album. Also recording in Vancouver, Aerosmith are constant companions, but Mötley guys also socialize with Bryan Adams, Jack Blades from Night Ranger, and Cheap Trick's Rick Nielsen and Robin Zander.

Nikki as devil doctor?

Kevin Estrada Collection

FEBRUARY 24, 1989 Mötley guest onstage at a Cheap Trick gig at the Pacific Coliseum in Vancouver.

MAY 11, 1989 Vince and Nikki join Skid Row onstage and help the band perform an encore version of "Live Wire."

MAY 19, 1989 Vince and country legend Willie Nelson play golf together, at a T.J. Martell fundraiser. The next day Vince squares off against comedian Sam Kinison in a softball game that is also a T.J. Martell event.

JULY 11, 1989 Vince undergoes surgery for a deviated septum.

AUGUST 13-14, 1989 Mötley play the massive *Moscow Music Peace Festival* in Moscow, a Doc McGhee antidrug rally arranged through his Make a Difference Foundation. As part of McGhee's penance for drug trafficking charges, he had been ordered to create the foundation, of which the concert was to be the crowning accomplishment. The mission for the extravaganza specifically was to promote world peace and to fight the drug war in the Soviet Union. The show featured heavyweights Cinderella, Ozzy Osbourne, Bon Jovi, Scorpions, and Mötley Crüe, along with baby band Skid Row and local favorites Gorky Park. Ego clashes abounded, with the bad behavior reverberating back to the US, helping to usher in, in popular folklore, the tired demise of "80s metal." In particular, Mötley Crüe was up in arms over McGhee's preferential treatment of Bon Jovi, who he managed along with Mötley at the time, resulting in Tommy Lee punching McGhee, quickly ending the band's relationship with Doc. The band convince Doug Thaler to also break with Doc. Thaler does, forming Top Rock Development Corporation, proceeding to continue on as Mötley's manager.

AUGUST 15, 1989 Aerosmith issue "Love in an Elevator" as an advance single from their forthcoming *Pump* album. Nikki's soon-to-be wife Brandi Brandt plays the elevator operator in the video, Brant also making the cover of the August '89 issue of Playboy, two years after her Playboy debut at eighteen years of age.

NIKKI SIXX ON MÖTLEY SPIRALLING OUT OF CONTROL:

You know, I said to Vince one day—and he was aghast when I told him—"Do you realize that the band is fucking over?!" After *Girls, Girls, Girls*. And he said, "What are you talking about?! We're not over. A sold-out tour . . ." And I said, "You don't realize, we just made two fucking abortions of records. We made two records that might have equalled one. And we can't do it again. We have to fucking get serious now." And if we hadn't gotten serious, I think we would've been over at that point. The fans like the fact that the band was like going to see a car wreck, or a car race. You know, we're waiting to see the crash. It's like *Use Your Illusion I* and *II*. There might be an EP there. You know, there might be an EP between *Theatre* and *Girls*.

AUGUST 28, 1989 "Dr. Feelgood" is issued as the advance single from Mötley's forthcoming album, backed with "Sticky Sweet." The track reaches #6 and stays in the chart for sixteen weeks. "Sticky Sweet" turned out to be the last track written for the album, while "Kickstart My Heart" became the first.

VINCE NEIL:

I knew it was a classic from the time I heard that very first "bomp bomp bomp bomp"— that intro just kind of grabs you. This song has been popular for twenty years. It was funny because I was watching VH1 and they had the Greatest Hard Rock Songs and "Feelgood" was fifteen or something. I was like, "Wow, of all time." Then you have Led Zeppelin and Aerosmith and AC/DC and "Feelgood." I was like, "Wow, that's cool." It's our signature song in some ways." (*Rolling Stone*, 2009)

VINCE NEIL:

I probably liked working with Bob Rock the most. A lot of producers say, "Okay, just go in and just do it," whereas he would actually . . . if I was singing something wrong, or not really wrong, as a producer, he's hearing stuff that I'm not hearing. And he'd stop me and say, "Try to sing it this way." And I would try, and nine times out of ten, it was better than what I was doing. So for a singer, he spent the time rather than just saying, go in sing it, and lay it down, okay, that's great. It was good to actually work on the vocals. But yeah, we love working with Bob. He's a musician and he's also a singer, so he brings out a lot of stuff in me that I didn't even think I could do. He has a confidence in me that I might not have confidence in, to even try, and he brings it out, and I go, "Ah man, that's cool!"

SEPTEMBER 1, 1989 Mötley Crüe issue their fifth album, the Bob Rock–produced *Dr. Feelgood* (working titles: *Monstrous* and *Sex, Sex, and Rock 'n' Roll*). Crafting the record sober and away from distractions, the band turn in what is to be their most critically acclaimed work since *Shout at the Devil*.

TOMMY LEE:

That was first time we worked with producer Bob Rock. We spent the time and money on it and that was a real signature time for us. Everybody was sober then as well and focused all their energy on writing a really great record which is what we needed to do at that point in our career.

SEPTEMBER 5, 1989 Vince punches Guns N' Roses guitarist Izzy Stradlin at the MTV Video Music Awards, as payback for his ill treatment of Vince's wife Sharise the previous month, at the Cathouse. What ensues is a feud between Axl and Vince where Axl repeatedly names a time and place for a fistfight, and then never shows up.

SEPTEMBER 12, 1989 Within a week and a half of the release of Mötley's record, Aerosmith issues *Pump*, which goes on to notch seven times platinum sales, with *Dr. Feelgood* reaching six times platinum.

OCTOBER 3, 1989 Ray DiMano at Elektra calls Tommy on his birthday to inform him that he has a #1 charting record on his hands.

OCTOBER 5, 1989 Mötley play a warm-up club show at the Whisky A Go Go, arriving at the show in an ambulance driven by Sam Kinison. Supporting the spirit of the band's newfound sobriety, Nikki goes the furthest, losing thirty pounds so that he could perform shirtless. The band would still be shooting up, only now it would be B-12 and B-6 supplements.

Garish satin pass for the *Dr. Feelgood* campaign. Author's Collection

VINCE NEIL ON RECORDING *DR. FEELGOOD*:

It was great, although a little tough because we had to live in Vancouver, and most of us basically just flew home on weekends, to LA. So it was hard having to travel back and forth between LA and Vancouver every weekend. But the studio was great, was fun being in there, Bob is a great producer, and it was also cool because Aerosmith was recording the *Pump* album right next door in the same studio and we were good friends with them forever, so it was kind of cool hanging out in the same studio. We were completely sober. We made a pact together and said if we're going to do it and survive as a band we're going to be sober. Because it was always like there was one guy sober and the other guys not. Everybody was kind of like up here, down there, up here, down there. This was the first time we were all in the same spot. So when we recorded *Dr. Feelgood*, we'd move out of LA, up to Vancouver for like nine months, so there were no distractions, just recording. It was good for us because we had Aerosmith right next door to us, and we've been friends with them for a long time, and they were going through the same thing.

OCTOBER 14-OCTOBER 30, 1989 The *Dr. Feelgood* tour opens in mainland Europe, support coming from Skid Row. With the Learjet back at home in LA, the band flies commercial, including some tiny planes, making for some tense moments for Mick Mars and his fear of flying.

OCTOBER 28, 1989 "Dr. Feelgood" becomes Mötley's first Top Ten single, peaking at #6 and going gold, the band's only single to do so.

OCTOBER 30, 1989 At the Zenith in Paris, France, Tommy and his cage are left dangling upside down when a power cord is severed. The accident, which required the removal of the drummer by ladders, also managed to knock out the lights and sound.

NOVEMBER 1-6, 1989 The *Dr. Feelgood* campaign moves over to the UK for five dates.

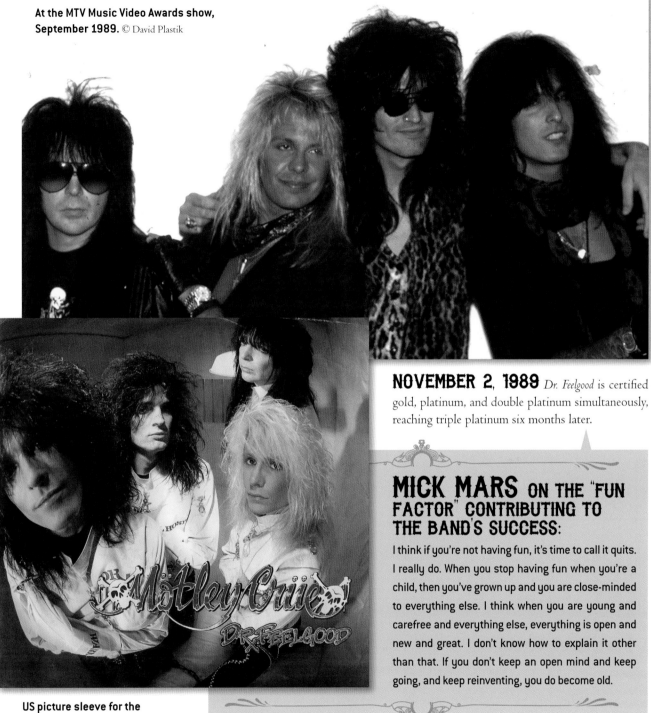

At the MTV Music Video Awards show, September 1989. © David Plastik

US picture sleeve for the trouncing title track from the band's comeback classic.

Tom Wojcik Collection

NOVEMBER 2, 1989 *Dr. Feelgood* is certified gold, platinum, and double platinum simultaneously, reaching triple platinum six months later.

MICK MARS ON THE "FUN FACTOR" CONTRIBUTING TO THE BAND'S SUCCESS:

I think if you're not having fun, it's time to call it quits. I really do. When you stop having fun when you're a child, then you've grown up and you are close-minded to everything else. I think when you are young and carefree and everything else, everything is open and new and great. I don't know how to explain it other than that. If you don't keep an open mind and keep going, and keep reinventing, you do become old.

NOVEMBER 15, 1989 *Shout at the Devil* reaches triple platinum.

NOVEMBER 16, 1989-APRIL 15, 1990 Mötley conduct the massive first leg of their American *Dr. Feelgood* campaign, after rehearsing for five days in San Diego. Support comes from Faster Pussycat and Warrant, and later, Tesla and Johnny Crash. The band lease a private jet previously used by Def Leppard on that band's *Hysteria* tour, outfitting the plane with an advanced home entertainment system and even a small studio.

The cavernous 55,000 seat SkyDome, but in half-sized "Skybowl" configuration. John Chronis Collection

You only tour that long if the record's a hit—and boy, was it a hit. Kevin Estrada Collection

German three-inch CD single for "Dr. Feelgood." Tom Wojcik Collection

Rare laminate dedicated to catering. Tom Wojcik Collection

Vince in his free MTV lid enjoying some downtime, 1989. © David Plastik

ACE FREHLEY:

I used to be kind of an amateur magician (laughs), besides a jokester. So I was in the dressing room with those guys, and I think Sebastian Bach was opening for them. I had come to see Sebastian and hang out, and then I went into the Mötley Crüe dressing room, and I ended up levitating a gallon of milk. And after I had levitated it, it fell over, and the whole floor got covered in milk. It was right before the show (laughs). It was funny as shit. But Mötley Crüe I always thought was a great band, and obviously some of the effects that they used, they got from us. You know, that's the way rock 'n' roll is. Everybody takes from everybody else. And the people that were before you, you get influenced by. But I never took it as an insult or anything like that. I think they're a great band in their own right.

NOVEMBER 20, 1989 The band issue "Kickstart My Heart" as a single, backed with "She Goes Down." The track—appreciated by Tommy for its similarity to Sweet's "Ballroom Blitz"—stalls at #27 but spends sixteen weeks on the charts.

DECEMBER 10, 1989 Mötley's show at the Meadowlands in New Jersey includes guest appearances from Sebastian Bach, Dimebag Darrell, and Ace Frehley, who join the band for a send-up of "Jailhouse Rock."

The '90s

The hair metal that Mötley helped cause and yet so vehemently denied—whatever—was dying a death as grunge so deftly pointed out the facile materialism and petulant diva-mad tantrumness of a genre about to die for good come September 1991 and the release of Nirvana's *Nevermind*. In essence, if musically what Soundgarden and Mudhoney were fed up with was Poison, Warrant, Slaughter, and a now unrecognizable Whitesnake, as people, the members of Mötley Crüe unfortunately were representing everything that was wrong with rock stars, from the wealth-flaunting to the trail of broken homes.

Mötley's response? From an artistic standpoint (glad to be talking about the art), it was actually quite admirable. First off, they toured hard their celebrated 1989 album *Dr. Feelgood*, and then issued a greatest hits album. It contained a new song, "Primal Scream," which has proven through history to be one of the dark-horse classics of the catalogue, and poignant as well, given that Nikki is writing there about his shattered childhood. Next we saw Nikki and Tommy blossoming as artists, as the two worked to push the band forward into the '90s and remain vital through change.

Vince, emblematic of the past, would be cast aside and right out of the band, while Mick would soldier on grumbling. Entering the fold would be a bold choice as replacement for Vince, relative unknown John Corabi. Inconsid-

VHS for the ill-fated Moscow debacle.
John Chronis Collection

erately wrecking things, spending stacks of cash, and learning nothing about the cause of the hating of their old music, the band nonetheless cranked out what is arguably their best album, *Motley Crue*—a grinding sprawl of gnarly modern metal smoked by wicked drums.

It failed commercially—failed meaning, it only went gold—but that's not the band's fault. They had changed their singer, sure (and I bet half the audience thought Vince was the leader of the band), but tastes change and the '90s were unforgiving for hard rock bands, especially bands so tied to the zeitgeist of the directly previous and hugely unfashionable decade.

Management and market forces conspired to coax the band to take Vince back, but lo and behold, after three years of pain, the band turned in another creative triumph in the layered and forward-thinking *Generation Swine*. As armies of detractors wielded pitchforks and declaimed and defamed the band, many of us longtime Mötley watchers were saying "Well played, Nikki and Tommy, well played." Fact is, every hair metal band was trying to make smart music, but *Generation Swine* proved that there were a couple of fearless artists in the band. Indeed, despite the tabloid lives they were leading (no doubt contributing to the band only getting two records out in the '90s), Nikki was quietly proving himself a lover and maker of art, and Tommy was showing enthusiasm as a sound collagist, thinking well beyond the boundaries of the acoustic drum set.

There'd be way more unsavory behavior to test the constitution of any Mötley fan before the decade was out, but back on the art (ah yes, the art): the band would close the decade the way they opened it, with a greatest hits album, this one actually called *Greatest Hits*. And in a second parallel, Nikki would strap some new music to the album, this time the band crafting two of its most joyous and hooky rockers of all time in "Bitter Pill" and "Enslaved." Gone was the overt electro texturing of the *Generation Swine* era, but gorgeously new was an elevated sense of pop hookery, perhaps hinted and tinted by Nikki's appreciation of Cheap Trick. It all bode well for the future of a band that unfortunately would spend the decade variably trying to stay current and just trying to stay . . . which Tommy didn't, announcing his departure from Mötley Crüe in April of 1999.

With late-to-the-hair-farm-party Warrant supporting.
Tom Wojcik Collection

1990

JANUARY 15, 1990 The day after a show in Houston, the band films a video for "Without You" at the Galveston Opera House, making use of a jaguar from a local wildlife refuge.

FEBRUARY 22, 1990 "Dr. Feelgood" fails to pull in a Grammy, beaten to the punch by Living Colour's smash hit "Cult of Personality."

FEBRUARY 28, 1990 America's premier metal magazine, *Circus*, publishes the results of their 1989 Reader's Poll. Mötley wins best band and *Dr. Feelgood* wins best album. Nikki wins best bassist and Tommy wins best drummer, while Vince takes fourth place for vocalist and Mick, fourth place as guitarist. The band also break the top five in the best single, best songwriter, best producer, and best long-form videocassette categories. Finally, the band rank as the #3 disappointment of the year, but also #1 comeback of the year.

NIKKI SIXX ON THE REBUILT MÖTLEY:

It's been so long since we've used anything that we don't really think about it. Everybody else mentions it. The most important thing is the music and the show—our intensity. And when people go, "You guys aren't partying anymore?" We go, "Oh yeah, we're not." It's not part of our lives anymore. We just don't dig the soapbox concept of sobriety. We do it because we want to. We did it because it was a challenge—we thought we could better the band, not for any other reason. If I didn't have the band, I'd still be using everything. Everybody—*everybody*—has tried to be the devil and tempt us, you know, and we're like, "But you don't understand, you can't tempt the devil." I mean, we were the fucking most evil motherfuckers there were when it came to drug use and abuse. And people go, "Come on, dude, just smoke a joint with me!" And we're going, "You don't get it, man. If I smoke a joint with you, I'm gonna spend all your money doing blow all night, I'm gonna wreck your car and I'm gonna fuck your girlfriend. You don't want me to smoke that joint with you, believe me!" (*M.E.A.T.*, 1990)

And it's back to Toronto's Skybowl with, apparently, no need to name the support act.

John Chronis Collection

Q107

Mötley Crüe Dr. Feelgood

SKYDOME. SKYBOWL
MONDAY JUNE 18, 7PM
Tickets $25.50 & $21.50 Plus S.C. Available at the SkyDome Box Office, (First Day, Cash Only), selected TicketMaster outlets, or call 872-1111 to charge
ON SALE THIS MONDAY
FOR MORE CONCERT INFO 538-0088
A CPI PRODUCTION

9598

SEC   ROW   SEAT

GEN. ADM.
JAN 18, 1990

ADMIT ONE THIS DATE ONLY

18

MÖTLEY CRÜE

MISSISSIPPI COLISEUM

BE-BOP PRODUCTIONS & MID-SOUTH CONCERTS PRESENT

JACKSON, MS

THURSDAY
7:30 PM
TAX INCLUDED

NO REFUND PRICE NO EXCHANGE

$17.50

SEC   ROW   SEAT

GEN. ADM.
9598

MOTLEY CRUE

$17.50

JAN 18, 1990

Tom Wojcik Collection

MARCH 12, 1990 Mötley issue ballad "Without You" as a single, backed with "Slice of Your Pie"; working titles for the B-side included "Slice of the Night" and "Slice of Your Life." "Without You" reaches #8 on the charts.

MARCH 21, 1990 *Dr. Feelgood* reaches triple platinum, and within another ten months, four times platinum. Four nights later in Augusta, Georgia, Tommy moons the crowd and is arrested onstage and charged with indecent exposure.

VINCE NEIL:

We got serious and cleaned up. When we recorded *Dr. Feelgood* up in Vancouver, we began to get close again as we were all living in apartments together, and each one of us were in the studio all the time together, whereas previously, one of us wouldn't be in the studio while the others were out—it wasn't like a band thing anymore. *Dr. Feelgood* was a band thing—I'd be singing and I'd look out and see the other guys and they'd be cheering me on, so it was like doing the first album again. (*M.E.A.T.*, 1991)

APRIL 7, 1990 In New Haven, Connecticut, Tommy receives a concussion when his complicated rope system fails at approximately 10:45 and he tumbles backward, butting heads with a concert-goer. He spends the night at Yale-New Haven Hospital, with a spokesman estimating that Tommy might have fallen as far as sixty feet in the mishap. Tommy recalls waking up out of the fall and trying to get back into his kit, only to soon realize that he was in an ambulance.

APRIL 27-MAY 15, 1990 After four months of US dates, the *Dr. Feelgood* tour moves to Australia for five shows and Japan for six. Tommy's wife Heather Locklear and his parents attend in Japan.

MAY 20, 1990 On the way back to the US from Japan, Nikki marries Brandi Brandt in Hawaii.

MAY 28, 1990 "Don't Go Away Mad" is issued as a single, backed with "Rattlesnake Shake." The track peaks at #19. The album's previous two singles had gone Top Ten by this point, pushing *Dr. Feelgood* to sales of 4.5 million only nine months after release. The video for the song features Nikki and Tommy with the sides of their heads shaved.

NIKKI SIXX ON THE VIDEO:

I can't believe the comments we're getting. Fred Coury called me yesterday after seeing the video, and said we look like some psycho punk rockers. I said, "We do?" We don't even think about it; we just do shit like that. We were bored— there's no master plan in rock 'n' roll. Nobody says you have to look any particular way. Maybe next week the whole thing will come off. It's not like we're doing anything new with our hair. Metallica and other speed metal bands have been doing it for a while. We don't really care as long as we have ourselves and the band. The music will pursue and be the most important thing. You see, we see ourselves as pretty normal, like a kid on the street. But I guess we're pretty animated. (*M.E.A.T.*, 1990)

MAY 31-AUGUST 5, 1990 Playing Hawaii on the way back to the US, Mötley continue their blanketing of America, while also incorporating a cross-Canada leg. After all the accounting is in, each member of the band will have amassed $8 million in income.

JOURNALIST STEVE MASCORD:

Lee's kit quivers and is lifted clear to the ceiling while he begins playing to sample tapes of the likes of AC/DC and Cream. The kit floats out into the audience and lowers frighteningly close to their collective heads. Lee, wearing a studded G-string and absolutely nothing else, puts one hand on a pole and leans out over the audience. He looks genuinely in awe of his situation, oblivious to the fact he does this every night. "Look how close I am to you fuckers, man!" he cries. He straps himself back in and keeps drumming. (*Kerrang!*, 1990)

TOMMY LEE ON STAYING SOBER:

It's probably the toughest thing I've ever done. It's like cancer. It's a stupid disease. Every day I want a drink. I feel like a time bomb, like I'm going to snap at any moment. I guess I didn't really love myself a lot. I didn't have very much self-esteem. And I'd just drunk myself into a coma and do massive amounts of other stuff. Heather really helped me. (*Circus*, 1990)

Mixing it up with a die-cut pass. Tom Wojcik Collection

Kevin Estrada Collection

WORKING PERSONNEL

I guess you could call this series of graphics another attempt at a band mascot. Tom Wojcik Collection

JUNE 18, 1990 The band receive their triple platinum awards from the CRIAA, for sales of over 300,000 in Canada. That night the band play Toronto's SkyDome, in half-capacity "Skybowl" configuration, to an audience of 24,000. Support is Tesla, credited with selling a substantial number of tickets on the Canadian leg of the tour, given the success of their second album *The Great Radio Controversy*, which reaches two times platinum. Skid Row's Sebastian Bach takes in the festivities from the press box.

JULY 11, 1990 Vince plays Bobby Black, lead singer of a band in Andrew Dice Clay's notorious *The Adventures of Ford Fairlane*.

JULY 31, 1990 "Same Ol' Situation (S.O.S.)" is issued as the fifth single from *Dr. Feelgood*, backed with "Wild Side." Peaking at #78, the track is credited to all of Mötley Crüe, a rarity in a band where Nikki Sixx takes most of the credits.

TOMMY LEE:

This is the part that sometimes throws people, but I've been singing and playing guitar and writing music like, since '84. No one knew about it unless you read the credits on the Mötley Crüe records. It's weird, like I sort of taught myself to play guitar and sing, because the other guys in the band would never come over to work. It's kind of crazy. So I've got to thank those guys for not showing up. It's like, "Hey man, I've got some ideas; why don't you guys come by?" And Vince would be doing his thing and Mick would be doing his. So it's like, fuck it, I'm going to teach myself to play guitar and sing. And eventually, if you do it enough, you get good at it and I was bringing in full-blown demos, all finished with vocals, drums, guitars, bass, everything, to the band. And at some point it was like, you know what? I can do this on my own as well.

SEPTEMBER 6, 1990 The band play "Don't Go Away Mad" at the MTV Music Awards, at the Universal Amphitheatre in LA.

SEPTEMBER 10, 1990 Nikki's AA meeting includes Rob Lowe, Steve Perry, and Harry Nilsson, soon to be the casualty of the four.

SEPTEMBER 19, 1990 Mick Mars marries Mötley Crüe backup singer Emi Canyn.

OCTOBER 22, 1990 Elektra releases *Dr. Feelgood: The Videos*, which goes platinum.

OCTOBER 30, 1990 Elektra issues *Moscow Music Peace Festival Volume 2*. This second of a two-part VHS campaign features Mötley Crüe, Gorky Park, Ozzy Osbourne, Scorpions, and the concluding jam. *Volume 1* featured Skid Row, Cinderella, and Bon Jovi. Mötley's set for the historical festival of August 13–14, 1989, consisted of "All in the Name of . . . ," "Live Wire," "Smokin' in the Boys Room," "Shout at the Devil," "Looks that Kill," "Wild Side," "Girls, Girls, Girls," and "Jailhouse Rock." The video release offers "All in the Name of . . . ," "Wild Side," and "Girls, Girls, Girls," with Vince also appearing in the festival-closing all-star jam.

1991

1991 The Scream, featuring future Mötley Crüe vocalist John Corabi, issue their first and only album, the Eddie Kramer–produced *Let it Scream*.

JANUARY 25, 1991 Nikki and Brandi welcome a son, Gunnar.

JANUARY 28, 1991 *Dr. Feelgood* wins a hard rock/heavy metal award at the American Music Awards, accepted by both Vince and Tommy. The band prevail over Aerosmith and Poison.

FEBRUARY 1991 Tommy and Heather move into a new spread, a country home on four acres.

FEBRUARY 20, 1991 Mötley is beaten at the Grammys, yet again by Living Colour.

MARCH 26, 1991 Vince and Sharise welcome a daughter, Skylar—Vince's third child, and first with Sharise. Vince, now getting heavily into auto racing, is also drinking heavily. The growing family move house, to Simi Valley.

It remains up for debate how punk rock any of the Mötley guys ever really were. Author's Collection

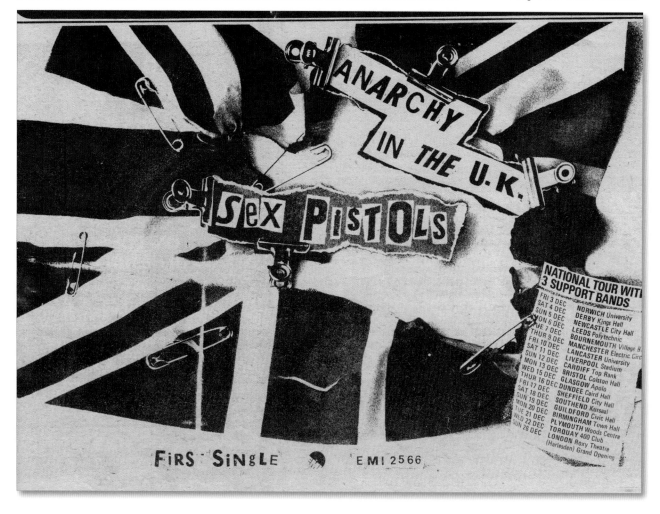

SUMMER 1991

BAND PERSONNEL

Note that the head reads AC/DC.
Tom Wojcik Collection

APRIL 1991 The band form Mötley Records, an imprint of Elektra. Geffen shows interest in luring the band away from Elektra.

VINCE NEIL:

It's Mötley Records now. We renegotiated our deal with Elektra Records, and part of it is that we now have our own record company. We are now able to sign bands and put them out on our own label. We're partners with our manager, Doug Thaler, and hopefully he'll find some acts and we'll stick them on our label. It's something for the future. Just the way things are going right now, we feel we'll have a long future, but we really just take it one record and tour at a time. We have been thinking a lot about it though—we'd like to have a career like the Stones where you're accepted by your old fans, and can make new ones too. It's like another goal of ours. We realize that in this biz, you can't be around forever, so with Mötley Records, we're thinking about our future outside of being a band. (*M.E.A.T.*, 1991)

MAY 1991 Manager Doug Thaler issues Vince an ultimatum over his drinking. After going on a bender with a porn star to Hawaii, Neil enters rehab in Tucson, Arizona.

JUNE 4, 1991 Tommy plays drums on one track on a Stu Hamm solo album, and provides backing vocals on an additional track.

JULY 2, 1991 Alice Cooper issues *Hey Stoopid*, featuring Nikki on bass on one track, plus a cowrite credit with Nikki and Mick on another.

AUGUST 3, 1991 Mötley shoot both tame and racy version videos to support the upcoming single release of funky heavy metal stomper "Primal Scream."

AUGUST 12, 1991 Metallica issues their Bob Rock–produced self titled album, commonly referred to as "the black album," which goes on to sell sixteen times platinum. Around this time, Bob Rock also produced albums for Electric Boys, Little Caesar, David Lee Roth, Blue Murder, Kingdom Come, and the Cult, with only the Cult's *Sonic Temple* joining ranks with Crüe and Metallica as clear commercial successes.

MICK MARS, SPEAKING DURING THE 2015 FAREWELL TOUR:

Probably my favorite song to play live is "Primal Scream." For me, personally, I thought that could've been a really good next direction for the band—but it was only the one song, and then I think we were off for a couple of years. So that didn't pan out. But I thought that would've been a really great step for the next record.

MICK MARS:

I remember shortly after the album was released, the Metallica guys went to see Bob Rock about working together. And when you first meet with Bob, he always goes, "So, what do you want?" And they threw down *Feelgood*, and said, "We want *that*." I think their album wound up doing okay, too. (*Guitar One*, 2009)

NIKKI SIXX:

Everybody was like, "You guys wanna go headline festivals?" And we are like, "No we want to play in the middle." "You want to play in the middle?!" And we were like, "Who is out there?" And they'd say AC/DC or Metallica. "But you guys aren't going to open for AC/DC or Metallica; you are bigger than them right now." And we said, "No we want to play in the middle. We want to play for sixty minutes." And it all came back to this conversation I had with our old manager in like '82, '83 when we were starting to get pretty hefty, pretty big, and we were really cocky, saying, "Why don't you go and get Ted Nugent or Aerosmith and have them open for us?" And he was like, "You don't want to do that." And I was like "Why?" And he said, "I've seen that before. A new band with like two hit singles has a band like Aerosmith open for them who has like fifteen years of history. And if the new band only gives them sixty minutes, they will blow them off the stage every time." So we took that concept and opened for Metallica and AC/DC and played sixty minutes in front of a 150,000 people a night. Slammed! How are you going to keep up with a hot rod that only has to run a quarter mile and everybody else has to do two hours? So we went out there, slammed, kicked ass, and went home and took a break. It was a good thing and it was a lot of fun. But then it all blew up after that (laughs) because we were so fried.

AUGUST 14, 1991 Mötley, billed as the Fourskins, play a warm-up club gig at the Marquee in London en route to eight Monsters of Rock dates where the band hits the stage after Queensrÿche and the Black Crowes and before AC/DC and Metallica. "Primal Scream," for which a video had been filmed the previous week, is played live for the first time at the Marquee show.

SEPTEMBER 1991 "Primal Scream" is issued as a single, supported by "Dancing on Glass," "Red Hot" (live), and "Dr. Feelgood" (live). The considerably heavy single reaches #63 in *Billboard*.

SEPTEMBER 17, 1991 The spotlight couldn't shine less bright on Mötley as arch-adversaries Guns N' Roses issue the long-awaited follow-up to *Appetite for Destruction*, a two-record assault called *Use Your Illusion I* and *Use Your Illusion II*.

VINCE NEIL:

Luck is a major factor in this business, and we've been pretty lucky. But we've been smart too. I think bands today make the major mistake of looking at what's happening at just this time, and try to do it, and then they try to change with the time. Now we're seeing metal bands put rap into their songs and shit like that, and that doesn't work, man. You have to be true to your own music first, and that's like the bottom line, because if you don't believe in your music, no one else will believe in it either. Bands today try too hard to be what they perceive is the rock 'n' roll life. (*M.E.A.T.*, 1991)

Somebody get me a doctor.
Tom Wojcik Collection

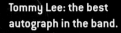

Tommy Lee: the best autograph in the band.
© Darkophoto.com

MICK MARS:

Your Firehouses, your Poisons, your Warrants, Great Whites, Dokkens . . . All those guys just went, woosh! Gone. I mean, they still played, but they didn't take that next step, in my opinion. They just kinda stayed in 1985. (*Guitar One*, 2009)

SEPTEMBER 24, 1991 Kurt Cobain and Nirvana issue their second record, *Nevermind*, which is credited as the record that shifted all attention away from Hollywood and hair metal toward the grunge movement of the Northwest. The smash success of Pearl Jam's *Ten* and Alice in Chains' *Facelift* seal the deal. Mötley respond to these market forces badly, losing their lead singer and taking five years to follow up on the comeback success of 1989's *Dr. Feelgood*.

NIKKI SIXX:

I remember going onto MTV and telling everyone on Headbangers Ball, "There's a brand-new band out. Their record's not out yet, but they're gonna blow your fucking skirt up. They're called Nirvana. Rock 'n' roll's over, baby." And it fucking happened. I'm not the poster boy for rock. I don't like most rock bands. I think most of them are Cheez Whiz and most bands in general are corporate fucking backwash. (*BW&BK*, 1997)

NIKKI SIXX:

For us it was the fact that we had been touring for another thirteen months, and the demand was out there to have the band go tour again. We were like, we have a couple of songs we're really into here, but we really didn't want to go tour. We just wanted to kind of cap what we had done so far, and take some time off and start the new phase.

OCTOBER 19, 1991 Mötley issue a hits pack with bonus rarities called *Decade of Decadence*. Three new tracks were recorded for the album: "Angela" (written by Nikki about his wife), "Anarchy in the UK" (a live highlight at the warm-up Marquee gig), and the aforementioned "Primal Scream." Remix track "Home Sweet Home '91" reaches #37 on the charts, and serves as the band's last Top Forty single. One other notable track was a cover of Tommy Bolin's "Teaser," which originated from the *Stairway to Heaven/Highway to Hell* compilation album generated for McGhee's Make a Difference Foundation.

BOB ROCK ON NIKKI'S CHOICE OF "ANARCHY IN THE UK":

He wanted to end the album with major 'tude. I was a little more tentative, but I think we got the right 'tude. It was one take, saved 'til last, and the guys were going, "Now Bob, can we finally do this, please?" We got that Twin Reverb/Marshall amp combination that Steve used with his Les Paul—it's just as irritating a guitar sound. Vince definitely discovered a part of his voice he never knew he had. I hope we'll be hearing more of it. (*Circus*, 1991)

OCTOBER 28, 1991 Soft rocker Richard Marx issues *Rush Street*, featuring Tommy's drum skills on a track called "Streets of Pain."

NOVEMBER 22, 1991 *Decade of Decadence* is certified gold and platinum simultaneously, rising to #2 in *Billboard*, held from the top spot by Garth Brooks' *Roping the Wind*. "Angela" is issued to radio as a promo single but not as a commercial item.

VINCE NEIL ON THE COVER ART FOR *DECADE OF DECADENCE*:

The memories were coming back when we were putting together the collage of pictures, which were from all of our scrapbooks. You know, when you're starting out, and you see your name in any mag or book and you cut it out, well, we have one hell of a collection. Some of the pictures were really cool, like Mick with Ozzy or me with David Lee Roth—these were taken before we even got signed. (*M.E.A.T.*, 1991)

TOMMY LEE ON "ANARCHY IN THE UK":

Steve (Jones) gave us a legit copy of the lyrics. After we recorded the music part of it, we found out that Megadeth had done a version and did the wrong lyrics. So we wanted to make sure we had the correct words. We used to crank up the Sex Pistols before we'd go onstage. For the vocals, Vince did it in one take. We filmed the "Anarchy" video in London, because it's their kind of song. It was totally out of control. (*Circus*, 1991)

Tom Wojcik Collection

Canadian chain Music World goes for the shotgun approach. Author's Collection

NIKKI SIXX:

Elektra really wanted to re-sign us, to be able to say, "We had this band throughout their career." To be honest, that wasn't as important to us. But Elektra knows how we tick. They know how to stay out of our bedroom—meaning the music. The president of another company offered us $30 million and they started talking about how we might want "creative control" clauses in the contract. But with Elektra, we've always had creative control, without ever having to write it into a contract. (*Musician*, 1992)

DECEMBER 1991 After nearly a year of tough negotiations, Mötley re-sign with Elektra for a rich $25 million advance and an abnormally high royalty rate as icing on the cake. The band immediately begins work on a darker, more experimental album, although Vince routinely begs off of the sessions citing fatigue or, say the rest of the guys, to attend auto race events.

DECEMBER 25, 1991 Heather acquires, at a price of $30,000, a guitar custom-made for Jimi Hendrix, and bequeaths it to Tommy for Christmas.

1992

FEBRUARY 8, 1992 Vince's birthday celebration at the Roxy devolves into a drunken brawl, topped off with Vince's wife hitting him in the face with a glass.

FEBRUARY 11, 1992 Vince, after much resistance due partially to the uncommonly stormy weather LA was experiencing, finally agrees to shows up at band rehearsals, arriving four hours late. He argues with Nikki, Tommy, and Mick and calls the new material they are working on stupid, upon which he is informed that they were thinking about getting a new lead singer.

VINCE NEIL:

The day I was fired was the only day I was ever late, *ever*. It was because of all the flooding that was going on—the freeways were all screwed up, there were sheets of water outside, people dying and shit. I mean, I'm always the only guy ever there on time. The day before, Nikki and Tommy were late two and a half hours, and Tommy has always been late. So it wasn't that. (*Circus*, 1992)

FEBRUARY 12, 1992 At a meeting at Nikki's house, the band decide to fire Vince, despite what it might do to their lucrative new record deal. Manager Doug Thaler informs Vince in a phone call. An official statement emerges two days later, on Valentine's Day.

Hmm, maybe this wasn't such a good idea. © Tom Wallace

VINCE NEIL:

It was just business as usual. We were rehearsing, and it just happened. It was really out of the blue and a big surprise for me. I don't know if they had been planning it for a while or what. I think what happened is that I didn't fit in with their idea of what they wanted to do in the future. When we were in the songwriting process, it was going more towards bluesy stuff, and I'm not a blues singer—I never have been and never will be. I think, rather than compromise the music, they just decided to get rid of me and get somebody who wanted to do that type of stuff. Driving home after it happened, I couldn't fuckin' believe it. I had never thought I'd ever be in this position, as I thought I was going to be in Mötley Crüe until I retired. All of a sudden, I found myself going, "What the fuck am I going to do now?" I didn't have a band, a manager . . . I didn't know if I even had a record company or a lawyer! I basically started from scratch. I just knew one thing, that I didn't want to be one of those guys sitting at a bar going, "I was in that band years ago!" (*M.E.A.T.*, 1993)

JOHN CORABI:

The Scream was what it was. I had a great time with those guys. For four guys that have never done a major album before and toured to great lengths like we did, we did a good job. I had never done a record. We got to go in. We worked with a guy named Eddie Kramer, which was a fucking blast for me. But it was weird. I was kind of disappointed at the time with the politics of the record business. So when Mötley Crüe called me and discussed things with me about coming down and jamming with them, I did it because I thought this would be an opportunity for me to do things that I hadn't done with the Scream. The other thing of it too, from a personal thing, I just found out, and anybody who knows me knows that I've got a son who's a diabetic. I had just found out that my three- or four-year-old son was diagnosed with diabetes and was in intensive care. I'm sitting there going, I'm making zip here with the Scream. This is a way for me to take care of my kids. Take care of my family and shit. When they asked me, I jumped at the opportunity. We went in and we started rehearsing. We were having a blast. We were having a great time.

FEBRUARY 17, 1992 John Corabi, who had impressed Nikki Sixx with his work with the Scream, meets the band for an audition at a studio in Burbank. Unfamiliar with the Mötley catalogue, they first run through the covers that Mötley do, and then ease into a few originals. The next day, after Kik Tracee's Stephen Shareaux also auditions, Corabi jams with the band some more, even playing guitar and collaborating on a bit of writing, and is asked to join the band.

FEBRUARY 19, 1992 Vince checks himself into rehab, once again same place in Tucson, after a four-night bender in Hawaii with porn star Savannah and a young groupie—Savannah ends up overdosed and in the hospital.

MARCH 1992 Vince signs a solo deal with Warner Bros. for $4 million, which kicks off with a $2 million advance for the making of his first record. At this point, Vince is living with Rob Lowe, with the duo partying hard around town.

MARCH 12, 1992 The *Decade of Decadence* video album is issued.

MARCH 29, 1992 Vince quits auto racing after crashing on the third lap in a race in Long Beach, California.

MAY 22, 1992 The *Encino Man* movie soundtrack includes Vince's first solo single, "You're Invited (But Your Friend Can't Come)." Its video would feature a cameo by Pauly Shore. Vince performs the track live at the MTV Movie Awards. The version of the song used for the soundtrack album is recorded before marquee guitarist Steve Stevens, ex-Billy Idol, arrives to record the album, on which the single receives a revamping. A total of four singles would be launched from the record (and to little avail). The video for the fourth and last single, "Can't Have Your Cake," features Pamela Anderson and Vince's only son Neil Wharton.

Decade of Decadence **proved a successful spot of product in terms of keeping the brand alive without a new record. Of course, it didn't hurt that the band came up with "Primal Scream."** Author's Collection

JULY 1992 Vince moves out of Rob Lowe's house into a West Hollywood hotel and takes a financial stake in a club and restaurant called Bar One, which becomes his next regular hangout. Meanwhile, Mötley Crüe, at Audible Sound in Burbank, is working full-time on material slated for their next record. The plan is to have the provisionally titled *'Til Death Do Us Part*—each of the band get that slogan imprinted, during a collective trip to Sunset Strip Tattoo—finished by the close of the year, cognizant of the fact that Vince's record is also imminently due.

Billy Idol's firecracker of a sideman, Steve Stevens. © Tom Wallace

VINCE NEIL: I was talking to a lot of different guitar players, but Steve was the first guy I had actually contacted, and that was through Billy Idol, who had called me up right after the breakup telling me I had to play with Steve. He then called Steve for me to find out what he was doing, and that's when I found out that he had just left the Jerusalem Slim thing. I had booked a week of rehearsal time so I could start auditioning guitar players, and a couple weeks before I started, Steve contacted me through our mutual friend, Ray Brown, who is a clothing designer, and Ray relayed the message that Steve was interested in talking about the band and gave me his number. I called Steve in New York, and told him what my vision was—the type of band, the type of music—and he came out the very next day. We rehearsed, wrote like five songs, and he's been out here ever since. Steve was the first guy that came to my mind, because I had been a fan of his for so long. I just wanted to put together a band that was really fucking good. I just got real lucky with Steve. I think a lot of people are really excited about us teaming up. (*M.E.A.T.*, 1993)

AUGUST 1992 Vince and ex-Billy Idol guitarist Steve Stevens work with producer Ron Nevison at the Record Plant on what will become Vince's first solo album.

AUGUST 21, 1992 Nikki rolls off the wagon again, this time in Jamaica.

AUGUST 27, 1992 John Corabi's generous pay packet with Crüe is set, including weekly per diems and $300,000 for his work on the upcoming record.

JOHN CORABI:

The first jam was interesting. I didn't really think that I was going to get the gig. I wasn't really familiar with a lot of their material. Being a singer, I'm really into listening to vocals and stuff, and no disrespect to Vince—they sold a lot of records with him—but I'm into Steve Marriott, Paul Rodgers, that kind of thing. I went down not expecting anything. So I jammed "Helter Skelter" and "Jailhouse Rock" with them and it was cool. I was the second person to jam with them. After they realized that Vince had pretty much bailed, they had Stephen Shareaux from Kik Tracee come down and then me. (*M.E.A.T.*, 1994)

SEPTEMBER 1992 John Corabi is almost killed in a mugging near his apartment in a bad part of town, where he is stabbed multiple times in the back and hand with a screwdriver. Mötley get him, his wife, and his son set up in the safer Thousand Oaks, also buying him a Harley Davidson.

OCTOBER 1992 Vince sues Mötley Crüe for damages, future royalties, and reinstatement into the band.

A sports look for a fairly athletic kinda guy. © Tom Wallace

VINCE NEIL ON THE MOTIVATION FUELLING *EXPOSED*:

I was out for revenge, but it was not only towards the guys in the band, but a lot of different people. The first thing I read after leaving the band was this thing in the *LA Times* calendar section. The headline was, "Put Your Money on Mötley Crüe," and they had all these industry insiders saying that I wasn't a proven talent, that I hadn't done this and that, and that Mötley Crüe could go on. And I was like, "Fuck you, people! Watch this!" So that really lit a fire under me to get this thing together and put out the best thing I possibly could. (*M.E.A.T.*, 1993)

NOVEMBER 1, 1992 Vince Neil's only recently hired manager Bruce Bird dies of a cerebral haemorrhage, age 44, during recording sessions for Vince's forthcoming solo album.

NOVEMBER 1992 Bob Rock arrives in LA to strategize about the new Mötley Crüe album, only to witness that Nikki and Tommy had relapsed. The band's rehab guru Bob Timmons quickly gets the situation under control and work continues sober. It is still not formally announced to the public that John Corabi is the band's lead singer. Rumors as to who was imminent for the gig included David Lee Roth, Stephen Pearcy, Marq Torien, and Sebastian Bach, who claims to have been offered the job and turned it down.

NOVEMBER 13, 1992 Sega Genesis pinball game *Crüe Ball* makes use of three Mötley anthems.

1993

JANUARY 14, 1993 Mötley Crüe official announce that John Corabi is their new lead singer.

TOMMY LEE ON THE BREAK WITH VINCE:

He came in about three hours late to a rehearsal. And to be very honest, we had new lead singer talks as far back as 1987. Anyway, we sat him down and said, "Look, man, you gotta show us some enthusiasm." But it just wasn't in Vince to write a song, or even care about music. He was very involved in everything else that came with the music: money, girls, cars, helicopter flying lessons, all the stuff that had nothing to do with music. (*The Toronto Sun*, 1994)

EARLY 1993 Sharise Ruddell files for divorce from Vince.

MARCH 1993 The band continue work on the first Mötley Crüe album of the John Corabi era. John contributes guitar work as well as lyrics, and in a show of extravagance, a sixty-three-piece orchestra is assembled for the string parts on "Misunderstood." By March, the band has burned through $1 million creating the still-unfinished album, an amount framed as more than all previous records combined. The claim is dubious, given that *Dr. Feelgood* had reportedly cost an estimated $600,000.

JOHN CORABI ON WRITING THE SONGS FOR THE ALBUM:

The majority of them were written before Vancouver. Actually, the single, "Hooligan's Holiday," came about there. Bob had to leave for the Bon Jovi tour to perform with Rockhead, so we came back home and relaxed. So we went back into rehearsal and wrote six new tunes while we were waiting. Up until the mastering process of this record, everybody was just coming to the table with new material. Bob actually had to tell us to stop writing. (*M.E.A.T.*, 1994)

APRIL 23, 1993 Mick files for divorce, claiming his wife had been romantically involved with the guitarist in her band.

Vince in solo support of Van Halen. © Tom Wallace

APRIL 27, 1993 Vince issues *Exposed*, the crooner's debut solo album. The record's '80s party metal sound is a slap in the face to the turning of the tide proposed by Seattle's grunge scene. Essentially, the record is more in the vein of classic era Mötley Crüe than the band without Vince would find themselves pursuing the following year. *Exposed* reaches #13 on the *Billboard* charts but fails to reach gold. The debut single "Sister of Pain" is supported by a video starring a porn star who at this point is dating Vince. The Japanese issue includes as bonus tracks "Blondes (Have More Fun)" and a cover of the Ramones' "I Wanna be Sedated."

VINCE NEIL ON CALLING THE ALBUM *EXPOSED*:

To me, it was like, "Here I am—I'm on my own and I'm vulnerable." I'm exposing myself in every other way for the first time, and I just thought it was the perfect title for the record. These songs came from the heart, songs that had been inside me for so long that might not have ever come out if this hadn't happened. I believe that things do happen for a reason, and I'm really happy now that it has happened. In Mötley Crüe, there were four guys in the band that did everything, so we were limited in the creativity. When I got out of Mötley Crüe, it was like this damn burst of songs. I've got this twenty-four-track studio in my house, and I just sat there and wrote and wrote. I'd come up with something, and have Steve and Phil come over. I also cowrote stuff with Jack Blades and Tommy Shaw. The ideas were just coming out—I wasn't trying to do anything special. Looking back on it, everything went really quickly because the stuff was there, and because the guys in the band are some of the best musicians I've ever played with. (*M.E.A.T.*, 1993)

Signed for the author at an interview backstage at the Molson Amphitheatre in Toronto. Author's Collection

MAY 1993 Vince's solo band play their first show, at the Roxy, under the pseudonym Five Guys from Van Nuys.

MAY 21, 1993 Vince and two girlfriends cart off to Hawaii to celebrate the release of his new record.

JUNE 1993 Tommy moves out of the house he shares with Heather, moving into a place on Malibu beach.

JUNE 25, 1993 Vince's solo act embarks on a high profile forty-two-date tour supporting Van Halen, who two years later, are still flying high off their *For Unlawful Carnal Knowledge* album. As the tour grinds on, two further singles from *Exposed* are floated, "The Edge" and "Can't Have Your Cake." Meanwhile, Mötley Crüe is still burning through money in Vancouver, and now drinking and drugging heavily again.

AUGUST 5, 1993 Heather Locklear files for divorce from Tommy.

SEPTEMBER 1993 After playing Japan, Vince's Australian and European tour plans disintegrate and he's relegated to playing clubs in the US.

OCTOBER 1993 Vince ups the ante by including four Playboy Playmates in the video for the fourth single from *Exposed*, "Can't Change Me." Meanwhile, Mötley Crüe wrap up the recording of their first album without Vince, amassing twenty-three finished tracks.

NOVEMBER 1993 Vince buys Sea Manor, in Malibu, moving out of the Bel Age Hotel. The new mansion doubles as an excellent place to shoot porn movies and spreads for *Penthouse*.

NOVEMBER 17, 1993 Tommy and Heather's divorce is finalized.

VINCE NEIL EXPOSED

Multi-Million album sales, a decade of chart dominating tracks and videos. And a reputation sealed in rock history.

Now, his solo debut on Warner Bros. Cassettes and Compact Discs.

Produced by Ron Nevison
Mixed by Chris Lord-Alge

Vince got a fair bit of label support for *Exposed*.

Author's Collection

Vince solo, in Barrie, Ontario, July 1993.

© Darkophoto.com

1994

FEBRUARY 1994 Vince and his strip club entrepreneur buddy take a bunch of cocaine-smuggling strippers onto two Learjets to the Bahamas for a yacht party, to be filmed. Amidst the mayhem Vince works on his relationship with his new girlfriend Heidi. Back home, the same month, Vince bides his time in a celebrity golf tournament as throat problems have sidelined his rock career.

FEBRUARY 1, 1994 Green Day issue their third album, *Dookie*, which eventually achieves RIAA diamond status. So-Cal or "pop" punk, aided and abetted by the likes of Rancid and the Offspring, is all the rage for a few years, further pushing all forms of heavy metal into the shadows as the '90s wear on.

Crüe with Corabi, July 13, 1994, in Darien Lake, New York. © Darkophoto.com

TOMMY LEE ON *MOTLEY CRUE*:

It is fucking heavy! Although there are quite a few pieces of really beautiful music. They're not heavy, they're gorgeous. There's a song called "Drift Away." It's one where you'll put your headphones on and pass out to it. It just takes you to another place. It's like looking at a piece of art where it just gives you a certain feeling. It's being sung from the heart, and played from the heart. Oh man, there are some fucking kickers on here. You know what, the album's so strong, I love them all. (*Live Wire*, 1994)

NIKKI SIXX:

The whole thing at that time was, we had a different singer in place, let's do something different. And as an artistic move, that was great, but as a career move, it was bad. Great album. Shouldn't be called Mötley Crüe. We went more for riff rock.

MARCH 15, 1994 Mötley Crüe issue their self-titled album (working title: *'Til Death Do Us Part*), featuring John Corabi on vocals. In actual fact, the album is only partially self-titled—there are no umlauts in *Motley Crue*. Originally released with the band name in yellow, later issues had it printed in red. The record features a radical shift in sound for the band, given John's lower, raspier singing style, but also a gritty, distorted production palette—in essence, the record presents Mötley as a grungier but more artistic band. At the same time, Elektra issues the mail-order-only *Quaternary* EP. The print run of 20,000 was designated to be sold only to those who had bought the *Motley Crue* album. Ordering details were included in the first one million copies of *Motley Crue*. Order forms would also be included in the tour program. Though it's out of print, all of the tracks became available on future reissues and compilations.

Promo picture sleeve CD for the self-titled album's pounding first single.
Author's Collection

JOHN CORABI:

Growth and change is what Mötley have based their whole career around. Their image has evolved always; they're on top of things. They know what kids want, because as much as Mötley Crüe is a big band, they're also fans. There isn't one person in this band who doesn't go out and see new bands and buy new CDs. The important thing is that a lot of bands who taste that bit of success lose that street thing—they lose the kid in them. If you listen to the new record, a lot of people are saying that it sounds real current, and as Nikki says, it's hard not to be motivated by something as powerful as new music. We just said, "Let's do the best that we can; let's really go out on a limb and experiment." And that's the coolest thing about Mötley—they experiment and they are fans of the music. As much as the fans change and turn with the times, Mötley does also. That's important." (*M.E.A.T.*, 1994)

MARCH 31, 1994 John Corabi's contract is changed, moving his pay structure away from weekly payouts to profit-sharing.

Nikki and John take a considerable leap of faith.
© Darkophoto.com

APRIL 1994 Vince cedes his ownership stake in nightclub Bar One.

APRIL 14, 1994 Nikki and Brandi have a second child, Storm Brieanne Sixx.

MAY 3, 1994 The *Motley Crue* album, which peaks at #7, is certified gold, a hollow victory given both the success of its predecessor and the fact that it had cost $2 million to make.

MICK MARS:

Honestly, in my heart, my favorite album is the *Motley Crue* album that we did with John. People have come to it twenty years late and now call it a great album, but you know what? They know that now—and that's good. I'm really happy and proud that they know that.

NIKKI SIXX:

I'm the guy in the band that if I had my way, we would sound like the Sisters of Mercy. It would be just a death, destruction, and doom band. I think that this album is a little more geared to where my head is. Most of the time, I think everyone else has synched up with that, Tommy, Mick, and especially John, who cowrote most of the lyrics with me. This is a dark time. For me it's been the best time it's ever been. Because that's where my head's always been. [*Late at Night* magazine, 1994]

JUNE 1994 Vince begins work on a follow-up to *Exposed*, using the Dust Brothers as producers, recording at NRG Studios. Meanwhile, MTV refuses to play Mötley's new video for the track "Misunderstood," as Nikki walked out of an MTV interview in April. The band's proposed stadium tour gets scaled back due to poor sales.

JUNE 9-AUGUST 29, 1994 Mötley embark on the American leg of their *Anywhere There's Electricity* tour, support coming from King's X and Type O Negative (House of Pain and the Ramones had been considered as well), the choices supporting the band's new "alternative metal" sound. With the tour losing money, Nikki and Tommy both pony up $75,000, with Mick not participating due to his recent divorce settlement and John giving up much of his paycheck instead.

JULY 19, 1994 Mick becomes a grandfather. The granddaughter's name is Shandi, named for an obscure Kiss song from 1980's *Unmasked* album.

SEPTEMBER 1994 Mötley breaks ties with manager Doug Thaler, hiring on Allen Kovac of Left Bank Management, who is first met with at his office in Beverly Hills by Nikki and Tommy. Meanwhile, also in the fall, Mötley issue "Smoke the Sky" as the album's second single, but MTV won't play it due to its controversial lyrics. Similar industry shenanigans affect the release of Vince's second album, with the record's modern rock direction causing a shake-up at the label and a delay in the release of the now finished record.

JOURNALIST MARTIN POPOFF ON MOTLEY CRUE:

Lo and behold, the Crüe update and correct for the '90s, scraping and scrapping through a slowburn collection of grimy street rockers, led capably by fresh vocalist (and songwriter) John Corabi, who roars his convictions (however tiring they might be), like Vince Neil never could. Despite the decelerated, almost deflated velocities, *Motley Crue* is no slouch, cranking a sort of valiant remedial skitter metal to the rotten core, managing a sort of ambition of bad taste, pulling lots of cheesy '80s moves, then slicing them together under a grinding grunge mix that is borderline hard to listen to. The result: decadent stadium rock with greasy hooks, "Hooligan's Holiday" an apt pick for lead single, initially dumb then infectious like the whole unwashed spread. (*BW&BK*, 1994)

"Anywhere there's electricity" became cruel commentary on the tour, indeed. Tom Wojcik Collection

OCTOBER 3-11, 1994 Mötley play seven dates in Japan. Tommy has with him his fiancé Bobbie Brown (who spanks Tommy onstage as a birthday present). Nikki's family flies out as well, and Nikki's son Gunner gets a samurai sword. After the last show of the tour, the band is presented with awards for gold sales of the *Motley Crue* album in Japan.

DECEMBER 1994 The band begin work on a follow-up to *Motley Crue*, vowing to be less dark and more straightforward. They also decide that Bob Rock, producer of the previous two records, is just too expensive for their tastes.

Nikki in fighting mode, defending his decision to soldier on with a new guy at the microphone. © Darkophoto.com

DECEMBER 6, 1994 Symbolizing how times have changed, Pearl Jam's *Vitalogy*, issued this day, eventually sells five times platinum, with the band's *Vs.* album from 1993 at six times platinum and debut *Ten* at diamond. The grunge explosion continues, eventually to be usurped by a format called hard alternative.

DECEMBER 21, 1994 The relationship between Tommy and Bobbie Brown deteriorates into a big fight over their inevitable breakup and the dividing of their possessions. Tommy kicks her out of the house but the police arrive and allow her to take her stuff. What's more, they arrest Tommy. When Tommy returns a few days later, the house has been stripped of pretty much everything not bolted down.

DECEMBER 31, 1994 Drinking and taking ecstasy at the Sanctuary club, partly owned by Pamela Anderson, Tommy becomes infatuated with Pam and before the long night is through, gets her number.

NIKKI SIXX: You know, people did what I refused to do. I refuse to put down the last ten years of music. You know, all the Soundgardens, Pearl Jams, and all those bands that came out were, "We're our own movement." All of a sudden, bands are getting this alternative thing. Whatever the title, just make good songs. All of a sudden, those newer bands are pointing at us like we did something wrong. And I was like, "Ex-squeeze me?!" We weathered the storm, we're on the other side and now everyone wants us to point at them and say they did something wrong. "They bored us. They were too serious. They were boring onstage. They're shitty performers." What the fuck's going on here? I'm not going to do it. I refuse to do it. I didn't like it when it was done to me. It was unjust and I'm not going to do an unjust thing to these other bands. The thing is if you go to these bands personally—Korn, Manson, the list goes on and on and on, Green Day—they'll tell you that Mötley Crüe's an influence. But they couldn't say it because they were categorized and they were told, "Look, you're different, man. You don't want to be in a rock band; you want to be alternative." Korn is like this heavy fucking rock band. Soundgarden is Black Sabbath. Pearl Jam is the Doors. What's going on here?

The photogenic and all 'round talented John Corabi. © Darkophoto.com

1995

JANUARY 27, 1995 Epic film *Highlander: The Fourth Dimension* makes use of an instrumental version of "Dr. Feelgood." (The song is also featured in the 2009 video game *Brütal Legend*.)

JANUARY 30, 1995 The band's show at Club Shelter in Pasadena proves to be John Corabi's last with the band.

FEBRUARY 13, 1995 Tommy follows Pamela Anderson to Cancun, Mexico, and finds the hotel she is staying at. From that point on they become inseparable. Five days later, he proposes marriage. A day after that they are married.

MARCH 3, 1995 A high-level meeting takes place in New York to propose getting Vince back in the band. Vince's daughter Skylar is rushed to the hospital, where doctors find and remove a large cancerous tumor. Over the months, more cancer is found and her condition worsens.

MARCH 28, 1995 Vince, using a Celica GT, comes in second place in a celebrity auto race sponsored by Toyota.

MAY 23, 1995 Nikki and Brandi welcome a son, Dekker.

JUNE 1995 Mötley continue to work on the follow-up to *Motley Crue*, provisionally entitled *Personality #9*, first in Tommy's living room and then moving to Nikki's home studio.

JUNE 5, 1995 *Theatre of Pain* and *Girls, Girls, Girls* are both certified four times platinum.

AUGUST 15, 1995 Vince and Sharise lose their beloved daughter Skylar to cancer, at age four. Vince's forthcoming album includes a track in her honor called "Skylar's Song."

AUGUST 28, 1995 Vince, overcome with grief over Skylar's death and drinking heavily, is finally coaxed into rehab, but quickly escapes and relapses hard.

SEPTEMBER 12, 1995 Vince issues his second solo album, *Carved in Stone*, which takes a comparatively modern rock approach versus *Exposed*, addressing both grunge and industrial metal, with production by the Dust Brothers. The album stalls at #139 in *Billboard* and sells under 100,000 copies.

OCTOBER 3, 1995 Pamela throws a surreal and decadent birthday party for Tommy that rings in at $300,000. Crüe play and so does Slash.

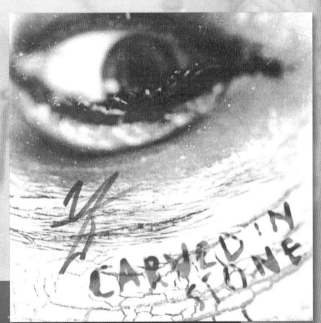

Vince's second album went over everyone's head. Too modern, too different from his first record and all the ones before it. Author's Collection

VINCE NEIL:

I love both those records. Looking back, it's one of the best things that has ever happened to me. Just to be able to go do solo records. Everything is on you. The songs, the cover art, it's all in your hands. Whereas in Mötley Crüe, everybody's an equal partner and we all talk about things and make decisions as a group. The first record was basically just pure a rock 'n' roll record, Steve Stevens playing guitar on it. And the next record, I just decided to experiment a little bit and it was a little bit ahead of its time. If it came out right now, it would be a fucking huge record. Back then, nobody ever thought about putting rock and rap together.

1996

FEBRUARY 13, 1996 Mick Mars contributes to Shrapnel Records' Jeff Beck tribute album, *Jeffology: A Guitar Chronicle*.

MARCH 1996 *Personality #9* is slated for release this month, but then word gets out that the band is a good year behind schedule. Meanwhile, Vince moves to Las Vegas and breaks ties with Warner as a solo artist.

APRIL 29, 1996 The *Barb Wire* soundtrack includes "Welcome to Planet Boom," a remix of Tommy's "Planet Boom" from *Quaternary*. Meanwhile, Tommy's got other problems as he's dealing with the theft of his and Pam's private sex tape.

APRIL 30, 1996 Relations between John Corabi and the rest of Mötley continue to degrade, wrapped up in the various artistic differences concerning the modern rock direction of the next album.

MAY 1996 Nikki completes most the work on material with his side project 1958 (later called 58) over the course of about a month.

JUNE 1996 Vince embarks on a summer tour as a solo act along with Warrant and Slaughter, surrendering to the idea that the fans want to hear '80s-style glam rock. The following month, he talks publicly about getting back together with Mötley for both an album and tour. Nikki denies that conversations with Vince had taken place.

JUNE 5, 1996 Tommy and Pam welcome their first child, Brandon Thomas Lee, who will be commemorated through song on the next Mötley album.

NIKKI SIXX ON "BRANDON," WHICH WOULD BE SUNG BY TOMMY:

It throws people for a big time loop, but it fits and flows. It really sets up good. We like *Day at the Races*, *Night at the Opera*. What those were, were songs that really sounded good with Roger Taylor singing and he sang it. There were no rules. It was really cool.

JULY 29, 1996 Nikki donates a Harley to the Hard Rock Cafe in Beverley Hills in grand style, driving it through the front doors, with his son Gunner perched on the gas tank.

AUGUST 30, 1996 Nikki and *Baywatch* star Donna D'Errico go on a blind date, set up by Pamela. Earlier in the day, Nikki talks about how the new album is coming along so well, it may turn out to be a double.

NIKKI SIXX:

I am the kind of person that likes to work with other artists. I can sit by myself and write songs and write lyrics. I don't really sing but I can get the idea down. I know how to run Pro Tools very efficiently. I could do all my demos at my house but in the end I feel like something's missing. I want to get together with other musicians. Working with Dave Darling was really exciting because Dave comes from R&B and traditional roots and I come from glam/punk/metal. We wrote the 58 record in a very short amount of time. For me there wasn't any, "I'm Nikki Sixx from Mötley Crüe and I've got to make something that sounds like *Shout at the Devil*." A lot of people did not get the 58 record. The bottom line is, I'm a huge Lou Reed fan. If that doesn't reek of Lou Reed and early Bowie, what does? (*Bravewords.com*, 2004)

Motley Crüe
Live 1983-1999: Entertainment or Death
Street Date November 23, 1999

℗© 1999 Motley Records/Beyond Music.
WARNING: Unauthorized duplication is a violation of applicable laws.

FOR PROMOTIONAL NOT FOR SA
BYADV-780

1. Looks that Kill (1985) 6:11 2. Knock 'Em Dead, Kid (1985) 3:32
3. Too Young to Fall in Love (1985) 4:04 4. Live Wire (1984) 4:20
5. Shout At The Devil (1984) 4:18 6. Ten Seconds to Love (1985) 4:45
7. Helter Skelter (1982) 4:17 8. Smokin' in the Boys Room (1985) 5:18
9. Home Sweet Home (1998) 4:18 10. Wild Side (1999) 6:03
11. Girls, Girls, Girls (1998) 5:03 12. Dr. Feelgood (1999) 5:20
13. Primal Scream (1998) 5:42 14. Same Ol' Situation (1999) 4:29
15. Kickstart My Heart (1999) 5:40

SEPTEMBER 13, 1996 John Corabi is informed, in a phone call to Nikki's home studio from Mötley manager Allen Kovac, that he's been fired as Mötley Crüe's lead singer.

JOHN CORABI:

I always kind of looked at things with Mötley as it could all end tomorrow. To be honest with you, even before we went on tour, fans were pissed off at Nikki. Touring-wise, we didn't do well. The record didn't do well. After we went on tour, I kind of thought that my days were numbered. I went and tried to do the best I could do under the circumstances and I think that, at that point in my life, that's when I had the most difficulty getting up in the morning, screwing my head on right and saying, okay, I'm going to write a song today. As much as the guys didn't want me to think that anything was happening—and I don't even know when this whole thing started to materialize—I just kind of believed and felt that it was going to happen. For the last year in the band, I was kind of uneasy. When they told me they were getting Vince back, I was actually relieved. I was just going to do my own solo thing. And then Bruce Kulick called. But I was actually really relieved that it was over. The bottom line of it is—and I told my girlfriend at the time—July 4th, we went to the Black Crowes concert down here. We were sitting there, watching the band. We're both having a beer. She goes, "As much as I love a lot of the music you come up with, I think you're in the wrong band." I'm like, "What do you mean?" She goes, "This is what you should be doing. This is what you're about. You love Zeppelin, the Stones, the Beatles. You're a hippie at heart. This is what you should be doing." When they told me, I didn't really feel like an odd man out. At that point, I had been in Mötley Crüe for five years. Love me or hate me, there's people all over the world who now know who John Corabi is. They didn't know when I was in the Scream."

Rich yet squandered asset to the band, John Corabi. © Darkophoto.com

SEPTEMBER 15, 1996 The four original Mötley members hold a summit at Nikki's home studio, at which time Vince is enlisted to do some preliminary singing work on the new tracks. Tommy is the least sure of the situation, meeting with John in an attempt to keep him on in the band at least as a second guitarist. Meanwhile, Mick isn't getting along with producer Scott Humphrey, who isn't digging Mick's guitar parts.

NOVEMBER 26, 1996 *Rolling Stone* reports that Vince is back in Mötley Crüe, and on his solo tour, Vince is feeding crowds information to the same effect.

JOHN CORABI:

I don't know if they were being sympathetic to the fact that I'm not in the band anymore or whatever, but all of the people that I talked to were like, "Corabi, man, that fucking record you did with Mötley was great." They're telling me that they felt the one mistake that we made doing that record was keeping the name of the band Mötley Crüe. Had it not have been Mötley Crüe, the record probably would have done way better. I'm like, that's cool. Everybody plays Monday morning quarterback. I'm kind of curious because I get a fifty-fifty reading on this whole reunion thing. Half the people I meet are, "Yeah man, nothing against you, dude, but I'm just glad the original Mötley's back together and they're doing okay and you're doing okay. It's all good." And they're excited for them. And then I meet another batch of people that go, "Well, if they think they're going to do the business Kiss did, they're mistaken. Nobody gives a fuck about Mötley Crüe anymore." It's just out of a curiosity thing. I would like to see them walk onstage and get the reception that Van Halen got with David Lee Roth.

SEPTEMBER 17, 1996 Mötley management tells John that his assistance is still very much requested, with respect to songwriting and possible guitar contributions to the forthcoming album, not to mention guiding Vince through some of the things he's done on the songs thus far as a singer. By October, relations have cooled and John is out of the picture.

NIKKI SIXX ON TAKING HIS TIME WITH THE REUNION PLANS:

We did want to do it until it was right. We didn't want to pop it until it was right. The other thing is working on a record is different from setting up a record. I want everyone to be aware that the record's coming. I want to have everything in place so that it's a really good experience. I've experienced the last-minute rushes because people are concerned with their percentages. We're like, "Look, let's just take our time, man. An extra couple months. Let's make sure the songs are perfect. Let's remix that first single again. Let's make it exactly the way we want it." It sort of just fell together. We were going through some legal stuff and got involved with some attorneys that got Vince wound up. And we had some attorneys that had us wound up. At one point, we were there doing bullshit and me and Vince were like, "Can you guys all just fuck off so we can talk?" We just sat down and started cracking up. We were like, "This is so silly." (*BW&BK*, 1997)

NIKKI SIXX ON STAYING CURRENT:

We've all got ears, man—use your ears. There's really good bands and there's really bad bands. You can't lump them all together. I've been getting, "Dude, man, rock's back, alternative's over." And I go, "God, I hope not. It's my roots." They go, "What do you mean, your roots?" I go, "Dude, I grew up in the '70s, man." CBGB's, the Sex Pistols, the Ramones, Dead Boys, old fucked-up heroin-shooting Steven Tyler, first three Aerosmith albums, the Stones' *Black and Blue* album. Come on, tell me alternative's over, I'll be sad. Why can't we go blow the fucking stage up with our fucking anarchic ways and be Mötley Crüe with pop songs? If we fucking want to wear makeup, who gives a fuck? Why can't we do what we do? Why? Who keeps doing this, man? It's sickening. It's just not cool. I think our fans are smarter than that. We gotta outsmart the record companies. We gotta get rid of labels. (*BW&BK*, 1997)

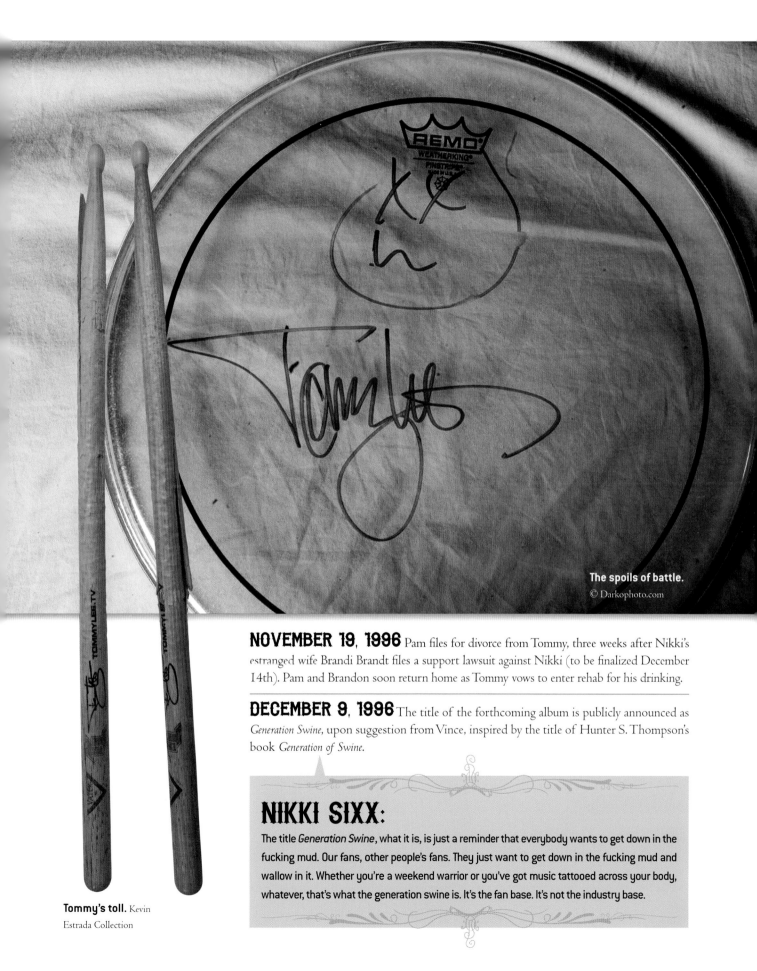

The spoils of battle.
© Darkophoto.com

Tommy's toll. Kevin
Estrada Collection

NOVEMBER 19, 1996 Pam files for divorce from Tommy, three weeks after Nikki's estranged wife Brandi Brandt files a support lawsuit against Nikki (to be finalized December 14th). Pam and Brandon soon return home as Tommy vows to enter rehab for his drinking.

DECEMBER 9, 1996 The title of the forthcoming album is publicly announced as *Generation Swine*, upon suggestion from Vince, inspired by the title of Hunter S. Thompson's book *Generation of Swine*.

NIKKI SIXX:

The title *Generation Swine*, what it is, is just a reminder that everybody wants to get down in the fucking mud. Our fans, other people's fans. They just want to get down in the fucking mud and wallow in it. Whether you're a weekend warrior or you've got music tattooed across your body, whatever, that's what the generation swine is. It's the fan base. It's not the industry base.

NIKKI SIXX ON THE BREAK WITH JOHN:

Songwriting wasn't clicking with John. It wasn't turning into the album we wanted it to turn into. John was doing something different. He's more of a jammer dude. We wanted to get the Mötley Crüe sensibility where you hear the song and go, "God, I love this track," and then put the depth on it. Between talking with Vince and realizing it wasn't working with John for some reason, it just happened. (*BW&BK*, 1997)

Vince in radio interview mode.
© Darkophoto.com

DECEMBER 12, 1996 The band quickly record three tracks for the forthcoming album, live in the studio.

NIKKI SIXX:

You know what? It's a journey. I found that the people that I've exposed to the record at this point, by the end of it, are saying, "Wow, man, can you put it on again?" It took you somewhere, but it didn't bore you in the meantime. It's definitely not linear. If I have to be cerebral about it, it's going to take me a week. If I just have to fucking trust my instincts, I'd have to say, it's a fucking rock 'n' roll record, man. It's just a rock 'n' roll record that's going to kick you in the nuts. (*BW&BK*, 1997)

DECEMBER 23, 1996 Nikki marries Donna D'Errico, in an intimate family ceremony at home. Meanwhile, the next day, Pam and Tommy renew their wedding vows with Tommy making his entrance in a suit of armor and on horseback.

DECEMBER 31, 1996 Tommy is significantly artistically inspired by a DJ set he witnesses at London's Ministry of Sound. A new musical direction for the Mötley drummer is hatched.

Hmm, I gotta get me some of that rap metal. © Darkophoto.com

1997

TOMMY LEE:

Yeah, John's cool. For awhile there, I was really upset because he went and sued us. And that's like taking money out of my children's fuckin' future. And that shit fuckin' bothered me. And for some reason I've accepted it a little bit more, because I know what happens is that managers get involved, and they start doing stupid shit, so everything wasn't coming from John. So part of it I accept, and part of it I'm still a little upset about.

1997 Mötley Crüe leaves Elektra Records and Mötley Records is now distributed by Beyond Records, which was under the umbrella of BMG. After the demise of Beyond, Mötley's distribution is taken over by Doug Morris' Hip-O Records, a sub-imprint at Universal. Currently, Mötley product in the US is distributed by Eleven Seven Music and Warner Music Group. Eleven Seven was founded in 2006 by Allen Kovac, Mötley's current manager. The company's roster includes the likes of Apocalyptica, Buckcherry, Hellyeah, Papa Roach, and Five Finger Death Punch.

JOHN CORABI, ON THE TURMOIL IN THE MÖTLEY CAMP AT THIS TIME:

The bottom line of it is, it was a political situation. They signed a huge record deal with Vince in the band for $30 or $40 million. A month or two later, they contact the record label and say, "By the way, we don't have that singer anymore. We got a new guy." In a quiet sense, it wasn't a big verbal disagreement or argument or anything like that. It wasn't even the staff at Elektra. I think it had more to do with the staff at Time Warner and WEA. Bob Krasnow, at the time, he was like, we support whatever decision you guys make. When our record came out, there was a five-year hiatus of Mötley Crüe, they changed singers, we still debuted in *Billboard* at #5. It wasn't bad. At that point, WEA and Time Warner stepped in and said to Bob, "You're out of here" and everybody else that was involved was fired too. I think they fired like sixty or seventy people. They got new people in there. When we were done with the tour, they talked to the guys and said, "Look, this is what we want." They had been harping on the guys for the better part of a year, year and a half to get Vince back in. There's $10 million lawsuits. There's just a bunch of political bullshit. It didn't have anything to do with how we were getting along.

JANUARY 14, 1997 Hits and rarities pack *Decade of Decadence* is certified double platinum.

JANUARY 23, 1997 The Skylar Neil Memorial Golf Tournaments fulfils a personal vow from Vince to contribute more to social causes, in the wake of Skylar's death. The celebrity tourney raises money for children with life-threatening diseases.

VINCE NEIL:

The music business is dirtier than the porno industry. I mean, everybody is out to fuck everybody else over. That's why we got out of Elektra Records and formed our own label. As a young band, yeah, you need a major label behind you because you obviously don't have the upfront capital to make your own records. But we're at the point in our career where we don't need to deal with any corporate bullshit, so it's good to have our own career in our own hands. It's in our own destiny.

TOMMY LEE ON HIS FAVORITE TIME TO WRITE MUSIC:

You know what? My favorite time of day is sunset. As the sun is setting down and the sky is orange, for some reason, that turns a switch on in me somewhere. That's my favorite time of day so my mood is pleasant, and that's when I seem to sit down and start writing music or lyrics or whatever. During the day, if it's a nice day, I'd rather be outside. But as the sun starts to set, for some reason, and it gets dark, that's when I feel most creative.

Reunited for some
press shots in Toronto.
© Darkophoto.com

JANUARY 27, 1997 The reunited Mötley Crüe performs for the first time at the American Music Awards, although Vince's vocals, for the re-engineered "Shout at the Devil '97," are prerecorded. The next day, strip club Girls, Girls, Girls, with involvement from Vince, opens in Japan.

FEBRUARY 18, 1997 Beck sends up Mötley's "Live Wire" video, in his treatment for his own song "The New Pollution." He appears in the video dressed as vintage Vince.

MARCH 27, 1997 Tempe, Arizona's 98 KUPD debut's "Afraid" from the forthcoming new Mötley album. Meanwhile, short clips from four songs had found their way onto the Internet, at this point still in its infancy with limited use.

NIKKI SIXX:

A song like "Afraid" is another pop song. And that's what Mötley Crüe really does best, whether it's the punkier edge of "Live Wire" from the first album or the funkier edge of "Dr. Feelgood." That's what we do, but we wanted to put some texture in there. Unlike the Bob Rock productions that were like full-force, in-your-face, and you go, "Okay, here's fourteen tracks of slamming Mick Mars guitars." I wrote "Afraid" about people who are—and I pointed to the opposite sex—about a girl who's afraid to live and to die. I have a firm belief in living and not just existing. There's lot of things that have been said lyrically about the album, as well as musically, that mean something to me right now, that when you take it into your gullet, it's like a whole different thing. And when your friend takes it, it'll mean another whole different thing. If I fucked your girlfriend in 1984, you probably don't listen with the same ears than if I didn't. It's Mötley Crüe. We're really one of those bands you really sink in and go, "This is really fucking honest" or you just really hate our guts. And I really love that. (*BW&BK*, 1997)

NIKKI SIXX ON "SHOUT AT THE DEVIL '97":

We had Jimmy "The Monkey" Cavalluzzo work on "Shout at the Devil." He did all the loops and stuff. We wanted to do an album, like a greatest hits album, where we redid every song. That's with that idea originally started from. We thought it would be great to do an EP with a fucked-up song from every album, or do a greatest hits album for a summertime tour, something really fun, but rerecord all the songs. We started talking about playing a song on the American Music Awards. We were going to play a new song, but the album wasn't going to be out in time, so somebody just said, fuck, man, what if we did "Shout at the Devil?" That got us back to the idea of updating it. It just fell together real quickly, and we put it on the album for some bizarre reason. Everybody thought, we should end the album with it or make it a bonus track. I said why? Because everybody else does? That's why we should put it in the middle of the album. (*BW&BK*, 1997)

Doing press at the Warehouse in Toronto, to discuss the reunion.

© Darkophoto.com

Mick at the Warehouse gig in Toronto.
© Darkophoto.com

VINCE NEIL:

We made some mistakes, you know? But nobody freaked out. We were rehearsing for weeks, but there's nothing like doing it live. I think we did a great job, and all of us had a hell of a time. When you get tight as a band, it's from playing together, and just being in a rehearsal studio for three weeks ain't gonna make you a tight, perfect band. Nobody got lost! Of course you make some mistakes, you get a little bummed, but in the overall picture, everyone was really happy. (*Metal Edge*, 1997)

APRIL 5, 1997 The reunited Mötley Crüe play their inaugural show at Livestock VII in Florida, to a crowd of approximately 30,000. Among the ten selections (including three of the as-yet unreleased new compositions), "Primal Scream" is played for the first time in front of a US audience. Opening selection to the one-hour set is "Shout at the Devil '97." Donna D'Errico, Pamela Anderson, and Vince's girlfriend Heidi Mark are all in attendance. Other bands at the Zephyr Hills festival included Jackyl, Type O Negative, Gravity Kills, Local H, Drain, and Helmet. AC/DC belter and Florida resident Brian Johnson guests onstage with local favorites Jackyl.

APRIL 27, 1997 The band embark on a promotional tour to Japan for the forthcoming new album, which had already shipped gold in advance of its release. Two nights later, Tommy and Nikki receive some new ink in their hotel room using traditional Japanese methods.

Nikki looks to the future, which is apparently hard right. © Darkophoto.com

NIKKI ON VINCE'S VOCAL WORK ON THE NEW ALBUM:
Vince has been really into experimenting vocally. He's got all sorts of bizarre ideas, left and right. That's what he really brings to the table. He's the vocalist. A lot of stuff like lyrics is really an essence of mind. Songwriting isn't so much his thing, but he's got this style. His style is very important. It's nice to see him taking his style, plus see him experimenting with it. We need that. We couldn't just have a rock singer. There's thing called chemistry. Chemistry works on different levels. Vince is a little fireball, I'm a fireball, and Tommy is a fireball. And Mick has his beliefs. That is what pushes the Crüe. (*BW&BK*, 1997)

MAY 9, 1997 The band hold a high-profile listening party for the new album at the Burbank Hilton in LA. Several hundred attend and they are mobbed for autographs, which spooks Vince. He cuts a quick exit, leaving Mick, Nikki, Tommy, and his wife Pamela to hold court.

MAY 15, 1997 *Shout at the Devil* is certified four times platinum while *Dr. Feelgood* attains six times platinum. Four days later, Vince participates in another celebrity golf tournament for children's charities.

MAY 20, 1997 Mötley is inducted into the Hollywood RockWalk, through the traditional cement handprint ceremony.

JUNE 9, 1997 MTV premieres the video for "Afraid."

JUNE 10, 1997 The band perform the entire new album plus select classics at a theatre show in LA to launch the album and tour. A Q&A is also part of the festivities and profits are donated to the Skylar Neil Foundation.

NIKKI SIXX:

There's no denying the pop sensibility of a song like "Afraid" or "Beauty." I've heard people say, "Oh man, anybody out there? It's like 'Live Wire' meets 'Anarchy in the UK.'" Yeah, it is. But if you really strip away the labels again, everybody walks around going, "I wanna be a dog. I wanna be your man." It's just a little snotty pop song and it's cool. I think that we'll get those short-attention span people because it's impossible for us to write riff rock. With John Corabi, we had a little different chemistry going on inside the band. John played guitar and songs were written from a guitar standpoint first. Tommy would lay down a groove and me, Mick, and John would start playing along. We were just in this sweatbox in the Valley somewhere just going, "This is fucking heavy. This is fucking great." It was so much fun. But then we'd listen to the tape back and get bored." [BW&BK, 1997]

NIKKI SIXX ON THE EXPERIMENTATION TAKING PLACE ON *GENERATION SWINE*:

Anything goes in the studio. If somebody says, "Let's grab a cellist and put him through the Polyfusion and then distort it and run it through a megaphone and then compress it and then put it backwards in the computer and chop it up into eighth notes!," "Okay" would be the answer. The other answer would be, "Done." By the time you got through telling Scott what you wanted, he was already done organizing the first half. What happens with that is so many accidents happen. I could say to the band, "Okay, everybody shut their eyes. Count to four and hit any chord you want and then just start following Tommy in that key." Mick would hit an E and I would hit an A. We'd go, "Fuck! That's insane!" And we'd drop that in the middle of a song. Just fucking splice it right in. A lot of these songs were written and just fucking Frankenstein-ed after. Just raped and pillaged and wrecked and fucked with, man. And the only way to get rubbers—that's what we call it when one note rubs against the other note and you go, "God, that's wrong"—is to just throw things against the wall. If it sticks, awesome.

There's something of a disconnect between this pass graphic and the idea of Mötley. Tom Wojcik Collection

Reunion show at the Riviera Theatre in Chicago, June 14, 1997. © Tom Wojcik

TOMMY LEE:

The *Generation Swine* album, Nikki and I pretty much wrote most of that record. That's when I was really pushing the pedal down as far as going in a new . . . not a new direction, but trying to push the envelope for us, take some chances, try some different things. And that album wasn't too well received, I remember. People expected Mötley Crüe to be a certain way. And I fucking remember that it was so frustrating. And the John Corabi album, I love that album too! It's insane, it's so fucking heavy! You know what? Those are probably my two favorite Mötley Crüe albums. And I just found that so frustrating. And I clearly remember that I couldn't work with Vince at some point. At one point it worked really well. We were all having a good time, then it stopped working. Then John came into the band—new blood, yeah! This is cool, heavier direction, and then Vince came back. And when Vince came back, that's when I said to myself, you know, this didn't work already once. This feels really forced and unnatural. And that's when I started writing music, and knowing I was writing for something else. That's when I started getting it together with my songwriting skills and playing a lot of guitar. I just knew I was going to move on to something else. But those two records, I don't know if I find like any of them better. They both had their really cool moments. One was really heavy and one was more punk rock and futuristic.

JUNE 24, 1997 Mötley Crüe issue *Generation Swine*, which marks the return of Vince Neil (the album sees Japanese release a month earlier and European release two weeks earlier). Previous lead singer John Corabi is credited on two tracks, although in the lead-up to the album, it was looking like he'd be included on six or seven songs. There had also been talk of him staying in the band as second guitarist. The launch finds the band in New York City, performing ten songs live in the street and appearing on *David Letterman*. There is also a band appearance at Tower Records for the midnight unleashing of the album. A highlight of the on-street performance is "Afraid." Vince is resplendent in red hair, sunglasses, and leathers and Tommy is aggressively pounding out the experimental song.

NIKKI SIXX:

It's deep; we wanted depth. What we wanted to do was mock our heroes. We all do. I was mocking the concept behind David Bowie's *Diamond Dogs*, which had pop songs with so much depth underneath them. And the only current record that I can put my finger on was the *Zooropa* album by U2. Pop songs are simple fuckin' ditties. A song like "Rocket Ship" is 1:57 long. And it's a pop song, but underneath it, there's all this texture and stuff. We wanted to go, "No, man, let's do one track, EQ all the bottom end out of it and throw some weird fucking filter cross it and bring that in for the verses. And on the choruses, let's go somewhere else." So the listener really went on a journey. What it all comes down to is the music. The listener who's out there waxing his car on a Sunday afternoon or throwing the football around in the park or drinking a beer with a buddy in a bar and it comes across the sound system, it's a song, man. Either you like it or you don't. All that other stuff is unimportant if the song's not good. So our first vision is to write great songs. (*BW&BK*, 1997)

Tom Wojcik Collection

JUNE 28, 1997 The band perform at the massive Roskilde Festival in Denmark, amidst a decidedly alternative rock roster, including Primus, Silverchair, Beck, Smashing Pumpkins, Radiohead, Pavement, and 311.

JULY 2, 1997 *Generation Swine* debuts at #4 in *Billboard*.

NIKKI SIXX:

With *Swine*, the production sometimes got in the way. Mötley Crüe doesn't write that kind of music. So it was kind of a battle between the band and the producer wanting to do something and us wanting to embrace new technology, but at the same time, try not to make Mötley Crüe sound like Filter or the Chemical Brothers or something. Mötley was trying, is trying, and will always be trying to live in the present. And to redefine ourselves every time. We hope to evolve into an Aerosmith or an AC/DC or a Rolling Stones. (*Extreme*, 2000)

Nikki in Toronto, dressed down for the semi-casual press day and gig. © Darkophoto.com

JOHN CORABI, ON THE RESOLUTION OF HIS LAWSUIT WITH THE BAND:

Let's just put it this way, we settled it, and Mötley's happy and I'm happy too, and it's gone. And the thing is, we went to the show, I took my girlfriend Lela with me, and we had a great time. Vince was very cordial to me; he came over and gave me a big hug, Nikki gave me a hug, told me he missed me, I told him I missed him, and that was nice and it was really cool. I got to see them play, it was a great show and it was sold out. And Nikki and I have talked to each other a couple times on the phone. I said there were a few songs left over while I was in the band that we didn't put on *Generation Swine*, and I thought they were great fucking songs. I would like to do some recording, put some songs together, like just to do a little solo thing. and I asked Nikki if he'd be into either writing or letting me take a look at some of those other tunes that we wrote together. He said, "Yeah, fuck, let's do it!" So, yes, I would be into getting together with Nikki and doing some writing. I think there are some songs during that period that really didn't get an opportunity to grow or breathe or whatever. Vince came back into the band and they opted for more . . . I don't want to say industrial, but they really went heavy with the Pro Tools. and I think there are some songs that really had a life but really didn't get a chance.

JULY 7, 1997 John Corabi files a lawsuit against the band and Elektra, citing multiple breaches.

JULY 18, 1997 The band visit Jay Leno and the Tonight Show to perform "Afraid." Meanwhile, "Beauty" is picked as the album's second single.

NIKKI SIXX:

That was a song that I wrote for my side project. I love of old Iggy and Sisters of Mercy, that whole fucking thing—Bowie *Low*—so I sing like that a lot. That was a song I wrote for 58 and everyone liked it and then Vince was like, "You know, Nikki, you should sing it." I was singing lead vocal on another song called "Find Myself." We were like, Tommy's singing on this song, I'm singing two songs, Tommy sings a part of this other song, we can't do this. We got Vince back in the band because we want people to hear his voice. He went in and sang that song, "Beauty," so cool.

AUGUST 16, 1997 The band perform two shows in Tokyo, and are presented with awards for *Generation Swine* achieving platinum sales in Japan.

AUGUST 26, 1997 *Generation Swine* is RIAA-certified gold in America, matching its predecessor, as plans for the futuristic stage set for the upcoming tour are finalized. "Beauty" stalls at mainstream radio with hopes pinned on the release of "Glitter."

SEPTEMBER 10, 1997 The band embark on a glitzy nine-stop press conference by private jet to announce the Apple-sponsored *Mötley Crüe Versus the Earth* tour.

NIKKI SIXX:

The last interview I did, asked why was there no melody that album? I hear that it's a hip-hop album and I hear that it's an industrial album and I even hear that it's a punk album. And I'm like, what?! We hear it's our best album and our worst album. It's our *Come Taste the Band*, which is my favorite album of theirs, and most people fucking hate it. People are like, "No, that ain't Deep Purple, man." It sounds different, too funky. But *Generation Swine* was just another growth process. I think having Scott Humphrey in there, a guy who had direct hands-on access to computers, made a difference. With stuff like *Dr. Feelgood*, and even stuff like "Primal Scream," we dumped them into a computer, did some sort of editing and playing around with it to get it really rhythmically tight. This was sort of *recorded* into the computer and then it was assembled. Which is what we did not do with "Bitter Pill" and "Enslaved."

SEPTEMBER 14, 1997 As Mötley grace the cover of the December issue of *Hustler*, tickets go on sale for the upcoming tour, selling briskly through nascent Internet channels.

SEPTEMBER 27, 1997 Nikki finds out that his father had died a decade ago, on Christmas Day. He and Donna locate and visit his grave in San Jose. Nikki gets closure with respect to his abandonment at three years old, by berating his father at graveside.

OCTOBER 3, 1997 Tommy and Pam take a Learjet to Mexico to celebrate Tommy's birthday, a week in advance of the much vaunted new Mötley tour dates.

OCTOBER 10, 1997 Mötley begin their tour in support of *Generation Swine* in Cedar Rapids, Iowa, with Cheap Trick—revered by the Mötley guys—as support. The band institute a $25,000 fine on each other to ensure sobriety on the tour. Vince soon has to shell out.

OCTOBER 19, 1997 Hardcore porn is "inexplicably" shown on screen before the band hits the state in Pittsburgh. Parents who brought their kids are incensed. A couple nights later, at Nassau Coliseum, Vince brawls with a fan in the crowd.

Pass for the Aragon Ballroom show in Chicago, November 14, 1998. Tom Wojcik Collection

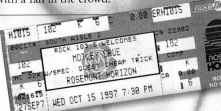

Tom Wojcik Collection

1998

FEBRUARY 9, 1998 Mötley begin work on a proposed covers album, provisionally titled *A Record to Crash Your Car To*. Three days later, Vince presents the second instalment of the Skylar Neil Memorial Golf Tournament.

FEBRUARY 24, 1998 Union issue their self-titled debut album; the band is the brainchild of John Corabi and Bruce Kulick.

JOHN CORABI ON HIS APPROACH TO VOCALS WITH UNION VERSUS MÖTLEY:

I wanted to do this, but I wouldn't say I always wanted to do this. Because when I did the Scream and the Mötley Crüe album, I did what I knew how to do, and that was just step up to the mic and start screaming. It's really strange, it wasn't like I was thinking about the future. But when we did the last record, I thought it's really, really hard to go out onstage every night and sing stuff like "Smoke the Sky" from that Mötley record. I mean, Brian Johnson, I got to tip the guy my hat. I don't know how he does it every night, night in, night out. And I just wanted to try some different things. I liked guys like Paul Rodgers, many different singers, so I wanted to exercise the lower part of my voice and give each song its own voice. If the song needed a low whispery-type voice, give it that. A lot of the time with the past, everybody went, "Cool, Corabi's a belter, yeah; just sing it as high as you can." And I'm like, "Well, I think we're kind of missing the boat here." So each song has its own personality or mood and I wanted to accentuate the music with whatever kind of voice I heard in my head. It's weird, because there are still some parts of songs where I am belting, but we chose to put it in the background.

Mick settles into the reunion with Vince. © Kevin Estrada

Legendary LA photographer Kevin Estrada's personal copy of *Greatest Hits*. Kevin Estrada Collection

FEBRUARY 26, 1998 Pam files for divorce from Tommy.

MARCH 13, 1998 Mötley extricate themselves from their deal with Elektra and as part of the arrangement, receive back their masters. They are now in total control of their catalogue, a rarity in the business.

APRIL 5, 1998 Nikki muses over releasing a book of poetry or perhaps a large cache of paintings that he has been working on, but most significantly, lets on that the idea of a covers album has been dropped. Additionally, he has been writing songs slated for use by Crüe, including "Erotic," "Bloodsucker" (variably "Bloodsuckers"), and "Americoma," which he has also tapped as the new name for a record label he wants to start. In more lurid news, both Tommy's and Vince's sex tapes are now widely available, Tommy's amidst a firestorm of press coverage for both the tape and his divorce proceedings with Pam. Nikki is enjoying domestic bliss with Donna and Mick is with a dynamic new girlfriend named Robbie Lauren Mantooth, an underwater photographer who also works in film.

BRUCE KULICK ON JOHN CORABI'S VOCAL PROWESS:

John's vocals are very versatile. Each song needs to be addressed a specific way. You know, sometimes John has that angry voice, and then he is more of an emotional singer. John does have a couple of different styles, ranging from Beatlesque to full-tilt, and I think you hear that full range. John's vocals as a result are very big and strong, and even if he is singing softly, he sounds really big.

APRIL 30, 1998 John Corabi's and Bruce Kulick's band Union play live for the first time, in San Diego. The *Motley Crue* album's "Power to the People" is included in the set.

MAY 15, 1998 Four days' worth of work gets done on new songs, including bed tracks and some guitars, to add to a proposed new Mötley Crüe greatest hits album, producer Bob Rock presiding.

MAY 20, 1998 Tommy is sentenced to six months in jail for spousal abuse, on top of three years probation. He is immediately led away to jail. Undaunted and having recorded rhythm tracks for some new songs, the band grinds on (with Nikki keeping in touch with Tommy every day in jail), with Mick working on guitars at Nikki's home studio and Vince and Nikki flying to Hawaii to work at Bob Rock's house.

JUNE 1998 Tommy keeps mentally fit in jail by voraciously reading, mostly psychology books on relationships, and planning material for a new solo album, calling in ideas to his home answering machine. Vince never visits him in jail and Mick, only once. Tommy soon gets a payphone installed in his cell and starts reaching out to his kids, Pam, and a life coach, but the payphone privileges don't last long.

AUGUST 25, 1998 Rob Zombie's *Hellbilly Deluxe* features Tommy drumming on two tracks, as well as coproduction by Mötley coproducer Scott Humphrey.

SEPTEMBER 5, 1998 Tommy is released from jail, having served just over three months of his six-month sentence, time reduced for good behavior.

TOMMY LEE:

I'm looking forward to the new year just to put all this bullshit behind me. When I got out, the first thing I did was sit in a jacuzzi at a friend's place right on the beach. Just looking up at the stars, I had a fucking anxiety attack. Seeing cars and traffic signals and people. I was just like, whoa! Decompression. I went from nothing, solitary confinement, to okay, we're back out in the world. Panic set in. So I just chilled at my buddy's house for a while and he eventually took me home. I put on some really fucking loud music, played my piano, played the drums, played the guitar. It was so great to hear music again. Eventually I got tired and went to sleep. A week or so after that I went to Hawaii. I've got three years' probation with drug testing and all that shit. For the last eight months, I've been sober, so I don't really miss the partying. I don't think about it. I've got two kids now. It's not just me I'm responsible for anymore. Things start to change in your life when you've got little guys that really depend on you. You've got to be up early in the morning and they play hard. They rock out, so I can't be fucking hungover and stoned and shit. (*BW&BK*, 1998)

TOMMY LEE:

I was in solitary confinement for my own protection. It was good in one sense, but I felt like I was in a fucking submarine. I went down and never came up. There was no one to talk to but the fucking cockroaches. It was a trip, but cool. In many ways, a fucking amazing learning experience. You start seeing things you love about yourself, things you hate about yourself. I dare people to sit alone for four months. Most people can't stand themselves, or they're afraid of themselves. I took that experience, and turned it from what could've been a bitter, negative experience into a positive. I read forty books while I was in jail. I did a ton of introspection on myself. I walked out of there a different person. (*BW&BK*, 1998)

SEPTEMBER 12, 1998 Nikki picks Laidlaw (previously Moonshine) to support the band on their next tour, with further backups being chosen through a battle of the bands called *Kickstart Your Career*. Nikki had been working with the band, who are to issue their album on Nikki's boutique label.

NIKKI SIXX:

If a band is thinking about getting signed, and they have under their belt that they won a battle of the bands to open up for Mötley Crüe, it brings some awareness to the band.

VINCE NEIL:

Yeah, with each city, instead of just having some people travel around with us and open up for us, let's give back to the bands. So we decided on this *Kickstart Your Career*, and have the fans vote on who to open up for us. And we're looking for acts for Mötley Crüe Records, so we can find some people. And you just give a shot in the arm to some local acts that haven't played in front of an audience like this. It gives them exposure in the same way that we got a break. So we're just helping some other people out too.

MÖTLE

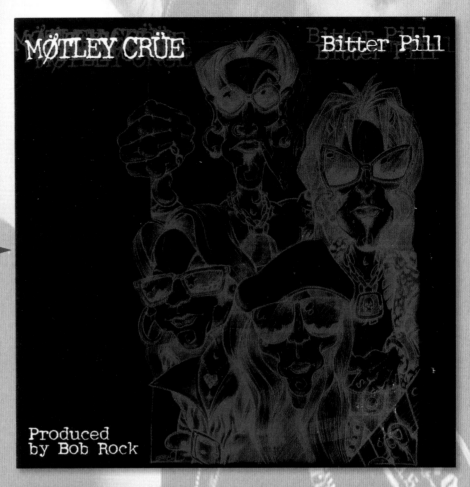

Cover of the promo issue of one of two new first-rate anthems featured on the *Greatest Hits* album. Tom Wojcik Collection

MICK MARS:

We always go to each other's houses. I mean all the fucking time. Even to visit, we always end up in the studio. We always write. I go over to Nikki's house and he tells me his idea. Tommy would come over and we would start fucking around; "Bitter Pill" comes out. And Tommy says he has an idea. So we all hustle over to Tommy's house and goof around and all this amazing stuff comes out. So we put them down on a DAT, send them to Bob Rock, and he says, "These fucking songs are amazing!" So enter Bob Rock and we go in the studio. That's basically how they came about. (*BW&BK*, 1998)

SEPTEMBER 23, 1998 The Bob Rock–produced "Bitter Pill" is released to radio, as the band begin rehearsals for their *Greatest Hits* tour. Tommy, fresh out of jail and some vacation time in Hawaii, is tentative about working with Mötley, having had his priorities vastly rearranged by his jail time.

TOMMY LEE:

Bob only had time to do a couple of tracks because he was in between Metallica and Bryan Adams. Really, there wasn't enough room for any more tracks time-wise on the CD. We only had time for two, really, because I had to go to jail and do time. I had a little window before I had to go away. And we cut the tracks real quick. When I went away, the guys finished doing some overdubs.

Anything called a Greatest Hits Tour is bound to see strong ticket sales. Tom Wojcik Collection

NIKKI SIXX:

The first time we played "Bitter Pill" and then the second night we performed "Wild Side," and a few of the guys who were big Mötley fans came up onstage, D-Generation X. They just came out and sang with me a little bit, and posed for the crowd and stuff. It was fun and all tongue-in-cheek—it felt good.

VINCE NEIL:

Wrestling and rock 'n' roll, there are so many similarities. It's the same fans, the same lifestyles. So we were approached to do it, and we were like, yeah! Same people, so it was cool. We've already shot the stuff. Tonight it's going to be "Wild Side."

OCTOBER 20, 1998 Mötley perform at WWF's high profile *Raw is War* in Madison, Wisconsin.

TOMMY LEE:

One of the wrestlers, the Undertaker, has come to see us play many times and there's always been a friendship connection there. The WWF asked us to come and do it. They've got thirty-five million viewers! That's fucking huge, man. It was a perfect opportunity. We've got a new record coming out, let's go play it. It was like a fucking rock show, man. We were tripping! You go there and they've got fucking pyros blowing up. There's 16,000 screaming fans in the audience in a big arena. It was perfect. They set up a stage at one end, the wrestling ring was in the middle, very cool. Those are some big motherfuckers, man. I'm 6'2" and those guys were fucking towering over me. (*BW&BK*, 1998)

OCTOBER 21, 1998–DECEMBER 20, 1998 Mötley execute the *Greatest Hits* tour, Laidlaw in tow, blanketing America with one Canadian date on October 27, at Toronto's venerable 2,200-capacity theatre venue Massey Hall, with the show attended by the author.

OCTOBER 28, 1998 Mötley appear on *Conan O'Brien*, performing "Dr. Feelgood" and a partial "Kickstart My Heart."

OCTOBER 29, 1998 Mötley play for MTV but a visit to Howard Stern is scrubbed when they can't get into the building. An intimate Beacon Theatre show takes place the following day followed by another cozy theatre stop in Boston on Halloween.

Rear Inlay for the promo "Bitter Pill" CD single. Tom Wojcik Collection

VINCE NEIL, ON WHETHER THE TWO NEW TRACKS REPRESENT THE BAND'S NEW DIRECTION:

I don't know. I think it might be that direction but a lot of things will happen between now and then, by the time another studio record comes out. But we are kind of back to our roots, back to where we need to be, because that's what Mötley Crüe is. We're always going to experiment with different textures, but I think we'll try to keep the basic roots there.

TOMMY LEE ON "ENSLAVED":

That one I wrote. But the way I wrote it, that's not the way it sounded. It was recorded very standard, very stock. The way I wrote the song, if you hear the demos, it sounds very different.

NOVEMBER 14, 1998 Mötley Crüe issue *Greatest Hits*, which peaks at #20 in *Billboard*. The album features, as the first two tracks on the album, two brand-new yet old school Mötley compositions, "Enslaved" (original title: "Slave") and "Bitter Pill" (the longstanding original title of the album was to be *Bitter Pills*). Into the new year, the album would moderately climb the charts, reaching #142, as the band continued to tour heavily behind it. The album saw release in Japan a month before its US release date, through Polydor, without the usual requisite bonus tracks. The cover art for the record features an illustrated caricature of the band, in homage to the cartoony Al Hirschfeld image Aerosmith used for the cover of 1977's *Draw the Line*.

NIKKI SIXX ON THE COMPLEX MELODIES WITHIN THE TWO NEW SONGS:

I think the complexity level goes up with any band as you grow musically. If you are a fan of music, you listen to more music and music revolves around you and you find yourself being influenced. Like when we first started out, we were influenced by our roots, which was somewhere between heavy metal and punk rock, and as you get older new influences come in. As a matter of fact, me and Vince happen to be big fans of the Eagles, so I'm sure at some point that sinks in. I like trip-hop and hip-hop, so that sneaks in, and industrial sneaks in. But it all kind of goes into a blender. We blend it all up and it becomes kind of what the band is all about. But it's never trying to be about something we're not.

NOVEMBER 19, 1998 Mötley experiment with retail, opening S'Crüe on Melrose Avenue, selling Crüe merchandise along with Vince's and Nikki's clothing lines. The shop closes by January of the following year.

DECEMBER 11, 1998 Nikki is pranked onstage in Florida for his fortieth birthday. First he is handcuffed to a wheelchair. Then two male strippers dressed as police officers perform a striptease, with the coup de grâce being a surprise visit from his wife Donna, also dressed as a police officer, who flashes him with a four on one breast and a zero on the other. The party continues back home in Malibu two days later with a lavishly decorated house and a nice family gathering.

DECEMBER 13, 1998 VH1's *Behind the Music* on Mötley airs, helping the revive the band's profile. The episode becomes the highest rated of the series.

1999

FEBRUARY 10-MARCH 28, 1999 Mötley conduct a second leg of their *Greatest Hits* tour, hitting mostly smaller markets throughout the US and Canada.

FEBRUARY 23, 1999 An Alice Cooper tribute album called *Humanary Stew* includes both Vince and Mick on a rendition of Crüe-worthy rocker "Cold Ethyl."

MARCH 16, 1999 Target retails a Mötley Crüe toy car, a black Firebird stamped with the old school Mötley logo. Another car is issued three weeks later, a Camaro with a *Decade of Decadence* theme. May brings a '75 Chevy Bel Air with a *Dr. Feelgood* theme.

MARCH 17, 1999 Vince and Tommy get into a physical fight at the airport in Las Vegas; Tommy vows to quit the band but Nikki talks him into finishing the tour, which now requires as much separation as possible between Tommy and Vince. Meanwhile Tommy has taken up with Carmen Electra, much to the annoyance of ex-boyfriend Dennis Rodman. Soon this transitions into warming relations with Pam.

MICK MARS, ON PLANS FOR A SOLO ALBUM:

I wouldn't call it traditional blues. There's a lot of percussion, a lot of horns, a lot of funk, plus that old R&B stuff. Not just your typical three chords. I love John Lee Hooker, but it isn't that, it's more aggressive. If you were to take an old Tower of Power song and add some scratching, you add a big-ass guitar onto it with a lot of mood, that's where I'm coming from. (*BW&BK*, 1998)

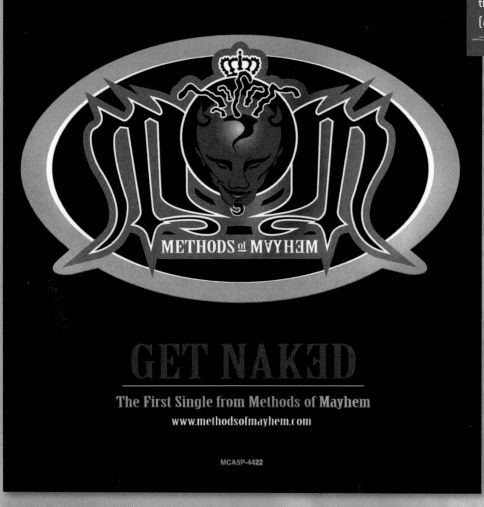

Picture sleeve cover art for promo issue of *Methods of Mayhem's* "Get Naked." Author's Collection

APRIL 13, 1999 "Kickstart My Heart" is included in a CD that is issued compiling the bands that were part of the *Kickstart My Career* promotion engineered to pick bands for backup status on the Crüe tour.

APRIL 16, 1999 Vince attends an auto race and promotes his Bad Bones clothing line, signing autographs and doing interviews. The following week brings the Third Annual Skylar Neil Memorial Golf Tournament, where Vince's son Neil wins runner-up.

APRIL 27, 1999 The celebrated Mötley edition of *Behind the Music* is issued on DVD, featuring ten additional minutes.

APRIL 29, 1999 Tommy Lee announces publicly that he's leaving Mötley Crüe. He wants to focus on his new project Methods of Mayhem as well as repair his family with Pam.

Mötley enter the era of the big double bills. Tom Wojcik Collection

VINCE NEIL:

Well, it's called, he wants to be a rapper (laughs) and we're a rock band. That's really it. He quit the band to be a rapper and you know, there's no rap in Mötley Crüe. He did not want to play drums any more and he did not want to be in rock anymore. I mean, if you don't want to play rock 'n' roll, then yeah, go do something else.

APRIL 30, 1999 "Shout at the Devil" is included in horror comedy *Idle Hands*. The same day, Tommy talks about his break with Mötley on KROQ while debuting a new Methods of Mayhem song, "Get Naked."

MAY 6, 1999 Mötley announce that Tommy's replacement is Randy Castillo, who had played previously in Vince's solo band.

Photo pass for a date on Maximum Rock; usually the rule is access to the photo pit for the first three songs.
Tom Wojcik Collection

TOMMY LEE:

Back when Vince got in the band, we tried to take on a new fresh perspective, the *Generation Swine* record—which I thought was one of Mötley's best records—and it wasn't received well with the fans. People weren't having it. They weren't accepting anything other than the same old version of Mötley Crüe and that's when I realized I gotta go do something else. Then we had management and stuff bringing in Bob Rock to get that same sound that was once successful on *Dr. Feelgood*, and all of it started to wear on me. (*Metal Edge*, 1999)

MAY 18, 1999 John Corabi's band Union issue a live album, *Live in the Galaxy*, which includes a rendition of "Power to the People."

NIKKI SIXX:

We're one of the few bands in history who got all of our albums back, the masters. We are forming our own label with BMG and Beyond. We have our *Greatest Hits* out and are going to be rereleasing all our albums, but with each one there's going to be songs that weren't released at the time, from those various eras. People are going to get stuff that was recorded in 1981, 1982. It's going to be a really cool thing for the fans. We're going to keep them limited. We don't want it to be like that's the way it is. There will be 300,000 or 400,000 of each one, and then after that it will revert back to the original album. I mean as a fan, if I could get *Get Your Wings* by Aerosmith, with two new songs from those sessions, I would be excited as hell!

Nikki opens up the vaults.

Author's Collection

JUNE 1, 1999 The first four Mötley Crüe albums see limited edition, remastered rerelease, with bonus tracks. *Too Fast for Love* adds "Toast of the Town" (unreleased track), "Tonight" (unreleased track), "Too Fast for Love" (alternate intro), and "Stick to Your Guns" (unreleased track). *Shout at the Devil* adds "Shout at the Devil" (demo), "Looks that Kill" (demo), "Hotter than Hell" (demo), and "I Will Survive" (unreleased track). *Theatre of Pain* adds "Home Sweet Home" (demo), "Smokin' in the Boys Room" (alternate guitar solo—rough mix), "City Boy Blues" (demo), "Home Sweet Home" (instrumental rough mix), "Keep Your Eye on the Money" (demo), and "Tommy's Drum Piece from Cherokee Studios." *Girls, Girls, Girls* adds "Girls, Girls, Girls" (Tom Werman and band intro—rough mix of instrumental track), "Wild Side" (instrumental—rough mix of instrumental track), "Rodeo" (unreleased track), "Nona" (instrumental demo idea), and "All in the Name of . . ." (Live—Moscow).

JUNE 17, 1999 Universal and Tommy sign a deal toward the release of his proposed Methods of Mayhem album.

JUNE 29, 1999 Three additional reissues plus a compilation add to the campaign commenced on June 1, with the expanded reissue of *Dr. Feelgood, Motley Crue,* and *Generation Swine,* plus a new rarities pack called *Supersonic and Demonic Relics. Dr. Feelgood* adds "Dr. Feelgood" (demo), "Without You" (demo), "Kickstart My Heart" (demo), and "Get it for Free" (unreleased track). *Motley Crue* adds "Hypnotized" (unreleased track), "Babykills" (from *Quaternary*), and "Livin' in the Know" (unreleased track. *Generation Swine* adds: "Afraid" (swine mix/Jimbo mix), "Wreck Me" (unreleased track), "Kiss the Sky" (unreleased track), "Rocketship" (early demo), and "Confessions" (demo—Tommy vocal). The track list for *Supersonic and Demonic Relics (Decade of Decadence, Quaternary,* and additional tracks) is as follows: "Teaser," "Primal Scream," "Sinners & Saints" (unreleased track), "Monsterous" (unreleased track), "Say Yeah" (unreleased track), "Planet Boom," "Bittersuite," "Father," "Anarchy in the UK," "So Good, So Bad" (unreleased track), "Hooligan's Holiday" (extended holiday version by Skinny Puppy), "Rock 'n' Roll Junkie," "Angela," "Mood Ring" (unreleased track), and "Dr. Feelgood" (live).

TOMMY LEE ON THE PROJECT'S HIGH-PROFILE RAP GUESTS:

Sometimes we would just let them take a big ol' pass at something, and we would go, "Yeah, that section and that section are awesome, boom, let's take those." So it was similar but different for each person. Style-wise, it's a free for all, just all the styles that are exciting to me and TiLo. We're combining, techno, hip-hop, metal, there's a bit of jungle in there, a few industrial flavors, there's just a little bit of all of our inspirations. In this project, I want to be on the fucking mic with TiLo, and I want to play guitar, and I want everybody to get fucking pumped. So yes, there'll be times when I'll be playing guitar and Stephen Perkins will be holding down the fort. I'm so excited about all this, I can't wait to start.

NIKKI SIXX:

There seems to be a resurgence on at this time. Somebody was telling us that the Kiss album, the Mötley album, the Sabbath album, they are all in the charts, so it's a breath of fresh air. Yes, our album just by being a greatest hits album will be one of the biggest sellers of the year, just because anybody, the country fans even, could go, I remember that song, I'm gonna get that. But there is no loyalty in this business. This album could sell five million copies, and next record can sell nine. That's what we've come to experience now in the industry. It's a very strange time. It used to be that you sell a million, then you sell two, then you three, then you sell four, then you sell five, and then you break up (laughs).

JUNE 29-SEPTEMBER 6, 1999 Mötley embark on the *Crucial Crüe* tour, tied to the reissue program of the same name. The band is supported by Flash Bastard, protégés of Nikki, and German rock titans Scorpions, who take an instant dislike to Flash Bastard and have them tossed off the tour within a week. Drummer for Mötley is Randy Castillo.

AUGUST 7, 1999 Vince is hit square in the throat by a tequila bottle onstage in Bakersfield, California. Unable to speak, it initially looks grave but he recovers and is able to complete the tour.

AUGUST 11, 1999 Nikki is thrown in jail for the night following the band's show in Las Vegas after nearly enticing a riot onstage as he reminded the crowd of the band's bad relationship with Las Vegas police force.

SEPTEMBER 7, 1999 Aerosmith tribute album *Same Old Song and Dance* includes renditions of "Chip Away the Stone" with Vince on vocals and "Sweet Emotion" with Randy Castillo on drums.

SEPTEMBER 22, 1999 *Greatest Hits* is certified gold, underscoring the fact that a band with history and legs can always sell compilations.

Japanese ad for the reissue series. Author's Collection

OCTOBER 4-15, 1999 Mötley tours Japan, dubbing the event the *Welcome to the Freekshow* tour.

OCTOBER 21, 1999 Mötley performs for *VH1 Hard Rock Live*, at Sony Studios in New York.

OCTOBER 26, 1999 Mötley tourmates Laidlaw issue their debut Nikki Sixx-produced album, *First Big Picnic*, on Nikki's label, Americoma Records.

NIKKI SIXX ON MÖTLEY'S MARKETING ACUMEN:

You are looking at the hotshot PR and marketing people right here (laughs). All of us brainstorm. We just had a few new ideas a few minutes ago. And what we do is take those ideas and give it to our management people Left Bank, who are a marketing company. That's what they do—they market. They say this is how we can make this happen and that happen. They are really brilliant in their own field, and it's just a great team. That's actually how the Beyond/Mötley Records association started, with Allen Kovac who, Left Bank is his baby. We sat down with him and said, "Our dream is to have our masters." Because we don't think anybody deserves to have them as much as the band who created them. And that was our goal. When we got our masters, that's when we said, "Okay, let's form Mötley Records." And Allen wanted to form Beyond Records, and he had some goals too. So together we took all of our power—his power and our power—and formed a relationship with BMG, and now we are basically set up in business to be our own power source. We can do what we want to do musically and visually. And like Vince said, we've been brainstorming and it's only going to grow. There will be offshoot companies. So Vince has companies he's planning on putting together. Me and Vince independently each have clothing lines. He has Bad Bones, and I have Outlaw, and we're very much into entrepreneuring. The problem with being with someone like Warner Bros./Elektra, is that they want to keep you under their thumb. "No, we only want you to do Mötley Crüe, we don't want to know about a Vince Neil solo album, we don't want to know about Nikki Sixx producing, we don't want to know about Mick Mars wanting to do a compilation blues album, we just want you to do this! Don't stray." And now we're in a position to do all this other stuff and put all our influences into the band.

NOVEMBER 23, 1999 Mötley Records issues *Live: Entertainment or Death*, a two-CD career-spanning live album which, amid controversy, seems to include much rerecording of Vince's vocals. Nikki had often voiced his opinion that he wasn't a fan of live albums, so it's understandable it had taken so long for the band to issue one. Liner notes are provided by top Mötley expert Paul Miles. The album debuts on the *Billboard* charts at #133. Guns N' Roses' much anticipated live album, *Live Era '87–'93*, issued the same day, doesn't fare much better comparatively, peaking at #45. Meanwhile Metallica's live-with-orchestra album *S&M*, issued the previous day, enters the charts at #2.

Promo sampler to celebrate the claw-back of the catalogue and the subsequent reissues with bonus tracks.
Author's Collection

TOMMY LEE ON HIS HARD BREAK WITH THE BOYS:

I haven't talked to them since I left, which is fucked, because I didn't want it to end that way. Vince and I got into a fistfight like nine shows before it was going to end, him being intoxicated every night. He was so dysfunctional that I couldn't handle it. Especially when fuckin' I'm trying to be sober, trying to fuckin' get my life together, and this guy is just shitty every night, "Fuck ya!, how ya doing?!" It's like if you go to a club and you haven't had any cocktails, and you have some drunk guy hanging all over you and pawing you, dude! Like that dude last night, shaking my hand and crushing it. It's like, dude, and he's punching me, and I'm like, I'm about to fuckin' fuck this dude up—you better get some security out here. I don't know, man, to be in a band with someone like that, I don't know how he can handle it. It's a relationship. Like me and him (points to *Methods of Mayhem* mate TiLo), we're fuckin' like each other's bitches in a sense, and we've signed our social security number after it—it's like we got married. If we want to be not married, we go to court. It's the same thing with the Crüe. When he left, I remember, he got the lawyer that is a Master P's lawyer, No Limit Records, which is a really big hip-hop label, and the band had like sixteen lawyers or something. It's crazy that it comes to things like that, you know. The other two guys, they were fine. They were their normal selves. That's the sad part. That's the part that bothers me, because I really like those guys. For the longest time, things have been really difficult. Vince is really just not a nice person, and it's hard to be around that.

DECEMBER 6, 1999 Tommy begins a one-month long VJ slot with MTV's *Return of the Rock.*

Author's personal copy, signed during a hotel room interview on Tommy's and TiLo's press stop in Toronto.
Author's Collection

Tom Wojcik Collection

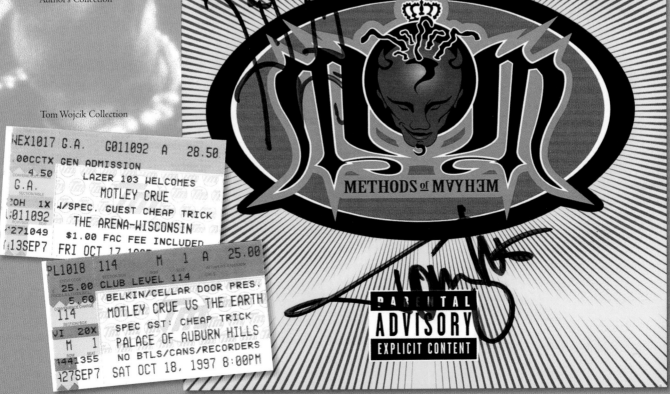

TOMMY LEE:

The *Methods of Mayhem* record for me was like a creative free-for-all. I was fresh out of the Crüe and I just wanted to do everything. I'm such a fan of so many different styles of music so that's why that album turned out very eclectic from track to track, full-on, tons of guest stars, just a creative free-for-all.

VINCE NEIL:

Well, me and Tommy went to high school together and we were great friends when we were younger. You know, I think Tommy just believes too much of his own press for his own good. He can be a really nice guy but all of a sudden, once he married Heather, he thought he was a movie star, and he thinks he still is. And I think he's just forgotten what his roots were, which is that he's a great drummer. But he refuses to play drums anymore.

DECEMBER 7, 1999 Tommy Lee's new band, Methods of Mayhem, issue their self-titled debut, which reaches #71 in *Billboard* and soon goes gold, starting the run with 40,000 copies sold in its first week.

METHODS OF MAYHEM'S TILO:

We listen to everything on the planet, from Jewel, Andrea Bocelli, the classical singer, to frickin' old AC/DC albums, Prodigy, the Beastie Boys, Chemical Brothers, Crystal Method, Snoop Doggy Dogg, We're fans from a lot of different kinds of music. You know where it comes from? For me, I have a big problem with like the authority kind of thing? Every time anybody is like this is the way it should be, I'm like no, no, I'm like MC Optional, the option to every situation. And for Tommy, finally this is an album where nobody is telling him that, well, you know, it's a great song, and it's a hit, but it's not Mötley. And I'm like looking at this and saying, fuck, he's bringing a killer song to the table, you're bringing a great song here, it's insane, but it's not Mötley. Imagine, with a Mötley album, and Tommy comes up with a Snoop Dogg, they wouldn't be that stoked. Oh, this is a little side-project, Tommy Lee, he's going to do his little something something, and it turned into *Methods of Mayhem*. He's quit Mötley Crüe. That's insane, dude, I mean, wow, that's really gnarly, that he would leave something that does work, that does good. It's really weird. You have to be a strong person to cut out of something like that.

DECEMBER 15, 1999 Mötley's official site allows an advance single called "1st Band on the Moon," from the band's forthcoming studio album, to be downloaded for free. On Christmas, "Time Bomb" and "I'm in Love with a Porno Star" (later truncated to "Porno Star") are also added.

"Music To Crash Your Car To" – Disc 2

Mötley Crüe

Reference – for audio program evaluation

1.	Toast Of The Town (CD Bonus Tune)	3:34
2.	Tonight (CD Bonus Tune)	4:26
3.	Too Fast For Love – alt intro (CD Bonus Tune)	4:18
4.	Merry-Go-...– live in San Anto... (CD Bonus ..)	3:56
5.	In The Beginning	1:14
6.	Shout At The Devil	3:16
7.	Looks That Kill	4:08
8.	Bastard	2:55
9.	God Bless The Children Of The Beast	1:31
10.	Helter Skelter	3:13
11.	Red Hot	3:22
12.	Too Young Too Fall In Love	3:33
13.	Knock 'Em Dead, Kid	3:44
14.	Ten Seconds To Love	4:17
15.	Danger	3:45
16.	Shout At The Devil – demo (CD Bonus Tune)	3:16
17.	Looks That Kill – demo (CD Bonus Tune)	5:05
18.	Hotter Than Hell – demo (CD Bonus Tune)	2:50
19.	I Will Survive (CD Bonus Tune)	3:22
20.	Too Young To Fall.. – demo (CD Bonus Tune)	3:04
	Total Duration Including Pauses:	68:51

Mastered by Gavin Lurssen

Discs are recorded to specifications set by Red Book standard

The Mastering Lab 6033 Hollywood Blvd.   Hollywood, CA 90028
Tel. (323)466-8589   Fax (323)465-7570
www.themasteringlab.com

Final Approved

Press advance CD insert for the box set sampler.

Author's Collection

VINCE NEIL:

I wasn't happy with the last album at all. We were with a producer who had absolutely no idea what he was doing. Tommy wanted to do hip-hop on the last record. A lot of the songs actually started out as great songs, but they were rewritten and rewritten. They changed titles three or four times. It was just a mess. We really got away from the Mötley Crüe sound on the last record. So this time we looked at ourselves and said, what made Mötley Crüe? What is the sound? We went backwards to go forward on this record. We've gone back to basics and it's turned out great. *New Tattoo* is like a cross between *Feelgood* and *Shout*. It's exactly what Mötley Crüe is. (*BW&BK*, 2000)

Ad from Japan's *Burrn!* magazine for Tommy's new project. Author's Collection

Tom Wojcik Collection

Tom Wojcik Collection

Tom Wojcik Collection

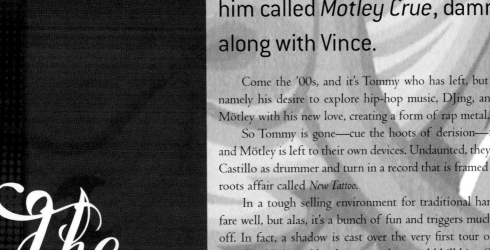

*I*n the '90s, the crack in the armor that had been a solid Mötley lineup was represented by Vince taking a holiday (many holidays, and with strippers). The result was, shockingly, an album without him called *Motley Crue*, damn the umlauts along with Vince.

Come the '00s, and it's Tommy who has left, but for more artistic reasons, namely his desire to explore hip-hop music, DJing, and essentially, by marrying Mötley with his new love, creating a form of rap metal.

So Tommy is gone—cue the hoots of derision—for Methods of Mayhem, and Mötley is left to their own devices. Undaunted, they adopt journeyman Randy Castillo as drummer and turn in a record that is framed as a no-frills, back-to-the-roots affair called *New Tattoo*.

In a tough selling environment for traditional hard rock, the album doesn't fare well, but alas, it's a bunch of fun and triggers much lucrative touring, on and off. In fact, a shadow is cast over the very first tour of the decade, with Randy Castillo debilitated by the cancer that would kill him. Samantha Maloney is hired on as brave choice for Mötley drummer.

As the decade wears on, Nikki will invent Sixx:A.M. on the wings of his confessional book, *The Heroin Diaries*; Vince and Tommy will discover a talent for reality TV; the band would have a surprise publishing-world hit with their raucous group

The '00s

Nikki 666, 2009.
© Chris Casella

Vince and Mick,
July 22, 2009,
First Midwest Bank
Amphitheatre,
Tinley Park,
Illinois. © Greg Olma

autobiography *The Dirt*; and Tommy would return to the fold, although fully awakened to the fact that there is art for him past any of this often rote-by-numbers Mötley activity. There are more books, side projects, Crüe reissues . . . there's a sense that the decade is a series of victory laps or at least the skilled fertilizing of a career.

The momentous event, however, in Crüe history concerning the '00s would be the creation of a new album marking Tommy's return to the fold. *Saints of Los Angeles* would become the band's most mature, polished, and self-aware album, aided and abetted in that cause by Sixx:A.M. singer James Michael, who would write and produce with the band, in effect, putting his skilled stamp on the proceedings. Also on board is song doctor Marti Frederiksen who, like Michael, helps the record become somewhat unassailable but perhaps, in a sense, too perfect.

As the decade comes to a close, Mötley Crüe is transitioning toward a classic rock act, a band of historical importance that can be celebrated through retrospective live shows even if the guys seem to be drifting towards other more personal projects to define their advancing years.

2000

JANUARY 11, 2000 "Get Naked," the first single from *Methods of Mayhem*, is issued on 12" vinyl, in two formats, Filthy Version and Instrumental Version. The following day, the album is certified gold—it must be said, to some degree because of Tommy's growing tabloid presence. Tommy keeps up the media assault—voluntary and sometimes not so voluntary—by presenting an award at the American Music Awards five days later.

TOMMY ON THE STANDARD VERSION VERSUS THE FILTHY:
It's fucking edited like crazy. It's cool, but I mean, there are big gaping holes in it. It's a little rough to listen to, because I know what's missing. But as a listener or fan, I hear it and go, "I want to go hear the real version." It's almost like you can't fuck it up because it makes the listener want to go hear the real deal. It's like a video with things blurred out; you don't want to see that, you want to see the real thing.

JANUARY 18, 2000 Coproduced by Mötley scholar Paul Miles, *Kickstart My Heart: A Tribute to Mötley Crüe* is issued. Cowriter of "Public Enemy #1," Lizzie Grey, plays guitar and sings on the rendition of that track.

Very likely Mötley's
classiest stage set;
2011 at the Hollywood
Bowl. © Kevin Estrada

FEBRUARY 14, 2000 Tommy (and TiLo) spend Valentine's Day finishing up a European promotional tour for *Methods of Mayhem*, with the album released this day in Europe, Australia, and New Zealand. Meanwhile, Pam tells Tommy on the phone that she won't be going through with their re-nuptials.

John Corabi proves once again his talents. Author's Collection

JOHN CORABI ON WRITING *THE BLUE ROOM*:

When Bruce and I write, we have a bunch of ideas and we put them together; he'll have a riff or I'll have a riff, or one of us will have a complete song, and will show it to the other guy. We'll twist it and turn it and add our two cents on each other songs. But it's weird. We don't really think of anything in particular. We like what we like. I like a lot of newer bands, but I like a lot of old bands. Probably about eighty percent of my collection is old shit from the '60s and '70s. I can't describe it. I just think it's very straight-ahead . . . you know, Bruce likes to call it meat and potatoes. It's straight-ahead rock 'n' roll. The two things we try to do is have really good lyrics and good production. And I don't really pay too much attention to style. I listen to new stuff, but I've come to the realization that I am what I am and that's it. If we sell records, great, if we don't, that's great too. I'm not going to make the next record sound like Limp Bizkit; although I like some of their stuff, that's not what I grew up listening to or doing.

FEBRUARY 22, 2000 Union issue their second studio album, and third overall, called *The Blue Room*.

MARCH 14, 2000 The industrial music–themed *Mötley Crüe Tribute: Shout at the Devil* is issued by Cleopatra Records, who also creates one of these around Van Halen.

MARCH 16, 2000 Methods of Mayhem begin their tour dates in Vancouver, British Columbia, at the venerable Commodore Ballroom, supported by Crazy Town. When they reach Toronto two weeks later, they will receive their gold discs for Canadian sales of 50,000 copies.

Tommy and TiLo in LA. © Kevin Estrada

BRUCE KULICK:

We created the whole album together with Bob Marlette, and there weren't as many preconceived demos per se. But generally, it was a bunch of guys getting in a room, checking out all the ideas, and developing a sound. We weren't trying to be anything that we're not. I think we've evolved, but I think it's still what Union has always been. I think we're powerful but melodic. One thing about the new album is I would say it has a very big sound, bigger than the first album, that's for sure. The first album touched upon that, but this whole album sounds large. There's just something very powerful about John's vocals all the time, and there are a lot of layers with the guitars. I'm very pleased with the overall vibe of us just sounding sonically very, very big.

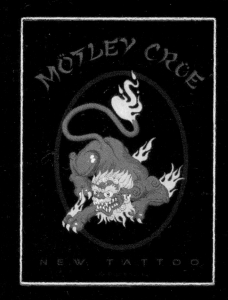

 WINTERLAND™

New Tattoo **sticker sheet.** Tom Wojcik Collection

VINCE NEIL:

It diversifies the crowd even more. You've got guys moshing right next to some guy with his family. It's really weird. But when you see Anthrax, Megadeth, and Mötley Crüe, you know it's a rock 'n' roll show. We just looked to see who was available and Megadeth was, so we gave Dave a call and said, "Hey, man, do you want to play this summer?" We've all been friends with each one of these bands for a while. It's a very cool vibe out there. We asked Anthrax very, very early on to do this, and they agreed to it. Then all these other bands wanted to do it. But that meant us telling Anthrax they would have to leave, which we weren't going to do. Every tour has a theme, and this year it's the streets of Holly-wood. We're bringing the streets out on the road with us. We have a strip club and a rock club and a tattoo parlor. There's tons of pyro and female backup singers. We're playing for ninety minutes and Megadeth is playing for ninety minutes before us. We're only playing one ballad on this tour, and that's "Home Sweet Home." (*BW&BK*, 2000)

APRIL 2, 2000 As recording gets underway on the next Mötley album, a photo shoot is conducted at LA's Lava Lounge, while *Maximum Rock 2000* tour dates in support of the record are announced, with Megadeth and Anthrax also on the bill.

MEGADETH'S DAVE MUSTAINE ON HIS MOTIVATIONS FOR JOINING THE PACKAGE:

Did you ever see their audience? Did you ever see all those tits out there? (laughs). No, just kidding. One of the things is that the money was really good. And you know, when we play in T.O., we're at the fucking Warehouse every time. You know, this is a great op-portunity for us to play the Molson Amphitheatre. We had to think, do we want to sit at home this summer? Or do we want to go with Mötley Crüe and play in sheds? And we can pick up new fans too because it's a different audience. I'll tell you what, the girls that are there to see Mötley Crüe, they say the difference between us and them, some of them are like ick!, and some of them are like yeah baby! And I'm digging that a lot of the Mötley Crüe fans that are guys are going, who are these Megger-deth guys? They're pretty heavy! A lot of people don't know who we are. Mötley Crüe does not sound like us. They are louder here because they have the P.A. clamped, which is part of the game that you play when you are the headliner. And they've got girls up onstage who are really re-ally terrific people and I think they are foxes. And I know them backstage without their costumes on and everything. And they've got the pyro and bombs and glitter and snow that comes from the ceiling and stuff. And personally, I mean, I like some of the Mötley Crüe songs—not all of them but I know some of them. And I think Vince is a very up-front kind of guy. He'll tell you what he's thinking. I guess he hand-picked us. He wanted to play with us for awhile. I'm flattered about that. But you have to remember, they were fucking enormous. And the reason we agreed to do this is because it's very similar to the Guns N' Roses/Metallica package—a glam band and a metal band.

From interview with author, Molson Amphitheatre, Toronto. © Martin Popoff

MÖTLEY CRÜE

Hell on High Heels

Picture sleeve for promo issue of "Hell on High Heels." Author's Collection

APRIL 10, 2000 Vince attends his second charity golf tournament in three weeks, with his own in honor of Skylar taking place two weeks later.

APRIL 11, 2000 Mötley is represented with a track on the *Ready to Rumble* movie soundtrack while Methods of Mayhem gets a song on the *Jailbait!* soundtrack. Meanwhile, the band's earliest rarity, "Nobody Knows What It's Like to Be Lonely" is unearthed as Randy's drum tracks are completed for the new record.

MAY 2, 2000 Randy Castillo is the drummer on an entire Def Leppard tribute album called *Leppardmania*.

MAY 27-28, 2000 Tommy spends the Memorial Day weekend in jail for violating his probation by drinking alcohol.

MAY 28, 2000 Vince enters into his third marriage, with Playboy Playmate Heidi Mark, after a seven-year engagement. Nikki serves as Vince's best man.

VINCE NEIL:

Parts of the song are almost ten years old, really just the guitar riff though. We found the song and rewrote the verses and chorus. The title of the song has been around that long. There's so many good songs on the record, we actually had to sit down with our managers and marketing people and listen to them all. It's a good thing when you have too many good songs. Usually when you do a record, you know, which song is going to be the first single. We really had no idea on this one. "Hell on High Heels" just turned out great. It's kind of like a "Girls, Girls, Girls" for the new millennium. Everybody voted on that one. (*BW&BK*, 2000)

JUNE 1, 2000 "Hell on High Heels" is released to radio, as the band begin tour rehearsals. Coincidentally, Methods of Mayhem (as Tommy completes five days in jail for parole violation) is also rehearsing for their next tour leg, kicking off at the Dynamo festival.

JOHN CORABI:

I heard the 58 thing Nikki did and I think it's fucking amazing! This guy, Dave Darling, I think he just produced the knew Meredith Brooks album, and he cowrote a bunch of songs with her. He's a great writer, great performer, singer, and he wrote with Nikki while I was in the band. So Nikki and him did this thing called 58, and it's fucking awesome, and I just freaked out. There's some really great songs on this record.

JUNE 20, 2000 Nikki Sixx steps out of Crüe for his long-incubating first side project, a record called *Diet for a New America*, under the band name 58, shortened from 1958.

JUNE 24-SEPTEMBER 3, 2000 Mötley embark on the exhaustive *Maximum Rock 2000* tour, which blankets America except for one Canadian date, in Toronto. With new drummer Randy Castillo falling gravely ill, the band replace him for these dates with Hole drummer Samantha Maloney, who not only is a huge Mötley fan but shares a birthday with Nikki as well. Meanwhile, opening night of the tour, Tommy is across the Atlantic presenting Methods of Mayhem to a crowd of 125,000 at Glastonbury.

VINCE NEIL:

Samantha has another gig. She's in Hole and they start recording soon. Courtney is actually shooting a movie; that's why she had time. Courtney actually came to the show at Los Angeles. She's a fan of the band and she's excited for Samantha, who's doing a great job. When this leg ends and we go to South America, Randy will be back with us. We didn't have any audition process. We just called her up and asked her if she wanted to do it and she was on the next flight from New York to Los Angeles. We actually met her when we were doing a show Hard Rock Live in New York City, and she came backstage to meet us because she's a big Mötley fan. And when we needed a drummer we just called her up. We already knew how good she was.

You definitely wouldn't see this wardrobe in a Mötley show. Methods of Mayhem, LA, 2000. © Kevin Estrada

JUNE 27, 2000 Lizzie Grey's Spiders & Snakes issue *London Daze*, which includes the London demo tape, featuring a pre-Crüe Nikki Sixx.

JULY 2, 2000 Methods of Mayhem begin their tour as part of Ozzfest.

VINCE NEIL:

The album—and the way people describe it, and I agree with them—is it's a cross between *Dr. Feelgood* and *Shout at the Devil*. It's got a lot of big elements to it, the big singable choruses, Mick's great guitar tone. So we kind of went backwards and recaptured what Mötley Crüe is all about. I really like "Hell on High Heels"—it's a great old sounding big rock tune. I like the one we do live, "Punched in the Teeth by Love"; just a good tune. "Treat Me like a Dog"—there are a lot of great songs on the album. When we knew we were going to be making a record, we did go to Bob Rock, but you know, Bob is a busy guy. He was already doing something else in the timeframe that we needed to record the record. But it was easy. You know, Mike Clink is an old school producer. He brought out the best of us on this record. He has great ideas. He knows how to get great sounds and he knows how to get the best performance out of each performer. And he's a cool guy and he has a great track record and he's made some big records. We're really happy with the way this record turned out.

JULY 11, 2000 Mötley Crüe issue their back-to-basics eighth album, *New Tattoo*. The lineup for the record is Vince, Mick, Tommy, and ex-Ozzy Osbourne drummer Randy Castillo, who does not tour the record. "Punched in the Teeth by Love" harkens back to the *Decade of Decadence* days, having nearly made the track list at that time; the song also finds Castillo included on the credits, his only credit on the album. "Punched in the Teeth by Love" is also the first new song one hears in the set list. Nikki's new songwriting partner James Michael is featured prominently across the album, with Nikki and James submitting songs to Sammy Hagar, Deanna Carter, and Meat Loaf (Marvin's daughter Pearl is currently a Crüe backup singer) as the germination of a side gig together. VH1 film the record's midnight release party in Plano, Texas, which is attended by the band and 3,500 fans.

JAMES MICHAEL, COWRITER OF SEVEN TRACKS ON THE ALBUM:

I think with *New Tattoo*, I guess, in some respects, when I look at a band like Mötley Crüe—and I think that Nikki and the rest of the guys would admit this—even though they would be considered to be a metal band, Mötley Crüe write pop songs. And they're fantastic pop songs. And then a very edgy, dramatic rock band performs those songs. So I've always been a bit miffed by people that refer to Mötley Crüe as a metal band. I just think that they're a rock 'n' roll band that is just all about attitude, great songs, great messages, and I think they really speak to an entire generation. So *New Tattoo* just kind of fell right in that category of a band that is not afraid to say things that make people uncomfortable. I mean, they built their entire career off of being able to just kind of piss people off. *New Tattoo* was just in a long line of records of a band that is kind of the notorious bad boys of rock 'n' roll.

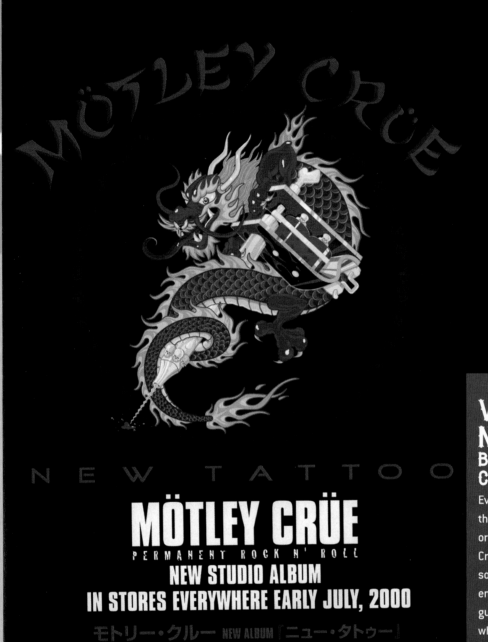

VINCE NEIL ON THE BAND'S NEW COLLABORATOR: Everybody contributes in their own way to the songs or else it wouldn't be Mötley Crüe. We just decided to do something a little bit different this time. We met this guy named James Michael, who is kind of like a Bryan Adams–type songwriting guy, but a rock guy. He's actually managed by our same management company, Left Bank. We got together with him and this guy's just brilliant. It was kind of good to have an outside ear on some stuff. He's classically trained; it was really a great writing experience. (*BW&BK*, 2000)

JULY 20, 2000 Mötley perform "Hell on High Heels" on *Jay Leno,* as the album opens at #41 in *Billboard,* moving 40,000 copies in its first week. Meanwhile, Anthrax drops off the tour due, as it turns out, to severe cuts in pay proposed to them given light ticket sales on the highly competitive tour circuit that summer.

JULY 25, 2000 *Bat Head Soup: A Tribute to Ozzy Osbourne* finds Vince belting out the vocal on "Paranoid."

VINCE NEIL ON GIFTS PROFFERED ON THE ROAD:

We get a lot of dolls. Nikki just had this doll made up just the other night. But nothing really too crazy. We get a lot of psychotic fans. There are two girls who came out on this tour and had been at every show. They sleep in their car, so we finally gave them some laminate passes so they can at least come in and eat with the road crew and stuff. It's just the fans having a good time. That's really it. Usually the audience is filled with a lot of good-looking girls with their tops off. As for crowds, they're all pretty much the same, every night between 15,000 and 20,000 people.

VINCE NEIL ON THE SITUATION WITH RANDY:

Something ruptured inside of Randy and they split him from his bellybutton up to his breastplate. It's a shame that he wasn't able to start the tour with us, but it's better that he makes sure everything is right. Randy can't come back too soon. Because if he does and something happens, he could be out the whole tour. This is a very long tour; we're going to be out 'til next summer. Samantha's great. She is amazing. It's working out, really, really well. She's really stepped up and the fans are really digging watching her play. (*BW&BK*, 2000)

AUGUST 3, 2000 Mötley play a house party in Pennsylvania, as part of a WXBE radio contest.

AUGUST 11, 2000 Mötley appear on *Live with Regis*.

SEPTEMBER 1, 2000 Ozzy is among the attendees at a huge Ozzfest-ending bash at Tommy's house.

OCTOBER 24, 2000 Wrestler Chris Jericho's metal vehicle Fozzy issue their self-titled debut album. Consisting mostly of metal covers, the album includes the band's take on "Live Wire."

NOVEMBER 3, 2000 "Live Wire" is used in the action flick *Charlie's Angels*.

NOVEMBER 5-19, 2000 Mötley play twelve dates in Japan, in support of *New Tattoo*. As is tradition for the band when visiting Japan, tattoos ensue.

DECEMBER 14, 2000 As rumors fly that Tommy will be the drummer on Ozzy Osbourne's next album, Randy has gone public with his cancer diagnosis. Meanwhile, Nikki hints of a long break for the band after the Japanese campaign and indeed, the band don't tour again until February of 2005.

Pass for the Alpine Valley Music Theatre show in Milwaukee, Wisconsin.
Tom Wojcik Collection

Pass for the New World Music Theatre show in Chicago.
Tom Wojcik Collection

2001

JANUARY 2, 2001 Nikki and Donna welcome a daughter, Frankie-Jean. The significance of the name Frankie is that Nikki is re-embracing his given name from his rough childhood. Shockingly, the couple announce their separation a month later, but strive to patch things up by spending time together as a family.

FEBRUARY 6, 2001 Both Mötley and Union appear on the soundtrack for motocross movie *Frezno Smooth*.

FEBRUARY 20, 2001 *Bulletproof Fever: A Tribute to Ted Nugent* includes John Corabi on album opener "Cat Scratch Fever" and Randy Castillo drumming on all tracks.

APRIL 18, 2001 Vince debuts his new solo band, live in St. Louis. The rhythm section is Union's Brent Fitz and Jamie Hunting. Union had effectively ceased to be when Bruce Kulick announced that he was joining Grand Funk.

MAY 22, 2001 Mötley and Neil Strauss publish their hit collective autobiography *The Dirt*. Meanwhile, Tommy's love life is fodder for public entertainment again due to Pam's association with both Tommy and Kid Rock. The book sells 70,000 copies in its first week of release, and as icing on the cake for Nikki, it seems like his marriage to Donna is again safe.

TOMMY LEE ON PUTTING TOGETHER *THE DIRT*:

We never sat down as a band, because at this point, I had left. So the writer, Neil Strauss, basically got together with each guy on their own and he put it all together. The discussion we did have about the book was, you know what? We're going to title this *The Dirt* and it's going to be exactly that. It's going to be wide-open, honest—whether good or bad (laughs)—and this will be an awesome book for a fan to read. And it will be the dirt, here it is, the scoop, all the shit, you want it, you got it. I think everybody did it openly, feeling that it should be told. It's crazy. Yeah, it's pretty crazy. I love how the book ends, with Nikki and I saying goodbye to our kids. Like, we just shook our heads in disbelief, like, a) we couldn't believe we were still alive, and b) wow, we're sitting here on the steps of the school, waving goodbye to our children. Did you ever think that this would happen?! And we just looked at each other and started laughing. Like this is fucking crazy. And I just thought it was a really nice way to end it.

JULY 3, 2001 Vince's two solo albums are reissued on his own imprint, VNS Records. Meanwhile Nikki is in rehab in Tucson after relapsing hard, Tommy is plotting his next Methods of Mayhem record, and Mick is cooking up a funk rock solo project.

JULY 17, 2001 Mötley issue *Lewd, Crüed, & Tattooed*, their first ever live DVD. The package celebrates both the making of the *New Tattoo* record and the subsequent tour for it.

VINCE NEIL:

Exposed was just a really cool rock record, lots of anthems, just rock 'n' roll, man. But with that second one, I really wanted to . . . you know, this is way before rock and rap ever meshed. I had the idea back then . . . this is like what? 1995? It's way before this stuff ever came out and I had this idea to do it and I mixed and matched the two and I think it just came out about four years before it should've came out, when I think it would've been more successful. I don't think people were ready for it. But it was basically an experiment and I thought it turned out pretty cool.

Letting it all hang out resulted in one very successful autobiography. Calling it *The Dirt* was a brilliant move as **well.** Author's Collection

Kevin Estrada Collection

AUGUST 26, 2001 Vince's new bassist is his original solo band bassist Phil Soussan, who cowrote much of *Exposed* with Vince back in 1992. But Phil is only required for three dates, as Vince and Jamie patch up their differences and resume working together.

AUGUST 29, 2001 Vince's third wife Heidi files for divorce, after fifteen months of marriage.

OCTOBER 3, 2001 Celebrating Tommy's birthday, Tommy and his new girlfriend skydive from 12,000 feet, with "Kickstart My Heart" playing as soundtrack to the jump. Weeks earlier, Tommy had lost his father to cancer.

NOVEMBER 12, 2001 With *The Dirt* selling in excess of 300,000 copies and foreign licensing deals being cut, the band turns to the idea of a Mötley Crüe biopic.

NIKKI SIXX: The depth of this band is special. We've always worn our emotions on our sleeves, but that book allowed people to see much deeper. A lot of people I've talked to have admitted that they feel like assholes for having called Mick out among their friends for him being "boring" or not "Mötley" enough. And now, because of that book, they finally fucking understand that, yeah, he doesn't move around onstage that much because he's living with a life-threatening disease! "Why doesn't Mick jump up and down?" 'Cause his fucking bones are falling apart, knucklehead. (*Metal Hammer*, 2005)

A sad but treasured bonus with this live and in-studio set was seeing the band work with Randy Castillo, soon to pass from cancer.

Author's Collection

NIKKI SIXX:

Randy was a great guy. And you know, he really saved our ass, to be honest with you, at that time, with Tommy quitting the band, when he wanted to go solo. Randy came in and . . . I don't know, it just feels like when Randy came in, he added this positive energy to the band. Like, he wanted to be in Mötley Crüe. He wanted to play those songs. He was happy every day to wake up and be on tour. It's just like, this is such a better energy than where Tommy was at, at the end of when he wanted to quit, because Tommy didn't want to be there. He didn't want to play those songs anymore. Now he's back, and I think everything is cool now. But at that time, Randy really, really saved our ass, I think, energy-wise, just with the spirit of who he was—and he was a killer drummer.

2002

MARCH 9, 2002 Vince and Tommy both participate in a charity celebrity golf tournament, having run into each other earlier at a private golf club and managed their way through a surprisingly cheerful conversation.

MARCH 26, 2002 Randy Castillo, drummer on Mötley's *New Tattoo* album, dies peacefully at home from the cancer he fought quite publicly and with grace. Both Nikki and Vince attend his service four days later.

MARCH 29, 2002 Tommy works on the video for his upcoming solo single "Hold Me Down," in which he works with Cirque de Soleil, flying a balloon through a forest.

TOMMY LEE ON OUTSIDE HOBBIES:

I've been goofing around on a wave board. Are you familiar with those? I have a dirt bike track on my property so every once in awhile I go tear it up there for a minute. I like to do relaxing things, because my life is pretty fuckin' crazy most of the time. I love to swim. I've been a water baby all my life and I love to just float around in the pool or be anywhere near the water, the beach. I find that most of the time when I have some free time, I really try take advantage of it and just relax, because there's not enough of that in my life.

APRIL 3, 2002 As Tommy mounts a promotional tour to radio stations, solo track "Hold Me Down" receives significant video play, helping propel the song toward minor hit status.

TOMMY LEE ON HIS FAVORITE LYRIC ON HIS NEW ALBUM:

There's a song called "Body Architects," and in the chorus it says, we all forget that we're the architects of the bodies we inhabit. And to me, that's just such a heavy statement. Because a lot of people are searching externally for religion; they're always looking for something when you don't even need to do that. It's all inside you. And I really believe that, that we all tend to forget that we are the architects. So, to me that's a strong message. I just said, I gotta write about this and remind people that you know what? Everything you need is just right inside you. You don't have to go looking for it. Generally, I just sort of pull from things I know about or things I've experienced, some truth about something. But I've never really looked at anybody else's lyrics and said oh, that's amazing. I don't spend that much time doing that. I always try to stay with truth, experience, events that are all real, because I have a hard time writing about fantasy (laughs). I'm never at a loss for content (laughs). But yeah, the way things are going right now . . . I just got a call from the label and my manager this morning. The track "Hold Me Down" just entered the Top Ten in all three rock charts, which is fucking amazing; like, I can't even believe this. So if that's any indication, I'll probably be on tour for quite some time this year. It'll be a while, because they're already talking about going to Europe, Australia, and Japan.

TOMMY LEE ON WHETHER HE WOULD GO BACK TO MÖTLEY CRÜE:

No. I keep telling everybody no. I actually asked Nikki to take it off the website. He's misleading people and that's not cool. It's strange, you know. He's asked me about it and I'm kind of like, I don't see that happening. And he's making statements like, "In 2003, when Tommy is done with a solo record, we're going to do this farewell tour." And I never said yes. So he's sort of taking liberties and I don't think that's very cool to the fans. They don't know. They just started e-mailing everybody like crazy and all of a sudden I'm doing a reunion tour. I'm like, I never said yes guys, stop, wait, hold on. On a creative level, I can't see myself playing that music anymore. It's just not where I'm at. I can't see myself doing that, and creatively if I'm unhappy I get miserable (laughs). And on a personal level . . . so there's two reasons, creative and personal. And on a personal level, Vince and I are cordial to each other when we see each other, but we don't like each other (laughs). At all. So no, I can't see myself doing it. Man, I really can't.

APRIL 8, 2002 Tommy gives as a gift, to his new drummer Will Hunt, the kit he used for 1994's *Motley Crue* album featuring John Corabi on vocals.

APRIL 29, 2002 A memorial concert is performed for Randy Castillo. The star-studded affair includes only one Mötley alumni, John Corabi. The next day a Guns N' Roses tribute album is issued with Randy drumming on all tracks.

MAY 2, 2002 Vince hosts the sixth annual Skylar Neil Memorial Golf Tournament, which he had created to help raise money for cancer research. His soon-to-be wife Lia Gerardini is also in attendance. Meanwhile Nikki has been doing some writing for Faith Hill and her husband Tim McGraw.

MAY 8, 2002 Live DVD *Lewd, Crüed, & Tattooed* is certified gold in the video category, for sales of over 50,000 copies.

MAY 15, 2002 Tommy's solo album is issued in Japan with two bonus tracks.

TOMMY LEE ON PLAYING GUITAR AND SINGING LIVE:

It's pretty much all the songs. It's definitely a guitar band. We like it heavy. Pretty much all the time. It is hard to do. I had a conversation with Dave Grohl from the Foo Fighters. Here's a drummer from Nirvana who goes and plays guitar and sings. And his band was rehearsing right next to mine. And this is when I was really nervous about all this, before I headed out on the *Methods of Mayhem* tour. I said, "Man, Dave, did you just have a fucking anxiety attack and thought you were going to fucking die?" And he said, "Bro, I'm telling you, I know exactly how you feel. I felt exactly the same way. The only thing I can tell you is that you'll get through it, you'll make some mistakes, but you will get through it and at some point you'll become very okay with it all." And he was right. I made mistakes, I had the anxiety attack (laughs), and I got through it man, I definitely got through it. And now, I'm not so freaked out about it. It's still difficult to know. Playing the drums, you can pretty much play the shit out of the drums and if you are to make a mistake, it's not so noticeable. But you play the wrong guitar chord and sing out of key, woooo! It's bad! So there's really no room for error.

You gotta admire Tommy for taking on this challenge. © Kevin Estrada

MAY 17, 2002 Vince, returning from a holiday in Hawaii, begins a solo tour, with a set comprised completely of Mötley hits.

MAY 19, 2002 Tommy's first show in support of his first solo album *Never a Dull Moment* is at a festival in Massachusetts in front of a crowd of 10,000.

TOMMY LEE ON HIS FAN BASE:

You know, I haven't really sat down and analyzed. I know there are some Crüe fans that keep up on what I'm doing and I know there are some new fans out there that are just coming on board. Last month I played with Sum 41 at the Palladium here in Los Angeles and I had fourteen-year-old girls coming up to me, "Tommy, can you take a picture with me?!" And I'm sitting there going, she's fourteen. Maybe even twelve. So to me, that's proof that there's a new generation out there, and my generation out there who are both hopefully enjoying the music I make.

VINCE ON KEEPING HIS VOICE IN SHAPE:

It's just singing every day. It's just like working out. The more you sing every day, the stronger your voice gets. It's actually worse after you take like a day off or a couple days off; that first day back, it's like going back to the gym after not going for awhile. It gets a little tough, but then like after the third day after three in a row, it's great. So basically, yeah, I've just got to keep singing.

MAY 21, 2002 Tommy Lee issues a solo album called *Never a Dull Moment*, which debuts at #39 in *Billboard*, selling 29,000 copies in its first week. The following night, Tommy performs "Hold Me Down" on *Jay Leno*. Meanwhile, producer Tom Werman files suit for unpaid royalties on Mötley's second, third, and fourth albums, plus songs from those records included on *Greatest Hits*. A settlement is reached in January of 2003.

TOMMY LEE:

When I started writing this record, in September of 2000, I had just gotten off the Ozzfest with *Methods of Mayhem*. I sort of locked myself up in my home studio here and started writing, and it's just where the music went. It didn't sound like Methods. It's modern rock, but just a little more focused and it had a common thread running through all of the music; it wasn't so eclectic and that was the one of the reasons just to call it Tommy Lee. I sat there with my producer one day and he said, "Dude, why don't you just call this what it is?" And I'm like, "What are you talking about?" He goes, why don't you just call it Tommy Lee? And I was like, nah, I don't think so. I don't know if I want to do that. And the more I listened to him, and my manager, and people at the label, they all had a really good point. They were like, you've been in the business for twenty-something years and everybody knows who you are—whether they like you or not they know who Tommy Lee is. And I sat there, and I was like OK, and I thought, to not use your own name is kind of crazy. It's like, *Methods of Mayhem*—you're starting over and trying to break some new thing. Why wouldn't you just use your name in an effort to help what you're trying to do? Magnify it. Use your name. And you know what? For me, I found that a little hard to swallow because I thought that sounds a little egotistical. I wasn't really feeling it. But the more I thought about it, it was like, these guys are right. They are absolutely fucking right. Why am I trying to . . . basically all the work that I put in for the last twenty-something years, and basically throwing it down the fucking toilet, because I'm trying to create something new that no one had really heard of yet. Uh, not smart, dude (laughs). Anyway, I wrote like twenty-three, twenty-five songs and the best eleven made it, so they're all my favorites. If anything, they are a lot more challenging because there's definitely more singing done on these. There are some really great melodies, a couple of really beautiful tracks.

TOMMY LEE:

If anything, I find it really hard to get excited about an acoustic drum set. So when I do play the drums now, Scott Humphrey, my producer and I, we absolutely go out of our way to make it sound new and fresh and tweak the hell out of it so it sounds crazy. So if anything, that would be my main objective these days, when I hear drums, is to try make them sound fucking amazing and not so stock. Because, I mean, I've been doing this for a long time and I just don't get excited about hearing an acoustic drum set anymore (laughs). Or sort of a stock guitar sound. We're always trying to push production to a new level.

Killer bill, but there's an element of career decline when this many bands have to get together to mount a successful tour. Author's Collection

JUNE 6, 2002 Ratt guitarist Robbin Crosby dies from AIDS. Robbin and Nikki had been tourmates, roommates, and co-users back in the mid '80s. In fact, Nikki has said the first time he ever took heroin was with Robbin.

JUNE 11, 2002 Nikki, Donna, and Nikki's songwriting partner James Michael are among the attendees at the launch party for Gene Simmons' new magazine *Tongue*. Also on this day, *Wildside: Tribute to Mötley Crüe* is issued, through metal label Artillery Music.

JUNE 21, 2002 Mötley issue, in Japan only, a box set containing eight original albums plus a CD of rarities and a DVD consisting of eighteen promo videos.

JULY 9, 2002 Butch Walker's *Left of Self-Centred* includes a track called "Into the Black," featuring Nikki on bass.

AUGUST 4, 2002 Nikki supports his interest in the rock- and ink-themed *Tattoo the Earth* tour with an appearance in Chicago, where he also maintains his ongoing role as a spokesman for JVC electronic equipment.

AUGUST 15-SEPTEMBER 8, 2002 Tommy Lee's solo band plays Ozzfest, Tommy reprising his Ozzfest 2000 campaign with Methods of Mayhem. The band is hired on as a main stage replacement for Drowning Pool, whose lead singer Dave Williams was found dead August 14th on the band's tour bus. Coincidentally, Nikki had been attempting to place some songwriting with the band. Williams had been a huge Mötley fan, and in tribute "Home Sweet Home" was played at his funeral.

AUGUST 31, 2002 Nikki and Donna attend the third-to-last Ozzfest show in San Bernardino, and catch up with Tommy at the end of tour bash later that night (there are in fact three more dates, in which Tommy is indeed included).

SEPTEMBER 18, 2002 Nikki Sixx and L.A. Guns' Tracii Guns have a new band unit under the working name Cockstar after putting aside both their main gigs. For a brief spell, they cede to complaints about the name and use Motordog before also considering Mortordevil and then settling on Brides of Destruction. The band's first rehearsal is conducted on this date, with six songs written within the few days that band are together. John Corabi attends the sessions, but it's unclear whether he will be included in the project.

NIKKI SIXX ON THE BRIDES SOUND:

Well, I guess it's pretty open to interpretation. The thing I always find interesting when people are interested in a band, they may say AC/DC, heavy metal. And of course we all say, well, if you know anything about AC/DC, you know it comes from the blues, and that's all those guys listen to. Everything they always tried to do is just be the blues. And I'm going, wow, I didn't hear that. "Highway to Hell," "Shot Down in Flames," "Back in Black" . . . where's the blues? But it's actually all through there. So with the Brides, it's interesting, because I'm going to say things, and some people would go, really?! I think it's pretty obvious. On "Shut the Fuck Up"— Cheap Trick, Black Sabbath, Buzzcocks, Aerosmith, Queen, and as much as I hate them, Zeppelin. Tracii just loves Zeppelin, and I'm just like . . . I'm fuckin' tired of it. Just tired.

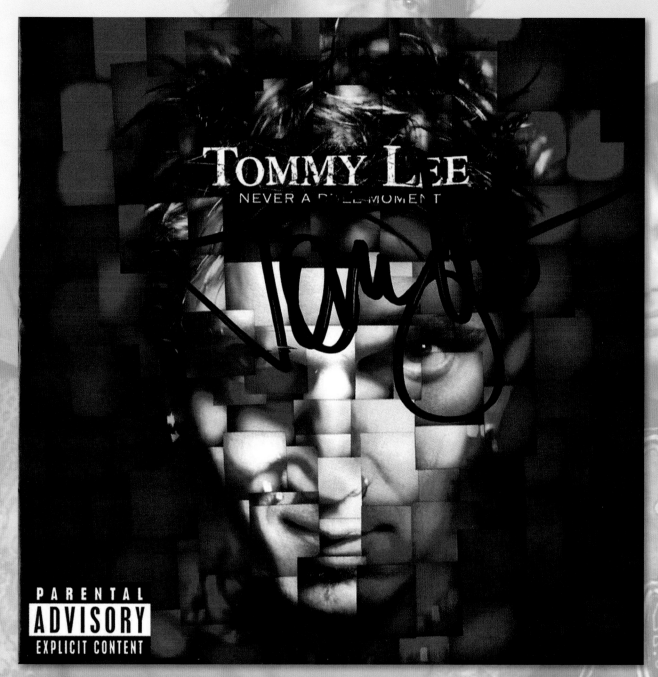

TOMMY LEE
NEVER A DULL MOMENT

PARENTAL
ADVISORY
EXPLICIT CONTENT

SEPTEMBER 23, 2002 *Tommy Lee: The Naked Truth* airs on VH1. Proposed as the start of a series similar to *The Osbournes*, it turns out to be a one-off.

OCTOBER 8, 2002 Tommy films an episode of *Rock the House*, where an unsuspecting fan gets showered with gifts and a partial home redecorating, at the hands of one of their rock idols.

OCTOBER 23, 2002 MCA and Tommy part ways when his solo CD sells in the region of 140,000 copies, a marked drop from *Methods of Mayhem*, which had gone gold. Three days later, Tommy plays Korea, which is broadcast on Korean TV.

OCTOBER 27, 2002 Video game *Grand Theft Auto: Vice City* makes use of "Too Young to Fall in Love."

Author's copy of Tommy's solo album, signed for him at the Rockstar Supernova gig at Massey Hall, Toronto. Author's Collection

NOVEMBER 4, 2002 Tommy's birthday party is a four-day affair in Morocco, with guests, including Diddy, flown over in two chartered 747s and then delivered in a fleet of Mercedes limos.

NOVEMBER 10, 2002 Vince participates in an early edition of *Rock 'n' Roll Fantasy Camp*, centred in LA.

NOVEMBER 12, 2002 Nu-metal act Saliva issue their gold-certified *Back into Your System* album, which includes "Rest in Pieces," written by Nikki Sixx and James Michael. The track is used as the second of the record's three singles.

DECEMBER 11, 2002 A judgement is rendered, ordering Internet Entertainment Group to pay Tommy and Pam $741,000 for their share of the profits of the sale of their sex tape. Two days later, in Las Vegas, Tommy and fiancé Mayte attend the opening party for the Sapphire Gentlemen's Club, the world's biggest strip club. Two days after that, Tommy puts his house up for sale, hoping to make a fresh start with Mayte, but soon he would break off the engagement.

DECEMBER 14, 2002 Nikki's Brides of Destruction (including John Corabi in the lineup) perform their first concert ever, including in the set covers of "Shout at the Devil" and "Live Wire." The band is in a support slot to Taproot and Mudvayne.

Kevin Estrada Collection

NIKKI SIXX ON THE EARLY POSSIBILITY OF SLASH JOINING THE BAND:

It started out that me and Slash were talking about doing a band. We talked about different singers—Josh from Buckcherry, Scott Weiland. The problem with a lot of musicians who used to be in bands that were really successful is there are a lot of managers that are attached to those artists in the hopes that those artists will someday go back to that original band, and then they get a piece. That's the dirty little secret of the business. So Slash had this guy, who is not managing him anymore, and he was adamant that Slash does this and has control of this much of the money. A bunch of that shit starts going on between the managers and me and Slash just wanted to get together and write songs. They're already doing the million-dollar tour projections and it totally sucked the life out of it pretty early on. Someone of Slash's stature and my stature, they were thinking if you put this guy and that guy together, we're talking the ultimate supergroup. I started getting a little bit uncomfortable about the concept of supergroup because it's going to feel bloated and machine-like, which is what I didn't want to do. I wanted it to be raw and simple so we could play a club and open for AFI. We could go out with Social Distortion. We could go to the Ozzfest or we could open for Aerosmith and Kiss—it doesn't matter. I just didn't feel inspired and I think Slash felt the same way. At the same time, Slash was hanging out with Duff, which he hadn't been doing in a long time, and they started playing. Velvet Revolver just organically happened. [BW&BK, 2007]

DECEMBER 31, 2002 After a family-oriented New Year's Eve at home, and with Mayte's parents present and consenting, Tommy proposes to Mayte shortly before midnight.

2003

JANUARY 9, 2003 Vince appears in the first season of pioneering reality TV show *The Surreal Life*. The nine-episode first season runs through February 20.

EXECUTIVE PRODUCER MARK CRONIN:

Vince Neil was a little reluctant. Although he's done a lot of reality. The thing about Vince is that I never thought of him to be chasing the scene very much. And he approached it almost like hey, I thought it would be kind of cool too, kind of like I don't know, it seemed cool. Seeing that it would be cool to live with some other people, meet some people. He didn't come at it from a promoting my ticket sales, or I'm promoting my new wardrobe line or anything like that. He was kind of pure about it, Vince was. He was excited to be there and meet MC Hammer and thought it would be cool to meet Corey Feldman, and he just really did it like, almost from a more genuine place than actually almost anybody.

FEBRUARY 15, 2003 Vince joins Scorpions onstage in Las Vegas for a performance of "Rock You like a Hurricane."

MARCH 4, 2003 *Greatest Hits* sees reissue through Hip-O/Universal. Meanwhile, Nikki, Tommy, and Pam are all talking about their clothing lines.

MARCH 18, 2003 The Brides of Destruction launch their website, allowing fans to hear full versions of eight songs that may or may not show up on the debut album. Of note, Bob Rock had met with the band in his hotel room a few weeks back and had declined to produce the upcoming record. Two weeks later, John Corabi announces an amicable split with the band.

NIKKI SIXX ON JOHN CORABI:

He was jamming with us. It was kind of cool. We recorded some songs and he loved the first set of songs we did which were "Natural Born Killers" and "Revolution." Then as we started becoming a band, we started to feel who we were and really where we wanted to go was more aggressive. That is who we are. We started writing stuff like "I Don't Care," "Shut the Fuck Up," and "2 Times Dead" as well as a bunch of other songs that are recorded which no one's heard yet that are even more punk-influenced. Tracii and I really have huge ties to punk. John was saying, "I loved where we were but I don't get where we're going." He's his own singer and songwriter so he just bowed out to do his own thing. We talk all the time. He's a great guy. I just don't think it felt right for him. (*BW&BK*, 2004)

VINCE NEIL ON TOURING WITH HIS SOLO BAND THROUGH THIS PERIOD:

The funniest thing was, Jason and Alan, they'd never done a tour like this before, so they're pretty overwhelmed by it all. And Alan, you know, staying at these nice hotels, he wanted to get his laundry done. So he thought it was really easy to send it down and have the laundry do it, you know at the hotel. He gets his stuff back and he doesn't realize how much they charge. It was $175! You know, $35 just to wash his socks, $80 for his underwear and another $70 something dollars for his T-shirts. That was pretty funny.

Mick soldiers on despite his advancing bone condition. ©
Kevin Estrada

APRIL 8, 2003 The Mötley catalogue—ten albums in total—gets rereleased, most for the second time, through Hip-O/Universal.

APRIL 18, 2003 Vince plays himself on the TV show *Greetings from Tucson*, while Tommy stars in an episode of Fox's *Fastlane*.

MAY 27, 2003 Vince issues an indie live spread called *Live at the Whisky: One Night Only*, consisting almost entirely of Mötley Crüe classics. In the press, Vince articulates his displeasure that Nikki is thwarting Mötley working together through his enthusiasm for Brides of Destruction, intimating that he's going to have to get lawyers involved. Nikki, for his part, says he'd like to see Mötley rocking again, but Vince would have to be back in fighting form.

VINCE NEIL:

I'm having a great time. "Girls, Girls, Girls" is a great song to sing because everybody sings along; "Same Ol' Situation" is another crowd favorite and it's fun to play, "Feelgood" is always a good one, "Home Sweet Home." The ones that have the big choruses in them are the most fun to play live because everybody just sings right along with you. I feel more sad for the fans, really that never got a chance to see us, or the fans that would love to see us again. But the other guys just don't seem to want to do anything and I'm the only guy who wants to go out and tour and make records. I don't really understand it myself. I'm very happy doing what I'm doing and I'll be making a new studio album, should be out early next year, and I'll be back out touring that again next summer.

Greatest Hits saw brand extension or stretch similar to what was accomplished with *Decade of Decadence*.
John Chronis Collection

MAY 31, 2003 At a benefit put on by Meat Loaf, Nikki says he expects to be reading a script for the rumored Mötley Crüe biopic, *The Dirt*, sometime soon.

VINCE NEIL:

He tells everybody that it's his movie. It has nothing to fuckin' do with him at all. Nothing. And each person in the band has input in that movie and Nikki has no more input than anybody else. But he likes to tell everybody that he does. And I don't think the movie is gonna get made anyway. (*BW&BK*, 2003)

JULY 10, 2003 A *Twentieth Century Masters: The Millennium Collection* compilation for Mötley is released.

VINCE NEIL ON HIS SUMMER TOUR AND RECENT LIVE CD:

We were playing the Whisky A Go Go and decided we'd roll some tape. It sounded pretty cool so we decided to make a record out of it. It wasn't made to sell a million copies. We're not even really promoting it; it's really kind of like a gift for the fans. If anybody collects any Mötley stuff it's kind of like a final tribute thing to get me singing Mötley Crüe stuff. The crowds are great. If you're a fan of '80s music, you're singing for like four hours with Skid Row doing their stuff and me doing mine and Poison. The tour is great for us too because I've been friends with both Skid Row and Poison for so many years that it just makes it a lot of fun. I mean I do what I do and I'll go out and be on tour next year again and I'll be promoting a new studio record and after that keep going. This is what I do and I'll continue to keep doing it. It's sad that Nikki would rather just do . . . you know, we were supposed to tour last year with Mötley and we were supposed to tour this year with Mötley, but he wants to sit on his fuckin' ass and not do anything. I can't do that. Yeah, I mean there's nothing to complain about. I just want people to know that I'm going to be out there rocking, so come out to the shows and I'm not retiring soon. I dig it too much. (*BW&BK*, 2003)

JULY 26, 2003 Nikki and Tommy talk at the one-year anniversary party for Nikki's clothing line N.SIXX. Three days later Nikki and Vince come to some agreement on the state of Mötley and manage to at least quell the bad-mouthing.

JULY 29, 2003 At a birthday party at the Skin Pool Lounge in Las Vegas, Vince tells patrons that a Mötley reunion is indeed in the cards.

AUGUST 15, 2003 Mixing of the forthcoming Brides of Destruction album is in progress, but the band has hit a roadblock. A Japanese deal is in place for the issue of the record, but an adequate enough US deal remains elusive. As well, Nikki is talking about putting tour dates on the hold, as attention turns toward the prospects of a Mötley reunion.

NIKKI SIXX:

I don't think we meant to but a lot of people have said that it's a bit like *Too Fast for Love*, meaning it's simple and raw. It's not overproduced. We didn't try too hard. *Too Fast for Love* is really a demo for Mötley Crüe's first record. This is sort of the same type of thing. When you do a demo, you go in and cut the songs. There's no bullshit. You don't think too much about the drum sound or the bass sound. You don't worry about doing the vocals exactly perfect. You just nail it so you have a reference and that's kind of what this record is. (*BW&BK*, 2004)

SEPTEMBER 7, 2003 Just another day on tour as Vince picks a fight with three out of four members of Poison, with only C.C. DeVille escaping his wrath.

VINCE NEIL:

Nikki's kinda single-handedly fucked up Mötley Crüe, and it's sad. We were supposed to tour last year, we were supposed to tour this year and he refuses to do it, and it's really screwed everything up. I don't want to sit around and wait for these guys anymore and he's making a lot of decisions without telling other people in the band, like these reissues and stuff. And so now I have to take him to court and sue him, and it's a sad thing when that happens. Yeah, I really have no interest. My Crüe days are over. Like I say, I'm having way too much fun not having to deal with those guys as personalities. It's fun just being out here and having guys that actually want to be onstage and are excited about it. You know, it's refreshing.

SEPTEMBER 22, 2003 Tommy appears on *The Sharon Osbourne Show*.

SEPTEMBER 23, 2003 Meat Loaf's *Couldn't Have Said it Better* includes two tracks written by James Michael and Nikki.

OCTOBER 4, 2003 Tommy jams with Sammy Hagar at Sammy's Cabo Wabo club in Mexico, along with Jerry Cantrell, the Chili Peppers' Chad Smith, and members of Sammy's band, the Waboritas.

OCTOBER 15, 2003 Warming relations somewhat, Nikki joins Vince onstage at his solo show at the Key Club in Hollywood. Bruce Kulick is hit by a stray bullet after the show.

NOVEMBER 11, 2003 A DVD compiling all of the band's videos called *Greatest Video Hits* is issued by Mötley/Universal, along with a four-CD box set called *Music to Crash Your Car To: Vol. 1.* Andy McCoy and Michael Monroe of Hanoi Rocks publicly protest the title of the box set, given the circumstances around the death of their drummer Razzle.

NIKKI SIXX:

Well, if it was malicious, I would feel a lot worse. But it wasn't malicious. I never even thought about it and I think things through pretty thoroughly. It was so, so long ago. Our lifestyle has encompassed a lot of tragedy and some of it has been glamorized but it's horrible. I've crashed a couple of Ferraris and Porsches in my time. Tommy's rolled a couple of cars, Mick's crashed a couple cars and we've all had motorcycle accidents. At one point, Tommy had written this song called "Music to Crash Your Car To." I thought that was a fucking cool title! That is kind or what Mötley Crüe music is—you're going really fast and it feels like that. Then he left the band and the next time I saw Tommy, we sat down and talked about the box set. We decided to use his title. That was it. Then I get a call from Vince. He says, "Dude, this isn't right. It's not cool. I've got all these people coming up to me saying, how could you do this?" Now Vince has his own manager. I make sure everything Mötley Crüe goes through his management. Personally, I don't think they showed it to him. A lot of times Vince just lets . . . he's not as involved in a lot of stuff. They might have said we're going to do a box set and he said cool. (*Bravewords.com*, 2004)

DECEMBER 10, 2003 Vince and his fiancé Lia, and Tommy and his current girl-friend Pink, are all at the 2003 Billboard Music Awards. Tommy presents and Pink performs.

DECEMBER 25, 2003 The Brides of Destruction's *Here Come the Brides* is issued in Japan, but the band is already working on material for a second record.

NIKKI SIXX:

I've talked to all the guys but there's one other thing missing from that equation and that's Mick. Mick was having construction done on his house, so he had been living with me for a month. He just moved back into his place. In that time we got to talk a lot more about how ill he really is. He plays guitar just like he always has but it's not easy for him to move around. So that's an issue in itself. That is more than anything else why if we didn't do it. If he can't tour comfortably, we're not going to bring in another guitar player. (*Bravewords.com*, 2004)

Actually a fairly decent cover for what is a most casual sonic presentation enclosed.
Author's Collection

A little more serious in the studio than he is live, especially as a solo act!
© Kevin Estrada

2004

FEBRUARY 24, 2004

Vince films his parts for his role as a tattoo artist for an upcoming episode of CBS' *Still Standing*.

MARCH 8, 2004 Brides of Destruction perform "Shut the Fuck Up" on *Jay Leno*, following up ten days later with a visit to Craig Kilborn's show. Meanwhile, Nikki has turned down tour dates with Kiss because Poison was also on the bill, preferring to try his luck with a headlining theatre tour.

"Maybe we should put out another album in four years."

© Kevin Estrada

NIKKI SIXX:

At the time when I wrote the lyrics to that, all the stuff with Osama Bin Laden and Saddam Hussein and George Bush and everyone . . . the newscasters on TV just fucking talking, talking, and talking. Shut the fuck up! I'm so sick of hearing you guys talk. Do something. Make a difference. But the big part for me is that I realized, in a lot of ways, that nothing I have to say really matters. It says that in the song. It's a feeling of helplessness. It's not too political. It could be geared towards a woman or an enemy or something like the media. It's sort of open for interpretation. [*BW&BK*, 2004]

MARCH 9, 2004 Brides of Destruction issue their debut album, *Here Come the Brides*, on Sanctuary. The lineup for the record, after a few changes since its 2002 inception, is London LeGrand on vocals, Tracii Guns on guitar, Scott Coogan on drums, and Nikki Sixx on bass, with Nikki also cowriting every track. John Corabi plays rhythm guitar on the album, but is out of the band before the record is issued. James Michael gets in three cowrites. The album stalls at #92 in *Billboard*, selling 13,694 copies in its first week.

NIKKI SIXX ON WRITING WITH BRIDES:

Well, it's very much like me and Mick Mars. Tracii brings in the riffs and I turn them into songs. Or I have songs, and he turns them into fucking muscle, and he changes this part, changes that part. So it ends up being right down the middle. It's like Tracii adds the meat and potatoes and I sprinkle the magic; it's a really good combination. I tend to write the lyrics mostly myself. London wrote some lyrics. Tracii had a couple things. It's not so much that I'm the lyrics-hoarder, it's that I think I deliver the right things a lot of times. People go, wow, that's cool. But London in his own right is a very good lyricist, quite different from me. It's not quite as easy to put your finger on what he's saying, which I find really interesting. You kind of got to listen to it and go, does he mean this? Or does he mean that? In music, I think that's great, because usually you want to have your own interpretation anyway. Personality-wise, I'm just sort of this dirty, grimy, pick up my bass and don't shower, and spit as much as I can while I play, kind of hang out in the corner and get cranky now and again. London is really like a peacock, very much so in the way that Vince has kinda taken on that role. As for the sound, this album fell like it needed to be underproduced. And we really didn't want to overthink it. It's the first album, a new band. We didn't want to get to analytical about it. We didn't want to get too long in the tooth about it. We just kind of want to get in, show people what we're about. If you like this, that's cool, because we've got more coming. The funny thing is, we have so much music that we've actually been contemplating what we're going to do for our next record. And right now, the loose game plan is that we're going to shoot for a double album. I mean, the creative juices are just flowing. Now, whether or not it happens, who knows? It's kind of a nice thing to shoot for, because if you're going to put twenty songs on an album, you have to write eighty, right? So if you shoot for eighty, you only get sixty, you got sixty to take ten from. Fuck man, it's all good. The listener is going to be very happy.

Prolific and always searching, Nikki looks to update his sound.
John Chronis Collection

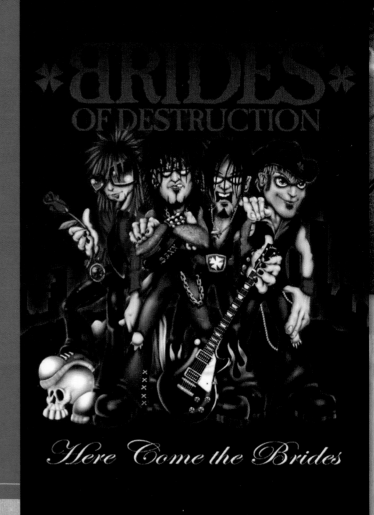

"It's me, Tommy." © Kevin Estrada

APRIL 9, 2004 Vince pleas no contest in response to an incident with a sex trade worker at Nevada's Moonlite Bunny Ranch. Meanwhile, Pam posts on her site that she is back with Tommy, following affectionate appearances at a handful of public events. This quells recent rumors that Tommy and Naomi Campbell are an item.

APRIL 30, 2004 Brides of Destruction embark on the four-week *Honeymoon from Hell* tour. Toronto is cancelled after the band couldn't cross the border. Meanwhile, Tommy is soon off to Canada for some DJing dates.

JUNE 1, 2004 Vince's second foray into reality TV is *Remaking Vince Neil*, in which Vince is implored to clean up and get back in shape for upcoming Mötley dates.

JUNE 29, 2004 Mötley Records/Hip-O issues *Music to Crash Your Car To: Vol. II,* a four CD set that comprises in full the *Dr. Feelgood, Decade of Decadence,* and *Motley Crue* albums, plus many rarities. There's also a comic book and poster.

NIKKI SIXX:

It's not meant for people to go and buy Mötley Crüe music they already have. When we left Elektra Records and started our own label, we rereleased all the music with those bonus tracks. That was, here's the music, if you don't have it, go ahead and get it. Then when we went to Universal Music, they're obviously going to change it from saying Mötley/Beyond to saying Mötley/Universal or Hip-O. The interpretation is: are you trying to get us to buy this shit again? Not at all, I just want it out there. There's a lot of new fans discovering Mötley Crüe. The idea of the box set is really just a crowning achievement in your career. If you're a collector, it's a cool thing to get. If you just like the first few years, then only get the first one. Box sets don't sell a lot, maybe 10,000 copies. Anybody that thinks bands put out box sets to make money don't realize that first of all, the box itself and all the artwork is very expensive. We basically break even. [*Bravewords.com,* 2004]

JULY 23, 2004 Vince has to cancel a show after breaking his ankle when he slips cleaning the window on his Ferrari; he plays a subsequent show in Colorado in a cast, from a sitting position.

AUGUST 4, 2004 Vince joins original rock 'n' rollers the Crickets for a rendition of "I Fought the Law," which he also sang on their collaboration album issued ten days earlier. Meanwhile, a meeting takes place between the band and their various managers (an ailing Mick not in person but by phone) to discuss a Mötley reunion.

Cello Studios, 6000 Sunset Boulevard, Hollywood, 2004.
© Kevin Estrada

THE '00s † 171

Hollywood tour kickoff.

© Kevin Estrada

AUGUST 8, 2004 Brides of Destruction play their last of two shows in Japan, the first territory to accept the band and a dependable stronghold for Mötley, before transitioning to Australia for three dates.

SEPTEMBER 17, 2004 Mötley has completed demos of four new songs, assembled in Las Vegas. Scratch guitar tracks, to be replaced by Mick when he recuperates from surgery, are played variously by DJ Ashba, Bob Rock, and Nikki.

MICK MARS:

As for as my AS, a lot of people call it a disease—I call it an inconvenience. Because it doesn't allow me to move as much as I would like to. It's just part of what it is. It's not life-threatening; it's more of an inconvenience. I can't turn my head, so I'm unable to drive a car now, you know what I mean? So it's that kind of a deal. It's just an inconvenience to me. The thing about this ankylosing spondylitis that I have, it's almost like, I don't want to sound weird, but it's almost like you're in a shell. If you move the wrong way, you can have little fractures, and it will just be painful, again, because you have to regrow where the AS has gone. It's hard to explain. Ankylosing spondylitis comes from a Greek word, which means . . . ankylosing means bent and spondylitis means fused. So you are bent and fused together. And so if you take a dead tree and bend it back, it's going to crack. You know what I'm saying? It's like, I take lots of—not lots; that sounds weird—but I do take medication for it, Celebrex NSAIDs, non-steroidal drugs. But nothing addictive—I was there before, like five years ago, and I hated it. It was the only thing that could get me through what we were going through at the time. Suddenly I went to the right doctor and got everything right, and that's it. So I take something like Celebrex. And anybody who hears this, I hope, who has the same thing as me, I say don't go for the quick fix.

OCTOBER 5, 2004 Mick Mars undergoes hip replacement surgery, due to complications from his advancing ankylosing spondylitis, a severe form of arthritis that attacks the spine and pelvis.

VINCE NEIL ON MICK MARS:

Mick is just Mick; he's never really changed. He doesn't socialize at all. He's the kind of guy who would much rather just sit at home and play his guitar, rather than get out on the road. Mick just follows whatever is gonna . . . Mick doesn't like to make any decisions (laughs); he just likes to flow. In terms of guitar, Mick always had his own thing going. He looked cool and he had some great tones out of his guitar and played some pretty memorable stuff on the records. I've always admired him as a guitar player.

NIKKI SIXX:

Mick's health is doing much better. I'll be honest with you. He's never going to be one hundred percent. He can't. I mean physically, it's impossible. But as far as getting better, he's still seeing doctors all the time. He's mobile and he's playing guitar all the time and his spirits are good. And we're going to do it if we can get everybody on the same page.

OCTOBER 7-NOVEMBER 12, 2004 Tommy enters the University of Nebraska. His education and exploits there are to be filmed for a new reality series called *Tommy Goes to College.*

OCTOBER 8, 2004 "Wild Side" is used in the film *Friday Night Lights*; it also appears in *Rock Star*, *Like Father Like Son*, and Dale Earnhardt documentary *Dale.*

OCTOBER 19, 2004 Tommy's autobiography *Tommyland* is released. Over the next few days, Tommy is on *20/20*, *David Letterman*, *Good Morning America*, and even *Larry King Live*, promoting it.

Relax, it's a video shoot.
© Kevin Estrada

OCTOBER 24, 2004 Barbara Coffman, in conjunction with Jacques Van Gool's Backstage Auctions company execute a successful auction of Mötley memorabilia from the late Allan Coffman's estate, including handwritten lyrics to every song from *Too Fast for Love*. Nikki vehemently objects, divulging that the Coffmans tried to sell the memorabilia to him for $10,000 and he had refused on grounds that it was his property to begin with.

DECEMBER 5, 2004 Tracii Guns is apparently banned from Mötley's official message board after vehemently dissing the band's new single, "If I Die Tomorrow," cowritten by Nikki and Canadian punk band Simple Plan, who had been working with Bob Rock. Nikki snipes back and it looks like the incident puts a knife in any future Brides of Destruction activity.

NIKKI SIXX ON "IF I DIE TOMORROW":

The way it happened was, I had taken my daughter to see Avril Lavigne. Simple Plan were opening. I'd never heard of them, but I was like, "Wow, these fucking guys have got some real fucking energy!" So I kind of became a supporter of the band. They were working with Bob Rock, who is obviously a longtime friend, and Bob said, "You know, a couple of the guys wrote this little riff— it's really cool, but they're not doing it because it's not really their thing." We changed the lyrics around, cut it, and made it Mötley Crüe. (*Revolver*, 2005)

Press conference at the Palladium in Hollywood to announce the Red, White, & Crüe tour. © Kevin Estrada

Jordan Berliant
10th Street Entertainment

Jim Richards
Clear Channel Entertainment

Tommy anticipates warming relations with Cuba. © Kevin Estrada

NIKKI SIXX ON OVERCOMING IMPEDIMENTS TO MÖTLEY WORKING TOGETHER:

Well, that problem is not really me or Vince or Tommy—it's managers. And you know, when artists have their own managers, managers can be self-serving. So sometimes Vince doesn't always get all the information, or he gets the information wrong. So it's just about direct communication. With Mötley Crüe, sometimes we don't talk for months and months and months and months. Other times we spend every single day together. I don't know why that is. I have a lot of friends like that, friends I won't see for a year, then I'll see them every single day for a month. Then I won't see them for a year again.

DECEMBER 6, 2004 Mötley Crüe lets it be known, in a typical hoopla-filled press conference, that they are reuniting for worldwide tour dates, entitled the *Red, White, & Crüe Tour 2005 . . . Better Live than Dead.*

DECEMBER 7, 2004 As the reunion announcement after-party—featuring DJ Ashba's band and a DJ set from Tommy at the Whisky A Go Go—winds down, the next day reveals that "If I Die Tomorrow" would be the subject of an innovative AOL Music and AOL Radio launch.

DECEMBER 9, 2004 Mötley revisits the notorious first Mötley house to conduct a photo shoot. Also this day, HardRadio cofounder, early Mötley business team member, and phone and e-mail friend of the author Bill Larson succumbs to cancer at age forty-four.

DECEMBER 10, 2004 Mötley perform "If I Die Tomorrow" and "Dr. Feelgood" on *Jimmy Kimmel*, who also supported Tommy on his book tour, three weeks earlier.

DECEMBER 31, 2004 Mötley appear on *The Tonight Show with Jay Leno*. Jay gets to deliver the scoop that due to huge demand for tickets, Mötley would be adding twenty-five dates to their reunion tour. The band play "Girls, Girls, Girls" and "Dr. Feelgood" while Vince breaks the no swearing rule, wishing Tommy a "happy fuckin' New Year."

2005

2005 Vince puts together his Off the Strip Poker Tournament, in Las Vegas.

JANUARY 9, 2005 Vince enters into his fourth marriage, with Lia Gherardini. The event is ministered by MC Hammer, by this point an ordained minister, in Las Vegas. Nikki and Tommy attend, but not Mick, understandably, given the advanced state of his affliction.

At dress rehearsals for the upcoming tour dates.

© Kevin Estrada

FEBRUARY 1, 2005 Mötley issue an expansive hits pack to correspond with the reunion called *Red, White, & Crüe*. Marquee tracks are "If I Die Tomorrow," a cover of the Rolling Stones' "Street Fighting Man," and new single "Sick Love Song," which was part of the cache of tracks considered for the Brides of Destruction project, but is credited to just Nikki and James. All three tracks are produced by Bob Rock, with "Street Fighting Man" featuring drumming by Josh Freese. The set sells 90,305 copies in its first week debuting at a healthy #6 on the *Billboard* charts and then moves briskly toward platinum as the tour progresses. A special edition was also issued, adding a greatest hits DVD. The regular version is a double-CD package, but there is also a single disc version, which, notably, doesn't include "Street Fighting Man."

FEBRUARY 14-MAY 1, 2005 Mötley's *Red, White, & Crüe* tour blankets the US and Canada, after kicking off with a show in San Juan, Puerto Rico. The usual support band slot is filled with a twenty-minute claymation video, after which the band pulls out all the stops with a circus carnival–themed show. The show becomes the sixth highest tour of early '05, grossing $21.3M in ticket sales, at a low average ticket price of under $50. The band will end the year as the eleventh highest grossing tour act of 2005 with total proceeds of $39.9M.

```
ACLB23   119      5    5        COMP
        0.00  LOUNGE E08           0.00
$                    GST # R126007780
CONVENIENCE CHARGE
119                    MOTLEY CRUE
SEC./SEC.
TM    8X          RED, WHITE, AND CRUE
5      5         BETTER LIVE THAN DEAD
ROW/RANGÉE SEAT/SIÈGE
MLA412C            AIR CANADA CENTRE
23DEC04      WED FEB 23 2005 8:00PM
```

Author's Collection

MARCH 3, 2005 Nikki and Tommy guest on *Regis & Kelly*, before the band's Madison Square Garden performance that night. A week later, the sale of Tommy's longtime Malibu home goes through.

MAY 6, 2005 A day after his ninth annual golf tourney in honor of Skylar, Vince gets his own wine, called Vince, produced by Adler Fels Winery from Santa Rosa, California (things develop quickly and an additional wine deal is announced two weeks later). One week later, Tommy and Nikki guest on *America's Most Wanted* concerning a missing Mötley Crüe fan.

MAY 30, 2005 VH1 airs *Resurrection: (Insideout) of Mötley Crüe*, which gives backstage access to the band as they engineer their reunion.

JUNE 4-25, 2005 Mötley play Europe, including a string of festival dates and a mini UK tour, with Killing Joke as support. Business interests in the UK had been instrumental in getting the ball rolling on the reunion, with these UK dates having been some of the first shows discussed.

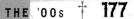

An admirable sense of creativity was applied to the Carnival of Sins tour. © Kevin Estrada

Mötley Crüe

RED, WHITE & CRÜE TOUR 2005

PLUS SPECIAL GUESTS

·KILLING JOKE·

TOMMY LEE   MICK MARS   VINCE NEIL   NIKKI SIXX

BETTER **LIVE** THAN DEAD

TUESDAY 14 JUNE
GLASGOW SECC
0870 040 4000

FRIDAY 17 JUNE
BIRMINGHAM NEC
0870 909 4133

SUNDAY 19 JUNE
WEMBLEY ARENA
0870 739 0739, 020 7287 0932, 020 7734 8932

WEDNESDAY 15 JUNE
MANCHESTER EVENING NEWS ARENA
0870 190 8000

SATURDAY 18 JUNE
CARDIFF INTERNATIONAL ARENA
029 2022 4488

24 HOUR CREDIT CARD HOTLINE
0870 060 6030
BUY ON-LINE: WWW.GIGSANDTOURS.COM

A METROPOLIS MUSIC PRESENTATION BY ARRANGEMENT WITH THE AGENCY   KERRANG! LIFE IS LOUD

A bill that raised a few eyebrows, to be sure. Author's Collection

JUNE 22, 2005 *Red, White, & Crüe* is simultaneously certified gold and platinum.

MICK MARS, ON THE BAND'S LONGEVITY:

When we started off, we didn't have the intention of sitting around and playing one hit. We wanted to keep writing and writing and writing—and the enthusiasm was there. And we just kept going like that. It was like well, it's been ten years already? Oh, it's been twenty years already? And we just keep going—the Mötley machine. Reinventing, rewriting, keeping up with the times, keeping current, as well as having the roots, the elements, still there, which made Mötley Crüe a household name in the first place.

JUNE 28, 2005 The RIAA ranks Mötley #84 in all-time US record sales at 22.5 million records sold.

JULY 2, 2005 Mötley play the poverty benefit *Live 8* at the Barrie, Ontario, location of the nine-venue event. Also on the bill are, among others, Deep Purple and Canadian rock ambassadors Bryan Adams, Gordon Lightfoot, Neil Young, Tom Cochrane, Our Lady Peace, The Tragically Hip, and Simple Plan, who the Crüe have an association with through "If I Die Tomorrow." Following *Live 8*, Tommy, Pam, and the kids go to Hawaii while Nikki and family go to Disney World.

JULY 22, 2005 Universal reissue *Too Fast for Love* on vinyl, with original mix and a bonus reproduction of the original 7" of "Stick to Your Guns" backed with "Toast of the Town." The package is offered in a numbered limited edition of 5,000 copies.

JULY 24-OCTOBER 16, 2005 Mötley conduct their *Carnival of Sins* tour, blanketing the US with limited Canadian stops. Support comes from Sum 41 (pop punk), Silvertide (old school), and the Exies (alternative). Mid-September, Vince tears a calf muscle onstage, but after truncating that show, he soldiers on and finishes the tour. October 12th in Wyoming, Tommy suffers burns from a pyro mishap.

"Next time, not so early, OK?" © Kevin Estrada

Somewhat of a Marilyn Manson vibe to some of the visuals associated with the band in 2005.
Tom Wojcik Collection

JULY 27, 2005 The hit stage production *Rock of Ages* premieres, in Hollywood. Nikki is adamant, against the opinion of Vince, that Mötley songs will not be part of the repertoire, in accordance with his longstanding disposition of not wanting to be considered part of the hair metal pack.

AUGUST 2, 2005 *Red, White, & Crüe* goes double platinum in Canada, which proves to be one of the band's dependable markets, due to their hard work hitting both large and smaller cities across the country over the years.

AUGUST 8, 2005 Tommy visits *The Tonight Show* and performs his new solo single "Good Times." Over the next few weeks he will also promote his multimedia assault on *Conan* and *Jimmy Kimmel Live*.

AUGUST 9, 2005 Tommy Lee issues a soundtrack album of sorts. *Tommyland: The Ride* is the star-studded companion piece to both Lee's autobiography *Tommyland*, as well as his reality show *Tommy Lee Goes to College*. *Tommyland: The Ride* opens at #62, selling only 16,000 copies in its first week.

AUGUST 16, 2005 Tommy Lee stars in the heavily scripted "reality show" *Tommy Lee Goes to College*, which consists of six episodes, concluding on September 13th. The theme song for the show, "Good Times," also serves as the second single from *Tommyland: The Ride*.

The larger than life Vince Neil, 2005. © Kevin Estrada

REALITY TV PRODUCER MARK CRONIN:
Tommy Lee, he's done a good job, kind of piloting himself into reality television. You know, the show wasn't super successful and I don't know that it was Tommy's fault. Reality television is always an experiment of some sort, a social experiment. And sometimes the experiment goes really well and sometimes it just doesn't. And I don't think he's been particularly blessed on that front. I think the show with Carmen Electra came a little closer to . . . did he do that one where they got married? Yeah, I believe that that one was a truer experience (laughs); that's what it was actually like for him and Carmen to have that romance they were having and plan that wedding. But the series where he goes back to school, it was mostly fake. It didn't seem very genuine to me.

Carnival of Sins tour, July 2005.
© Kevin Estrada

AUGUST 19, 2005 Nikki makes good on his plans to create a charity for homeless and underprivileged teens, announcing Running Wild in the Night, in conjunction with Covenant House.

SEPTEMBER 10, 2005 Mötley participate in a Hurricane Katrina benefit from Nashville, with a lavish version of "Home Sweet Home." The performance is followed up by a rerecording, with all proceeds going to charity.

SEPTEMBER 13, 2005 Brides of Destruction issue, on Shrapnel, their second and final album. The Andy Johns–produced *Runaway Brides*, however, finds Nikki replaced by Amen's Scott Sorry, as Nikki had been called back to Mötley for a reunion tour and relations with Tracii had soured.

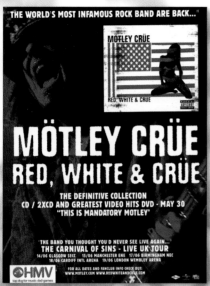

Canadian ad for the new (tour-inspired?) compilation. Author's Collection

OCTOBER 25, 2005 Mötley issue a concert DVD called *Carnival of Sins*, in conjunction with Clear Channel.

OCTOBER 30-NOVEMBER 1 2005 Mötley play two shows supporting the Rolling Stones, in Seattle and Portland.

NOVEMBER 8, 2005 Limp Bizkit include a bastardized, ersatz cover of "Home Sweet Home" on their gold-selling *Greatest Hitz* album.

NOVEMBER 9, 2005 Tommy performs a charity DJ set in the UK and also appears on a talk show with old buddy Ozzy Osbourne.

NOVEMBER 19-DECEMBER 14, 2005 Mötley conduct a tour of Japan and Australia, closing it out in Hawaii on the way back to the US. A preamble to the Australian dates finds the *Carnival of Sins* DVD playing in theatres for contest winners.

DECEMBER 31, 2005 Mötley celebrate the New Year with a one-off show in Detroit. The band cover U2's "New Year's Day," much champagne is doled out, and Mick ends the night requiring medical attention after he is yanked offstage by a female fan.

Red, white, and neon. © Kevin Estrada

2006

JANUARY 25, 2006 Mötley receive a star on the Hollywood Walk of Fame, cheered on by 600 fans.

FEBRUARY 4, 2006 Nikki's auction raises $60,000 for his Running Wild in the Night charity. Meanwhile, Tommy is in Detroit for Super Bowl weekend partying with Fergie, Jenna Jameson, and Diddy, while getting in a little DJing on the side.

Kevin Estrada Collection

Have bass, well traveled.

© Kevin Estrada

"Time out, time out. I forgot the words." © Kevin Estrada

FEBRUARY 7, 2006 Mötley issue the CD version(s) of their Grand Rapids, Michigan, *Carnival of Sins* set, in two volumes, exclusively through Walmart.

FEBRUARY 10-APRIL 13, 2006 Mötley reprise their *Carnival of Sins* tour for another pile of US and Canadian dates through mostly what are known as "B" markets (i.e., smaller cities).

APRIL 5, 2006 With Tommy's tendonitis flaring up as the band swing into Red Deer, Alberta, Mötley give fan and local bar-band drummer Harvey Warren the job of drumming the gig. Tommy follows up by having his solo band drummer Will Hunt take over to play the last two shows on the tour, Canadian dates in Lethbridge, Alberta, and Regina, Saskatchewan.

APRIL 25, 2006 The six episodes of *Tommy Lee Goes to College* see release on DVD.

APRIL 28, 2006 Donna files for divorce from Nikki.

MAY 5, 2006 The tenth annual edition of Vince's golf tourney in honor of Skylar raises $175,000 for medical research.

MAY 25, 2006 Tommy plays drums on "God of Thunder" at the *VH1 Rock Honors'* celebration of Kiss. Vince and his wife Lia are in attendance.

JULY 5, 2006 Gilby Clarke, Jason Newsted, and Tommy Lee are the majority of a supergroup called Rock Star Supernova, assembled for a reality TV show called *Rock Star: Supernova*, premiering on this date. The mission of the show is to find a suitable lead singer and conquer the world.

JULY 11, 2006 Vince does the 2006 ESPY Celebrity Golf Classic in Simi Valley, California, the next day guest-starring on *Criss Angel Mindfreak*.

JULY 22, 2006 Vince plays celebrated classic rock fest Rock the Park in Kitchener, Ontario, and then hops a plane to Cadott, Wisconsin, to perform with Crüe, who are headlining a festival date there on the same day.

AUGUST 18, 2006 Mafia film *10th & Wolf* hits theatres this day, with Tommy Lee in a minor role playing Jimmy Tattoo.

SEPTEMBER 5-DECEMBER 13, 2006 Mötley embark on the *Route of All Evil* tour with co-headliners Aerosmith. Nikki spends his downtime healing from the breakup of his marriage (the house goes up for sale October 3rd), feeding his interest in photography, and working on music, with guitar wizard DJ Ashba joining him on the road for a week, during which they write songs, amassing an album's worth over time.

NIKKI SIXX:

I was married with children and I thought we were going to all live happily ever after. Then my wife files for divorce. We go through a very difficult divorce. I have to start my life over again with my children in the midst of doing a Mötley Crüe tour and I've got to look at this thing and it fucking hurts! What does Nikki Sixx do when it hurts too bad? Historically, pain reliever. And I didn't do it. I stayed sober. I didn't become my father. I'm going to be present for the kids. I'm going to be the best I can be 'cause I shit like everybody else so fucking stop the madness. So maybe part of the story that might be good for somebody else is, you can be a rock star and you can be unhappy, or you can just be a regular guy going through a difficult divorce, but you don't have to act out. And acting out is a lot of different things. You can just be a fucking asshole. You cannot be willing to look at other people's side of it. You can just be a bad person. Or you can use drugs and alcohol to escape, or sex and gambling. You have to look at yourself and say, am I doing the very best and honorable thing I can do? (*BW&BK*, 2007)

Heating up the Hollywood Bowl, November 7, 2006.

© Kevin Estrada

OCTOBER 2, 2006 At the Mötley/Aerosmith stop at the Air Canada Centre in Toronto, Tommy is guest drummer for Aerosmith's "Last Child." A month later, Mick joins the band onstage for Aerosmith rarity "Stop Messin'." For the closing date, in Vancouver, Nikki joins Aerosmith for a rendition of mutual cover "Helter Skelter."

OCTOBER 31, 2006 US release date for Meat Loaf's gold-certified *Bat Out of Hell III: The Monster is Loose*, featuring two James Michael cowrites and one Nikki Sixx cowrite, on the opening title track.

NOVEMBER 3, 2006 Vince opens Vince Neil Ink, a tattoo parlor, inside a casino in Las Vegas.

NOVEMBER 7, 2006 "Shout at the Devil" is included on Play-Station 2 game *Guitar Hero II*.

NOVEMBER 21, 2006 *Rock Star Supernova* is issued on this date, by the band featuring original members Gilby Clarke, Jason Newsted, and Tommy Lee plus new lead singer Lukas Rossi, a Canadian unknown picked from three finalists and 25,000 initial applicants worldwide. The band soon loses Jason Newsted to a shoulder injury as he tries to break the fall of a bass head tumbling down upon him. First week sales of *Rock Star Supernova* in the US are a paltry 17,000 copies (resulting in a #101 *Billboard* chart placement), with slightly more than that selling in Canada, due in large part to the winner of the contest being Canadian Lukas Rossi.

NIKKI SIXX:

I just found the original hand written lyrics to "Shout at the Devil." I wrote it in one stream of consciousness and it was done. For me being a lyricist, it's about waiting until you're ready and just letting it flow. It's not about the rhyming dictionary. When I write lyrics, a lot of the time I'm very spontaneous. Vince has a singing style where some words may not sound right. The producer or myself will say, "Hey Vince, try this." But I don't really write out my lyrics and study them. (*Bravewords.com*, 2004)

GILBY CLARKE:

I've admired Tommy since he started Mötley Crüe. I saw those first shows. I always thought he was an incredible musician. So this is all just part of the journey. So many people . . . whatever opportunity is out there. He wrote a lot, he plays guitar, he plays piano. When this came together, it was kind of strange, because he had brought in a bunch of songs. His songs were fairly complete; they were already recorded. Not with melodies, but musically, there were pieces. So basically what I did was, I took the guitar parts and changed it into how I would do it. Where some stuff would be detuned, I took that out and said, "Well, this is how I would play it." I like things detuned every now and then, but for the most part, I don't. It was interesting—the grooves, the sounds, it was great. With Tommy, I learned how well-rounded a musician he is. You know, look, I'd heard his solo records and I'd heard what he brought to Mötley Crüe, and I didn't hear, you know, how good he was at making pieces of music, loops, and all that kind of stuff, and how he never takes no for an answer. There is always a way. And I like that persistence. That's pretty incredible."

JASON NEWSTED:

Tommy was trying to figure out, you know, like a meeting of stars somehow. Some kind of definition for this thing. And he found in the dictionary the meeting of stars in the sky, and when they meet or collide, they make a supernova. So that's that. A bunch of stars coming to a meeting and creating a giant burst.

DECEMBER 31, 2006 Having drummed for Mötley in Detroit last New Year's, Tommy Lee spends this year's last night as the backbone for Rock Star Supernova, as the band performs its first live gig ever, at the Joint in Las Vegas.

2007

JANUARY 15, 2007 The last day of Vince's four-day Mötley Cruise between Miami and the Bahamas. Amidst much partying and a set by Vince's solo band, $20,000 is raised for the T.J. Martell Foundation and the Skylar Neil Memorial Fund. Meanwhile Nikki and DJ Ashba are both in LA now and able to work more seriously on music, along with James Michael.

JANUARY 29, 2007 Rock Star Supernova performs on *Regis & Kelly*.

Good crowd at Massey Hall in Toronto to support the Canadian winner of the front man job. Author's Collection

FEBRUARY 20, 2007 Vince follows Sammy Hagar and launches his own tequila, Tres Rios. A party celebrating the event takes place in Guadalajara, Mexico, where Vince performs with a local band. In a few days, Vince is off to a wine and food festival to promote the brand, followed by a return to rehab.

MAY 22, 2007 With an album of material essentially finished and in the mixing stages, Sixx:A.M. release the video for a debut single called "Life is Beautiful." A week later, amidst business in New York related to the new band, Nikki plots rehearsals with Crüe and meetings with partner Kelly Gray with respect to their new fashion line, Royal Underground.

JUNE 1-12, 2007 Mötley play festivals in Europe, plus select UK dates. Mick and Fai McNasty (Seraina Schönenberger) become an item, meeting when the band performs the first date of the tour in Zurich, Switzerland. Due again to Tommy's tendonitis, Will Hunt is enlisted to drum the last show of the tour, in Manchester, after which Mick is off to Zurich (and then to Stockholm, to work with neo-hair metal band Crashdiet) while the rest of the band heads home.

JUNE 16, 2007 Sixx:A.M. play their first live show ever, at Crash Mansion in LA, as part of a lavish press conference and sneak preview of both the forthcoming album and Nikki Sixx book.

AUGUST 7, 2007 Drowning Pool, now under the same management as Mötley, issue *Full Circle*, which includes "Reason I'm Alive," written solely by Nikki and produced by Nikki and DJ Ashba.

AUGUST 21, 2007 Nikki Sixx's side project Sixx A.M. issue their debut album, *The Heroin Diaries Soundtrack*. The album debuts at #62, selling just under 11,000 copies in its first week.

> ## SIXX:A.M. VOCALIST, COWRITER AND PRODUCER
> # JAMES MICHAEL:
> Nikki and I tend to react to the same types of songs. You know, 10cc, Bread, the Babys, real strong '70s pop stuff, and then of course it goes all the way over to the heavier rock stuff. He would have his long list of bands, but my influences were about five years later. But we found a lot of common ground on bands like Queen, for instance, which I would say is my absolute favorite rock band of all time.

AUGUST 24, 2007 Tommy, who had been spotted in public being very affectionate with Pam repeatedly over the months, is now romantically linked with Rod Stewart's daughter Kimberly, with Rod's blessing. On this day, it is reported that Tommy has bought a new house, which, as described, would make it the most ostentatious mansion purchased yet by a Mötley member.

SEPTEMBER 9, 2007 Tommy and Kid Rock get into a physical confrontation at the MTV Video Music Awards. Las Vegas police issue a citation to Kid Rock, ascertaining that he was the aggressor.

> # NIKKI SIXX:
> It's very hard to say the things that I'm saying and be careful how I'm saying them. I don't want to have the effect on anybody that I felt when somebody was trying to tell me what to do. My hope is in reading the book and listening to the record, people can just take the information and do with it what they feel is right. It is their life. (*BW&BK*, 2007)

> # NIKKI SIXX:
> The project, the album, was inspired by the book, and we only put the band together because radio wanted to play the music. It was very freeing as a bass player—because Mick and I talk about this all the time—there are certain things you can do that are trademarks, and part of what feels really great, like Mötley Crüe. And then there is stuff that, you know, I'm just a smart-ass bass player. I'm not going to play classical-style note progressions in Mötley Crüe! (laughs). But Sixx:A.M. has moments that call for that.

Cover art for the band's debut, band being the "edgy" configuration of a trio with non-specified drummer.

Author's Collection

SEPTEMBER 13, 2007 The stress over a huge legal dustup between his personal manager and other Mötley mangers has Tommy feeling that his status in Mötley is uncertain, but he wants to work it out. Essentially, there is valid resentment on the part of those representing the band entity that all of Tommy's solo and reality TV exploits, as well Rock Star Supernova, have certainly weakened Mötley's prospects through delays and diminished workload, and arguably damaged the brand as well. For his part, Tommy's manager says he's doing what he's supposed to do, managing Tommy.

NIKKI SIXX:

To me, a big part of revealing this was the honesty that comes with not just the diaries but the commentary from other people. Letting people feel comfortable in getting their point of view out there. They're real true feelings. Not buffering that, letting them really say, "He was an asshole" or "He was a dictator" or "He was difficult" or "I was scared," whatever it was they felt compelled to say and not to edit that, gives the reader a clear view of what that snapshot of that year is about. I've done a lot of digging. I've peeled the onion many times and will continue to do so in my life to discover why I was compelled to do the things I did and to find myself with my feet firmly planted on the ground. Moving forward, you can only accept it as fact. In other words, nothing they said surprised me and I didn't want them to lie. I didn't want them to say, "Aw bro, I love you; it's okay, that was a long time ago." Why would we want a fluff piece? In Mötley Crüe, I love the fact that Mick, Vince, and Tommy have balls the size of a bull and that they're willing to do such things. It was amazing for Slash to come forward. Vanity is an evangelist now and it was difficult for her at times, but she did rise to the occasion. Record company executives and managers coming forward with their side of the story. And I'm going to tell you, all their points of view, I don't necessarily agree with. That doesn't matter! It is their point of view. I'm able to look at the story and write the overview and really get in there. (*BW&BK*, 2007)

SEPTEMBER 18, 2007 Nikki issues a book called *The Heroin Diaries*, a diary/memoir of a year in the life of Nikki—Christmas '86 to Christmas '87—in which he documents his heroin addiction as well as the *Girls, Girls, Girls* recording and tour cycle. The title of the book recalls Jim Carroll's classic memoir *The Basketball Diaries*, which was most notorious for its documentation of heroin addiction. Nikki's charity Running Wild in the Night is slated to receive twenty-five percent of all royalties. The Borders branch trusted with the book launch sells out of their entire stock of the title. A New York City book launch a week later, in the evening after a visit to Howard Stern earlier in the day, is just as successful, with the Virgin Megastore moving 600 copies.

OCTOBER 3, 2007 Crashdiet's *The Unattractive Revolution* contains two cowrites with Mick Mars, with Mick playing on both tracks. The band is Swedish, with a Mötley look, and they record for Universal, who have ties to Crüe.

OCTOBER 23, 2007 The previously Walmart-exclusive *Carnival of Sins* live set is now reissued as a double CD album.

OCTOBER 25, 2007 Sixx:A.M. play their second show ever, and first in a conventional larger rock setting, opening for Korn, who had planned to include their take on "Shout at the Devil" on their oft-delayed and then shelved *Korn Kovers* album. The same day, Nikki's and Donna's Agoura Hills home is sold.

NOVEMBER 11, 2007 *Rock 'n' Royalty: A Very Special Tribute to Queen* includes "Calling All Girls," with Vince on vocals. The previous night, Vince performed at the anniversary party for his Las Vegas tattoo parlor, Vince Neil Ink, on the heels of his third annual Off the Strip Poker Tournament a week earlier.

DECEMBER 31, 2007 Tommy spent New Year's Eve '05 playing with Mötley in Detroit, New Year's Eve '06 playing with Rock Star Supernova in Las Vegas, and now spends New Year's Eve '07 DJing with his buddy DJ Aero in Minneapolis.

NIKKI SIXX:

I found my other self, you know what I mean? That girl is so perfect for me, and I'm so perfect for her. It's awesome. Will she be joining me on tour? You know, the other day, we both looked at each other and we were like, I'm leaving on tour, she's starting her third season on *LA Ink*, and we're like, well, we always wanted to be in a relationship with somebody else as driven as each other, and now that we've got it, it fucking sucks (laughs). Because will we ever get to see each other? But you know what? Love is stronger than a little bit of time away from each other, so we'll be all right. I've got my other family out there on the road. I'll have my kids, and we'll be with the guys in the band, and me and Mick want to start writing music as soon as we get out there. It's going to be a blast.

2008

JANUARY 4, 2008 Vince performs at an Animal Rescue Foundation fundraiser, along with Mr. Big's Eric Martin and members of Y&T.

JANUARY 19, 2008 Vince plays a free solo show to mark the opening of his Dr. Feelgood's restaurant in West Palm Beach, California. A week later he's off on Mötley Cruise 2008, a four-day rock 'n' roll cruise between Florida and Mexico.

JANUARY 30, 2008 Nikki announces that songwriting for Mötley's next album, *The Dirt*, is now complete. He begins work on what will become Mötley's summer tour package, *Crüe Fest*. As well, Nikki and Kat Von D become a super-couple; on August 25, 2010, Nikki will issue a statement that it's over.

Backstage at the Avalon.
© Kevin Estrada

MARCH 5, 2008 Famed addiction specialist Bob Timmons, who had worked extensively with Mötley members, dies of respiratory failure at age sixty-one.

MARCH 25, 2008 Mötley's new single "Saints of Los Angeles" premieres at radio. Two weeks later it's issued as a exclusive stream at Spinner.com.

MARCH 29, 2008 The *Carnival of Sins* DVD is issued on Blu-ray.

APRIL 8, 2008 Country artist James Otto issues his second album, *Sunset Man.* The leadoff track is "Ain't Gonna Stop," written by James, Big & Rich, and Nikki Sixx.

Tommy's prank post that *Carved in Stone* just went gold works famously. © Kevin Estrada

JAMES MICHAEL, COWRITER AND COPRODUCER OF THE SONG AND ALBUM:

I'm really, really proud of *Saints of Los Angeles*. it's one of those things, when there's so many moving parts to something, and you're dealing with a band that has such a reputation already, and had so much success under their belt, and then for somebody like me to come along who's . . . you know, I have a track record, but it's not like I have a long, long history with Mötley Crüe. It was a daunting task to even take that one on and roll up my sleeves and be a part of that. And while it was a huge honor, it was scary, to be honest with you. And I was just so determined to make it a celebration of what we all love about Mötley Crüe. And from that angle, it's a very proud moment for me, because when I listen to that record, it's exactly what I hear. I feel like those guys all came back into the studio and recorded that record like they were a hungry band that was just starting out. And yet they've all had such a beautiful backdrop of an amazing career to base it on. And it was a magical time. And when I listen to "Saints of Los Angeles," that song in particular, I just feel like we nailed it. Other highlights on that record, for me, I love "Down at the Whisky." It tells such . . . That's my recollection of Mötley Crüe, and their legacy. And I think that there's just something on that record for everyone that's been a lifetime lover of Mötley Crüe.

APRIL 11, 2008 Mötley issue the Grammy-nominated title track from the forthcoming *Saints of Los Angeles* album as a single. The video for the song includes cameos from members of bands picked to be on the upcoming summer's *Crüe Fest* tour package.

APRIL 15, 2008 The band hold a press conference to announce the upcoming *Crüe Fest*, at which time they also debut the video for "Saints of Los Angeles," performing the new track as well, along with "Kickstart My Heart."

MICK MARS:

We always do something really cutting edge, modern, hip, new, unseen, and that's all about all I can tell you (laughs). None of us in the band really like to give anything away, so that when you come and see us it's a complete surprise. It's like trick-or-treating and finding out you're only getting a Tootsie Roll or something.

NIKKI SIXX:

The song "Saints of Los Angeles" is the time in the story where we signed our life away to the record companies, and we were willing to do anything to get out of here, to get out of Los Angeles, because we were a big fish in a small pond. Or we had become a big fish in a pond that looked small to us and we wanted to take over the world at that time in the story.

NIKKI SIXX:

It feels nice that people got the book and got something out of it, that's the best part. For me, it's like every time someone has the book, they really went on a journey; they feel disgusted or they feel inspired. I feel like every time one of those books leaves the bookshelf, something powerful's going to happen. (*Bravewords.com*, 2011)

MAY 9, 2008 Nikki is feted at a Covenant House awards gala at which he presents a cheque for $250,000. The substantial size of the donation is due to the success of *The Heroin Diaries*, part of the proceeds of which go to his Covenant House charity Running Wild in the Night.

JUNE 10, 2008 Sixx:A.M. issue, as digital download only, their *X-Mas in Hell* EP, which presents "Life Is Beautiful" in three versions.

JUNE 20, 2008 Mötley appear on *Larry King Live*. Two days later they are headlining Heavy MTL in Montreal, Quebec. Meanwhile, after years of false starts, the band pull the plug on their current partners with respect to the long-delayed film version of *The Dirt*.

Backstage at Crüefest rehearsals. Author's Collection

NIKKI SIXX:

Saints of Los Angeles, the thing is, the album is loosely based, thematically—and I do mean loosely based, because it's not really a concept record—but *Saints of Los Angeles*, you can plug in the story into the Mötley Crüe book, *The Dirt*. So it starts one place, and it ends pretty much where we're at now. It starts right when we form the band, and it ends where we are at right now, which is obviously not the end of the story. Anybody I've played it to, they've gone, well, it's like Mötley is back! But it doesn't sound dated. I don't know what that means, but the guitar tones are heavy, the drums are thick, the bass is aggressive, the vocals are right up front. The songs are Mötley Crüe songs; the lyrics are good. Some are funny, some are serious, some are just in-your-face. It's like Mick was saying, it is diverse, but it's like a typical successful Mötley Crüe record, where it's got a lot of different things going on through the record.

MICK MARS:

It's a very diverse album. It goes from radio-friendly to full-on like shred, kicking butt. It does all sorts of stuff. Also all types of music—Mötley music of course (laughs), and I think it's a great album. Also it's modern and hip-sounding. It's old school Mötley, but modern—it doesn't sound 1980s.

JUNE 24, 2008 Mötley Crüe issue their ninth and (at press time—never say never) last album, *Saints of Los Angeles*, which debuts at #4 in *Billboard*.

JAMES MICHAEL:

When we got to *Saints of Los Angeles*, I think there was more of an autobiographical challenge there. It was very important that we began to kind of tell the story of the band and celebrate that a bit. My goal with *Saints of Los Angeles* was to celebrate a genre of music that the band had really been at the forefront of. And so it was important to me that we created a feel of a band that had come back together and was writing and creating songs that really reflected the genre that they were known for. But I needed *Saints of Los Angeles* to have a very modern sound, because it was very important at the time that we didn't make a record that sounded dated. We knew that the songs were going to have a very kind of '80s/'90s feel to them, as far as songwriting goes, but it was important that the record sounded very today, very cutting edge, because we needed it to be able to compete with the active rock sound at the time. And I think that album really turned out the way that we intended, because it really does sound like vintage Mötley Crüe in spirit, but it is definitely competitive with other records of the day.

JUNE 25, 2008 Mötley/Universal in Japan issue ten Mötley Crüe albums in cardboard sleeve versions.

Mick offers a peace of his action.

© Kevin Estrada

JULY 1, 2008-AUGUST 31, 2008 Mötley Crüe embark on *Crüe Fest*, supported by Papa Roach, Buckcherry, Trapt, and Nikki's side band Sixx:A.M., who take on as touring drummer Papa Roach's Tony Palermo.

Cool lighting helped gin up Crüefest.

© Kevin Estrada

NIKKI SIXX:

We wanted to do a festival for a long time. Rather than just doing it, we said that we would wait for the right time, something that we felt would be a celebration around it, rather than just the festival itself. So me and Mick were talking a while ago, and we thought, hey, this is our first full-length record in ten years, and that felt like a really important time for us. The band has been sort of like re-embraced by the public. We have a really young demographic as well as our own demographic, so our demographic's now teenager to forty-year-olds. So what a perfect time to do a festival, with that kind of demographic of fans, and our first full record in ten years. There are always these people who go rock is dead, rock is over. It's like constantly, people are always out to kill rock 'n' roll. I don't get it—we're like the ugly stepchild of the music business. And yet, we're the one brand of music that continues to be viable—and valuable. So one of the things for us was, we want to go out and stand up for rock 'n' roll. It's not like rock is back. Rock never left! It never left. And we are a rock 'n' roll band, Buckcherry is a rock 'n' roll band, Papa Roach, Sixx:A.M., Trapt . . . these are all bands that are about guitars. Guitars and sexy lead singers and snotty rock 'n' roll music, and let's put them all together and put them in front of tens of thousands of people and kick it around the country. It's something to be proud of.

JAMES MICHAEL ON MARTI FREDERIKSEN, ADDITIONAL COWRITER OF EVERY SONG ON THE ALBUM:

Marti is a fantastic songwriter and he's a real workhorse. I brought Marti into that fold because the challenge was extreme. The responsibility and pressure to make it an amazing record was there and with us every single day. It was a very stressful challenge. I've known Marti for a long time. He's a consummate pro, he's an incredible songwriter, and he operates much like me—he operates really well under pressure. And I just needed a team of very capable people to help, you know, make sure that this giant ship was going in the right direction. So he's the kind of songwriter that I can bring in for just about any type of project, and I know that he's going to deliver. And of course, he's kind of from the same era, had his experience with Aerosmith, and he gets the importance and the responsibility of working with a band that has such a big legacy, and honoring them, being able to work comfortably in that.

JULY 15-16, 2008 Footage from Mötley's two shows in Detroit and Chicago, respectively, are used for the video to support "Mutherfucker of the Year," the second of three singles from *Saints of Los Angeles*.

NIKKI SIXX ON THE CONSTRUCTION OF THE NEW ALBUM:

You know, the studio is a different environment now. Mick can write a riff at his house and e-mail it to me, and I can fiddle around with some lyrics and send it back to him with a bass line on it, and we can take the hard drive over to James Michael's house, who was the producer on the record, and we can put down drum patterns and build up the demo and kind of get the songs built. And then you can cut the song, however you want to cut it, whether you want to cut it live in a room, drums, bass together, and then guitars at a different session. There are so many ways of doing it. But one thing that I felt with this album, this album reminds me of our successful albums, and what I mean by that is, it wasn't four guys sitting in a room scratching their heads, trying to figure out a song. It wasn't songs that were written, and then a band that turns them into Mötley Crüe. This is more what *Shout at the Devil* is, what *Too Fast for Love* is, what *Dr. Feelgood* is, what our successful albums are. When we got into jam mode, like when we did the John Corabi record, it's hard to focus—even the *Generation Swine* album. It wasn't songs first. You know, Mick has an encyclopaedia full of rock riffs, unbelievable classic rock riffs, and all I need is an afternoon with Mick Mars, and you can rape and pillage that library, and begin the process of writing songs. You know, the songs have to have verses and choruses and catchy lyrics and twisted melodies. So to me it's about the song first now, and with technology, it's so fucking exciting. I think songwriting is getting better because people are focusing on writing songs and then capturing the song.

JULY 31, 2008 The City of Los Angeles' mayor's office declares every July 31st moving forward as Mötley Crüe Day.

Laminate for the loudest show on earth. Kevin Estrada Collection

TOMMY LEE:

For a long time we were playing for people in our age group. All of a sudden we look out and see a guy my age with his seven-year-old on top of his shoulders throwing up the horns singing "Shout at the Devil." When I look out now I see all ages, colors, it's pretty wild. It's a sign of longevity. When little kids are coming to check you out, you know you're doing something right. We're still going. (*About Entertainment*, 2008)

AUGUST 8, 2008 The band's show in Las Vegas is broadcast for free over the Internet.

AUGUST 3, 2008 Tommy and Ludacris cohost the TV series *Battleground Earth*, in which the two acts go on tour and see who keep their rolling revues the most environmentally friendly. Tommy goes on *Jimmy Kimmel Live* four days later to promote the show.

SEPTEMBER 30, 2008 Mötley/Eleven Seven (Nikki is now label head of the latter) reissue all of the band's studio albums.

OCTOBER 3, 2008 Mötley play Guadalajara, Mexico, for the first time ever and Nikki's dressing room burns down. A week later, the band play Argentina for the first time (headlining the Pepsi Music Festival), followed by their first ever Singapore gig five days later.

OCTOBER 19-26, 2008 Mötley perform six dates in Japan.

All in the family. © Kevin Estrada

OCTOBER 28, 2008 *The Heroin Diaries* is issued in paperback, a rite of passage for a successful hardcover.

NOVEMBER 4, 2008 Hinder's second album *Take It to the Limit* includes Mick Mars soloing on the title track.

HEAVY MTL

SATURDAY JUNE 21
Parc Jean-Drapeau

SOMEWHERE BACK IN TIME

IRON MAIDEN

DETHKLOK · TYPE O NEGATIVE · MASTODON · HAMMERFALL
HATEBREED · SYMPHONY X · 3 INCHES OF BLOOD
OVERKILL · UNEXPECT · LAUREN HARRIS

SUNDAY JUNE 22
Parc Jean-Drapeau

MÖTLEY CRÜE

DISTURBED · THREE DAYS GRACE · ANTHRAX · VOIVOD
SHADOWS FALL · DROWNING POOL · PRIESTESS · REV THEORY

FOR FUL LINEUP

WWW.HEAVYMTL.COM
TICKETS : 514 790-1245 WWW.GEG.CA

Mötley brought the fun to what was otherwise a fairly heavy metal lineup. Author's Collection

Toast of the town.
© Chris Casella

NOVEMBER 25, 2008

Sixx:A.M. issue *Live is Beautiful*, an EP of eight live tracks recorded during *Crüe Fest*. It is issued as part of the deluxe edition of *The Heroin Diaries Soundtrack*, also issued on this day, as well as separately. Also on this day, five Mötley albums, including the new one, are issued on vinyl.

JAMES MICHAEL:

Sixx:A.M. is in an odd situation. We're not a normal touring band. We're not a "make a record, do a tour, make a record, do a tour" type of band. So it was important to us that we made things available for the fans that did show that that's in our hearts. That live performance is something that we can, and *do* do, and intend to do more of in the future. We needed something that was going to compensate for the fact that we're not out there in people's faces. We're not out there on the road every summer. And I think that, also, you know, we'd gotten together and we had done *Crüe Fest* once, and we had rehearsed this thing that at the time was not a band and kind of became a band during that period. And we had so much fun, it was just such an amazing time for Sixx:A.M., and we wanted something to document that. And maybe, possibly, to remind us that we need to get back out there and do that again.

2009

Kevin Estrada Collection

JANUARY 6, 2009 Downtown Music Publishing signs a deal for Nikki's publishing as well as the administering of the Mötley masters.

JANUARY 31-MARCH 18, 2009 Mötley conduct an American dates campaign (plus two shows in Canada) in support of *Saints of Los Angeles*, with support from Hinder and Canada's Theory of a Deadman.

MÖTLEY CRÜE

PYRÖ ROOM

NO SMOKIN

JOURNALIST **AARON SMALL** ON *SAINTS OF LOS ANGELES*:

Each of the thirteen songs on Saints was inspired by events detailed in the band's best-selling biography, *The Dirt*. "Just Another Psycho" grooves and twists while "Face Down in the Dirt' claws and scratches and "Saints of Los Angeles" is the undisputed rock anthem of the summer. Without fail, each of these rough and tumble rockers will scar you in one way or another. After all the greatest hits packages, box sets, live albums, DVDs, books, and side projects that have been issued since *New Tattoo* in 2000, it's beyond exciting to have this brand new bunch of sleazy, intoxicating Mötley Crüe tunes to sink your teeth into.

FEBRUARY 8, 2009 Mötley lose out to the Mars Volta in the Hard Rock Performance category at the Grammys.

FEBRUARY 15, 2009 Mötley play Rockford, Illinois, home of band favorites Cheap Trick. Rick Nielsen jams on "Jailhouse Rock" with the band, after which Nikki is a guest in Rick's home, where he gets to enjoy Rick's legendary guitar collection.

MARCH 2, 2009 Vince opens a Dr. Feelgood's in Miami Beach, which, along with his locations in Las Vegas and California, make it three spots in three states.

MARCH 16, 2009 Mötley arrive for their New York press conference in a vintage Cadillac ambulance, bookended by two Goth gals dressed as nurses. The occasion is to announce upcoming *Crüe Fest* dates and accompanying bands.

MICK MARS ON HIS GUITAR SOUND:

I do have my own style of playing. My sound that I have offstage, if you put like any guitar player on my amplifier . . . if it's Jeff Beck, he's going to sound like Jeff Beck. No matter what he plays through or whatever, you know what I'm saying? Eddie Van Halen or all these guys are going to sound how they sound. I think it comes more from my hands than anything else, which may sound a little weird, but it's true. It's like, I can play through a little Pignose amp and if you turn your back, you can tell I'm playing. Edward's in the room, you can tell he's playing, you know what I mean?

MARCH 24, 2009 Mötley issue the *Crüe Fest* DVD, with the band captured live on disc one, mostly from the Molson Amphitheatre show in Toronto. Disc two features tracks from the festival's other acts. The same day, *Crüe Fest* band Papa Roach issue their sixth album, *Metamorphosis*. "Into the Light" features a cameo from Mick Mars, who supplies a guitar solo.

NIKKI SIXX ON PICKING THE BANDS FOR *CRÜE FEST*:

We were fans of some and friends of others. Some of both. There were about thirty bands we were looking at, and some bands had one hit, and some band was like the new band on the block and everyone was excited about it, and we liked them as well. So when it boils right down to it, I think what we miss out of festivals whenever we play on them or go, is, when we see festivals that have a very condensed amount of bands with hit singles, and you know, it becomes a long day—you want to hear songs you know. So we were looking at Buckcherry because of their history, and how much radio airplay they have, and that they are a killer performing band live. Papa Roach, Trapt, they have so many hits at alternative radio and that's great for us, because we fluctuate between rock radio, mainstream radio, active, and alternative. So, some of the bands that we have are stronger in different formats, and we felt that it was a great opportunity to bring a lot of different audiences together, for a great ticket price.

"Let's get crazy, Chicago!" © Greg Olma

Size matters. © Greg Olma

MARCH 26, 2009 Cineplex presents the *Crüe Fest* DVD in theatres, one night only. The package debuts at #2 in *Billboard*, selling 7,000 copies in its first week.

APRIL 2009 James Michael and Nikki Sixx are in the studio, recording what will become the second Sixx:A.M. album.

APRIL 14, 2009 Nikki coproduces the *What Gets You Off* album by the Last Vegas, Sixx also cowriting on two tracks.

MAY 14, 2009 All four Mötley members guest on Fox series *Bones*, performing "Dr. Feelgood."

JUNE 2–JULY 1, 2009 Mötley tour Europe, kicking off with two dates in Russia, the first time back since the notorious Moscow Music Peace Festival in 1989. Support, variously, includes Hardcore Superstars, Backyard Babies, and Loaded, featuring Nikki's longtime buddy Duff McKagan, who had also recently played with the band in Japan.

JUNE 30, 2009 Aerosmith drummer Joey Kramer issues his autobiography, with a foreword written by Nikki.

JULY 15-17, 2009 Production rehearsals for the upcoming *Crüe Fest 2* dates reveals a massive overhaul to the stage set.

JULY 19-SEPTEMBER 5, 2009 The band embark on the US-only *Crüe Fest 2*, support coming from Charm City Devils, Drowning Pool, Theory of a Deadman, and Godsmack.

AUGUST 14-19, 2009 Sevendust's Morgan Rose fills in on drums for five shows after Tommy injures his left hand. It seems, in celebration of his girlfriend's birthday, Tommy thought it would be cool to light up forty-odd sparklers and hand them out to fans hanging around outside the tour bus. The injury occurred as he tried to speed things up by lighting too many at once. Street Drum Corps' Frank Zummo covers for Tommy on an additional three dates.

SEPTEMBER 21, 2009 *Dr. Feelgood* sees release as a deluxe two-CD reissue.

OCTOBER 29, 2010 In a month in which Vince drops the puck at a minor league hockey game and attends the opening of a new Hard Rock Cafe in Las Vegas, and Tommy DJs in Vegas, Mexico, and Australia, the big announcement concerns a new radio show for Nikki for January 2010, commandeered by Premiere Radio Networks.

NOVEMBER 17, 2009 *Greatest Hits* is reissued, also seeing release on vinyl.

DECEMBER 22, 2009 Vince is busy recording tracks for an upcoming solo album, having done much of the writing over the fall months.

Mötley lording over the Whisky, the Sunset Strip, and Nickelback.

© Kevin Estrada

The visionary in the band, Nikki Sixx, triumphs yet again with a fresh visual representation of the mind space of Mötley. © Greg Olma

Mad Max meets the military. Nikki, 2010.
© Kevin Estrada

The '10s

Mötley just *is*, as the new decade alights, with tour dates arising and echoing with a various amount of hubbub. Nikki continues with his coddling and growing of Sixx:A.M. while Vince makes some waves with his covers album and attendant autobiography, *Tattoos & Tequila*, tying book to album just like Tommy and Nikki had.

The big news occurs, however, in early 2014, where the band announces that they are signing contracts to close out the existence of the band with one more, long, long, long tour. It is no secret that the guys hadn't gotten along over the years and that reality becomes a subtext that no one talks about as the publicity machine comes to life around the band's *The Final Tour*. And, as Mötley history should have taught us by now, the publicity is effective, with tickets selling briskly based on the fact that every time Mötley hits your town, it's the last time you're gonna be seeing them—"Home Sweet Home" indeed.

It's bittersweet, it's melancholy, it's plain sad, but for more reasons than it being the last Mötley show in your town. While Nikki is excited about Sixx:A.M., having just issued the band's third album, *Modern Vintage*, at the end of 2014, one doesn't get the sense Vince is all that interested in music beyond the end of Mötley. Tommy, at this point . . . we haven't heard much enthusiasm for projects either, despite Lee being the band's second most creative entity. Mick's condition continues to worsen, but it's inspiring how valiant he is with his struggle.

In a sense, it's almost fitting that Nikki is the most fired up creatively, given the fact that it was his multimedia vision that created Mötley Crüe in the first place, more than thirty years ago in an environment of abject, dead-end desperation and very real life-and-death poverty. Where it goes from here is anybody's guess, but one thing seems clear: the execution of this band's farewell tour in particular has been carried out with a panache typical for this organization. Each night is magical, and each night is greeted with a sense of finality by band and fan alike that is touching and raw for all involved.

Vince was always able to carefully put together a look that isn't one. © Kevin Estrada

2010

JANUARY 12, 2010 Vince announces Vince Neil Aviation, followed, on the next day, by the launch of Tres Rios tequila—in the Caribbean, after using his new company's jet to get there. Three days later, Vince is in Florida to play a show celebrating the second anniversary of the local Feelgood's.

Methods of Mayhem only in name, this one came and went without much impact. Author's Collection

Nikki, with a bass made out of an old theater . . . of pain!
© Kevin Estrada

```
AC0204    102      28    2      COMP     EAC0204
                 SEC./SEC.  ROW/RANGÉE  SEAT/SIÈGE  PRICE/PRIX

F= 0.00  ALL GATE ACCESS      0.00      20:05
$                                                 CN 3171 6
  CONVENIENCE CHARGE  LIVENATION.COM/R126007780
 102                                              102
TM 94X SEC./SEC.  MOTLEY CRUE                      TMMLA406
FC         AIR CANADA CENTRE
  28    2   THE DEAD OF WINTER TOUR                 28
ROW/RANGÉE  SEAT/SIÈGE  GREATEST HITS OUT NOW      C    0.00
MLA406C                                                      2
 4FEB1C    THU FEB 04 2010 8:00PM                SEAT/SIÈGE
```

The author attended this show and can confirm that it was definitely taking place in the dead of a Toronto winter.

Author's Collection

JANUARY 23-FEBRUARY 5, 2010 Mötley embark on the cross-Canada *Dead of Winter* tour, supported by Joe Perry and Airbourne.

MICK MARS ON THE BAND'S DURABILITY:

"I think it means that we're just together, and we want to be together. We're set up to be together like since day one. There's a lot of bands that have been together for like three or four or five years and they've done their run. We're one of the kinds of bands that keep going, and are changing; keeping up with the times and just keep moving on, like Aerosmith or U2 are bands like that. It's like we had the intention when we first put it together, to keep going like this, and not be one of those fly-by-night one-hit wonder bands.

NIKKI SIXX:

There were some scheduling problems; James lives in Nashville now, to add just another thing in there. We sort of did it when we could do it. A lot of the songs we wrote together out on *Crüe Fest*. James came out on the road and hung out with me sometimes and we wrote some songs; we wrote "Smile" out on the road. Then DJ would come back and we would get together and have writing sessions. We'd cut guitars for thirteen songs in three or four days and he'd be out, then we'd edit those together, I'd do the bass tracks. It was really done like that. The thing is we are producer/songwriters; we're not a band. So we don't really rehearse in that sense. (*Bravewords.com*, 2011)

FEBRUARY-MAY, 2010 Sixx:A.M. continue to work, on and off, on the recording of what will become *This Is Gonna Hurt*.

FEBRUARY 8, 2010 Nikki's radio show "Sixx Sense with Nikki Sixx" launches.

FEBRUARY 24, 2010 Vince and his band conduct a solo tour of South America; transportation includes the Gulfstream from his new company Vince Neil Aviation.

MARCH 25, 2010 Tommy copresents, with DJ Rap and Roger Sanchez, the International Dance Music Awards.

MAY 27, 2010 Nikki completes his bass tracks for the forthcoming Sixx:A.M. album.

It's a book, an album, *and* a guitar. © Kevin Estrada

JOURNALIST AARON SMALL:

The album opener and title track to Mötley Crüe vocalist Vince Neil's new solo effort is a breathtaking blast of sleaze rock, bound to become a staple in strip clubs the world over. *Tattoos & Tequila* is the feelgood rock album of the summer. Vince's backing band on this disc of debauchery consists of bassist Dana Strum, guitarist Jeff Blando (both of Slaughter), and drummer Zoltan Chaney. Considering the musical magic generated by these four, it's a pity they only wrote one song together: the remainder of *Tattoos & Tequila* consists of cover songs and one leftover Mötley tune. The Crüe track in question is "Another Bad Day," a ballad originally penned by Nikki Sixx, which just missed the cut for *New Tattoo* back in 2000. Like it or not [the covers] are songs that inspired Vince throughout the years and that's why he poured his own Tres Rios—no salt or lemon required—all over them. (*Bravewords.com*, 2010)

JUNE 19, 2010 Vince jumps up onstage with Scorpions at their M3 stop in Maryland to perform "Another Piece of Meat" with the band—one of the many covers featured on his upcoming solo album.

JUNE 22, 2010 Vince issues *Tattoos & Tequila*, an album of mostly classic hard rock covers that also serves as the soundtrack to his book of the same name. Vince borrows three-quarters of Slaughter to form his band for the project, just like Kiss guitarist Vinnie Vincent did twenty-five years earlier. The album reaches #57 in *Billboard*, as well as #14 on the US Rock and #7 on US Indie charts.

San Manuel Amphitheater, San Bernardino, August 14, 2010.
© Kevin Estrada

Horns up, California.
© Kevin Estrada

NIKKI SIXX ON TOURING NOW VERSUS THEN:

It's less lonely. Because with the Internet, you can communicate with people a lot easier. Cell phones, iChat . . . I could talk to my kids any time I want and see them. In the old days I remember going days and days and days without talking to anybody. I would write them a letter, and they would get a letter a week later, and we would make phone calls from truck stops at three o'clock in the morning and reach people's answering machines and leave a message. Now you're not so isolated out there. I think that had a lot to do with how much drinking and drugs we were doing. I mean, you just get straight-up bored.

JUNE 27, 2010 Tommy plays drums with Ludacris, and others, at the BET Awards in LA.

JULY 31-AUGUST 7, 2010 The band play four festival dates in Europe, with a closing date in Finland cancelled due to a storm.

AUGUST 3, 2010 It is reported that Vince and Lia have separated.

AUGUST 11, 2010 The band play the massive Sturgis Motorcycle Rally, reinforcing their ties with the biker class, dating back most significantly to the cover art of *Girls, Girls, Girls*.

AUGUST 14-24, 2010 Mötley play Ozzfest dates in the central and eastern US.

AUGUST 31, 2010 Murderdolls issue their second (and so far last) album *Women and Children Last*, on which Mick Mars cowrites and plays on two tracks.

SEPTEMBER 21, 2010 Methods of Mayhem issue, with very little publicity, their second album, *A Public Disservice Announcement*, on Loud & Proud/Roadrunner. The album's novel construction consisted of Tommy and coproducer Scott Humphrey gathering audio files from fans around the world and using them as building blocks upon Tommy's original drum tracks. The lone single from the album is "Time Bomb," which saw release as a video two weeks previous.

SEPTEMBER 22, 2010 Methods of Mayhem perform "Time Bomb" on *Jay Leno*, drummer for the occasion being Sevendust's Morgan Rose, who had stood in for Tommy on a handful of live dates recently.

SEPTEMBER 23, 2010 Vince issues his autobiography, *Tattoos & Tequila: To Hell and Back with One of Rock's Most Notorious Frontmen*.

NOVEMBER 22, 2010 Vince appears on *Skating with the Stars*, skating with Jennifer Webster. The busy fall months for Vince include the Off the Strip Poker Tournament, playing ShipRocked, and an awareness initiative for The Skylar Neil Memorial Foundation, shared with The Pablove Foundation, also a childhood cancer charity. In November and into December, Nikki also participates in a charitable initiative, supporting AIDS efforts in third-world countries.

DECEMBER 31, 2010 Tommy finds himself in Jakarta, Indonesia, for New Year's, performing a DJ set.

2011

JANUARY 26, 2011 Vince pleads guilty to a drunk driving charge, after arrest incidents in 2007 and 2010, resulting in fifteen days in jail and fifteen days of ankle-monitored house arrest. He's out after ten days, February 25, on good behavior.

You can't help but be inspired by Mick for continuing to pound out those big nasty riffs despite his physical obstacles. © Kevin Estrada

NIKKI SIXX ON "LIES OF THE BEAUTIFUL PEOPLE":

Have you seen *People* magazine's "100 Most Beautiful People?" I don't know; it unnerved me. It was really a peak creative time for me. I was in the studio, immersed in the writing and the photography and the lights; I did everything myself, it was very intense. I popped my head out for a second at a gas station and I see this thing (*People* magazine) and it was like everything froze for me. It was like, really? How could that moment have happened? Life's so interesting. I've seen that magazine a million times and never really even opened it, but that time it really stopped me in my tracks. It must have been because of what I was going through, seeing some of these people that I was photographing tell me their stories. I'm thinking, God, I wish I was half as strong as you. (*Bravewords.com*, 2011)

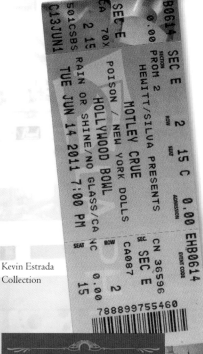

Kevin Estrada
Collection

FEBRUARY 25, 2011 Sixx:A.M. issue "Lies of the Beautiful People" as an advance single from their second album, after Nikki had debuted the video for it on his radio show a week previous.

MARCH 10, 2011 Nikki serves as an industry speaker at Canadian Music Week in Toronto.

APRIL 11, 2011 Mick writes with Zappa alumni Terry Bozzio (drums) and Mike Keneally (over to bass from guitar). Still, a solo album seems a distant hope (a few weeks later he jams with jazz great George Benson), as does an autobiography, Mick being the only member without his own book.

APRIL 4, 2011 Nikki's book *This Is Gonna Hurt: Music, Photography and Life Through the Distorted Lens of Nikki Sixx* is issued, with promo beginning with a book signing in hometown LA.

APRIL 20, 2011 The rising-in-stature Revolver Golden Gods Awards bestow upon the Crüe the first ever Ronnie James Dio Lifetime Achievement Award, presented to the band by Slipknot's Corey Taylor.

MAY 3, 2011 Sixx:A.M. issue their second album, *This Is Gonna Hurt*. Like the debut, it's a companion piece to a Nikki Sixx book; this time, reflective of his photography coffee-table tome issued a month earlier. The album enters the *Billboard* charts at #10, moving 30,000 copies in its first week.

NIKKI SIXX:

For me, the photos came first and then I was able to sort of dissect them. A lot of it obviously is a premeditated assault on the senses. When I'm shooting certain stuff, I have already in mind what it is that I'm trying to say. Sometimes I wasn't necessarily sure and it took the writing process to find that out, digging the tomb so to speak. (*Bravewords.com*, 2011)

NIKKI SIXX:

It's all about the songs. We don't sit in a room and play. We build this music up around concepts and standards and to elevate ourselves to some of the music that inspired us. It's just a different process. It comes out swinging, then it gets really mellow. Kind of like a record from the '70s—I feel like you should have to flip it over. (*Bravewords.com*, 2011)

Nikki is excited about his future with this band that also allows him outside writing possibilities with each of his two bandmates. Author's Collection

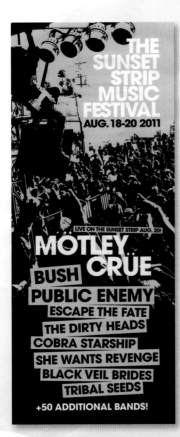

Mötley and Public Enemy!

Kevin Estrada Collection

Life is good. © Kevin Estrada

NIKKI SIXX:

Mick's always been the guy who doesn't like anyone knowing anything about him. In fact, he's got more birthdays than anyone I know. I get e-mail to tell Mick happy birthday. I go to Mick, "Was yesterday your birthday?" He's all, "No." A month later, it's "Happy birthday, Mick." "Mick, is it your birthday?" "No." He's got so many birthdays, I don't know when his birthday is. He said he was from Newfoundland because he figured, "If I'm from Newfoundland, nobody will know anything about me." I don't know anything about this man. I've never seen him with his socks off. Never seen him with his shirt off. I mean, this guy's a mystery.

MAY 5, 2011 Mick turns sixty, but it's Nikki that gets to meet President Obama on this day.

MAY 14-27, 2011 The band play Mexico and South America, returning home just in time for Rocklahoma on May 29.

JUNE 7-AUGUST 20, 2011 Mötley's 2011 summer tour blankets America, with one Canadian date in Toronto.

AUGUST 20, 2011 The Sunset Strip Music Festival attracts a crowd of 17,000, headliner for the event being Mötley Crüe (eleven songs, plus solos), other luminaries including Bush and Public Enemy, with a host of bands slated for the legendary venues around the strip for the three-day fest. The next day, Vince is honored with a lifetime achievement award in Las Vegas.

A busy Mick and a happy Nikki on home turf at the Hollywood Bowl, June 14, 2011. © Kevin Estrada

Woo-hoo! Laundry night!

© Kevin Estrada

SEPTEMBER 8, 2011 Mick continues to collaborate with people for a proposed solo album, writing with Twiggy Ramirez, ex-Marilyn Manson, after working in the summer with Andy Biersack, vocalist for Black Veil Brides.

SEPTEMBER 21-OCTOBER 5, 2011 The band log three dates in Australia, followed by six in Japan. Rivals Poison are also on the bill, along with reunited openers the New York Dolls.

NOVEMBER 15, 2011 The video game *Saints Row: The Third* makes use of both "Shout at the Devil" and "Live Wire."

NOVEMBER 22, 2011 On the heels of the band reissuing select product in various formats the previous week, a deluxe edition of *The Dirt* is released, featuring hi-tech cover and additional material, to commemorate the band's thirtieth anniversary.

DECEMBER 5, 2011 Sixx:A.M. issue their acoustic 7 EP.

DECEMBER 6-DECEMBER 14, 2011 Mötley mount a short six-date UK tour, a co-headlining stint with Def Leppard, supported by hair metal send-ups Steel Panther. In conjunction, *Greatest Hits* sees UK reissue, in four formats.

DECEMBER 7, 2011 *New York Post* fashion insert Alexa publishes a '70s glam-inspired fashion spread (and cover image) shot by Nikki.

DECEMBER 31, 2011 Following up his DJ set in Indonesia the previous New Year's Eve, this time Tommy finds himself not far from there, DJing at a festival in New Zealand.

Sixx:A.M.'s DJ Ashba, Nikki Sixx, and James Michael. © Kevin Estrada

2012

FEBRUARY 3-19 Mötley set up for a circus-like, twelve-date Las Vegas residency at the Hard Rock Hotel & Casino. At the band's show on the 8th, Vince celebrates his birthday by riding Tommy's custom drum roller-coaster. Geographically related: in March, Vince opens Deja Vu Presents: Vince Neil's Girls Girls Girls, also in Las Vegas.

MICK MARS:

The Elvis Presley of metal; that's pretty funny. I believe that we are the very first metal band that has done a twelve-day residency. This will set another milestone for Mötley Crüe. We are like the metal Rat Pack. Vegas has changed a lot and rock bands are now wanting to play there. We got lucky and we got this residency at the Hard Rock. I have to say, and I am guessing, but I really think we are the first rock band to do that. (*Classic Rock Revisited*, 2012)

Irvine California,
August, 2012. ©
Kevin Estrada

LA press conference to announce the tour dates with Kiss. © Kevin Estrada

NIKKI SIXX, COMPARING MÖTLEY WITH SIXX:A.M.:

I feel Mötley Crüe is built to insult you. We're here to assault you. I'm not interested in snuggling and a kiss. I just want to get right to fuckin'. And it's like, Sixx:A.M. is a seductive, sexually charged, beautiful evening out under the moon that ends up making love. Fortunately in a graveyard. Mötley Crüe, it's just like fucking a nasty stripper that's probably gonna give you a disease. And I'm proud of that. I don't want us to be tame. (*Powerline*, 2012)

FEBRUARY 5, 2012 Mötley (and "Kickstart My Heart") feature in a Kia commercial, which airs during the Super Bowl.

FEBRUARY 7, 2012 David Lee Roth is back in Van Halen for the creditable *A Different Kind of Truth* album. The ensuing tour does well, but the album fails to catch on, pulling up just short of gold status in the US.

FEBRUARY 26, 2012 The band lay down tracks at Tommy's studio for new song called "Sex," designed for use on the band's upcoming co-headlining tour with Kiss.

APRIL 11, 2012 Sixx:A.M. perform a rare live show (albeit two songs only) at Revolver's Golden Gods Awards, at Club Nokia in LA. Nikki receives the Paul Gray Best Bassist Award, named for the deceased Slipknot bassist.

JUNE 5-23, 2012 Mötley mount a European tour of mostly festival dates.

JUNE 19, 2012 North American release date for Lita Ford's *Living Like a Runaway*, which includes a Nikki Sixx/David Darling song (written for their band 58) called "A Song to Slit Your Wrists By."

JULY 17, 2012 Mötley issue a new single called "Sex," debuting the track on SiriusXM radio four days earlier. Three days later, the band begins a massive US tour—called *THE Tour*—co-heading with Kiss, adding one date in Toronto and one in Mexico City, through September 29.

NIKKI SIXX:

We happened to have this song everyone was really excited about, so instead of saying, "Let's add it to the pile of songs we have and we'll sort 'em out later," we were, "Hey, let's finish this one up." We got it out there for the fans, for the tour, and it's exciting for the band to play something new. The way the song is connecting with people feels like the way the music used to connect with people when we were a baby band and just had our first record out. The song really seems to work. (*Billboard*, 2012)

AUGUST 8, 2012 Kiss and Mötley play Denver, pledging to donate $100,000 to the victims of the Aurora, Colorado, theatre shooting massacre. They follow up in Nashville with a pledge of $50,000 to veterans charity Operation Homefront.

SEPTEMBER 5, 2012 The band's pyrotechnics truck crashes en route to a scheduled Detroit show, which needs to be postponed a day. A week later, Vince breaks his foot onstage in Cleveland.

OCTOBER 10, 2012 Tour with Kiss completed, Vince is one of the music workshop stars in this year's version of Rock 'N' Roll Fantasy Camp in Las Vegas. A month later he's at Lee's Discount Liquor, still in Las Vegas, launching his new vodka Tatuado.

NOVEMBER 13, 2012 John Corabi's *Unplugged* album includes acoustic versions of "Loveshine" and "Hooligan's Holiday" from his one album with the band, *Motley Crue*.

Uh, next question.
© Kevin Estrada

"I didn't do it!" © Kevin Estrada

Kevin Estrada Collection

EVENT CODE VWA08 4 $XXX.X $

SECTION/AISLE ORCH P ROW/BOX 6 SEAT 155 ADMISSION COMP PKG X.XX

SECTION/AISLE ORCH AC 6 6 155 YLBC80 13AUG1

KLOS COMPANY PICNIC
KISS AND MOTLEY CRUE
THE TOUR 2012
VERIZON AMPHITHEATER
KISSONLINE.COM-MOTLEY.COM
TUE AUG 14 2012 7:00 PM

EVENT CODE EVWA YL001 CN O OI AC C CXXX

2013

JANUARY 26, 2013 Nikki announces his partnership with Schecter, who issue a Schecter Sixx signature bass, ending Nikki's long period of loyalty to Gibson basses.

FEBRUARY 28-MARCH 16, 2013 The band notch eight dates in Australia.

MARCH 7, 2013 Doing press in Australia, Nikki raises the spectre of a farewell tour. A medical drama in Australia finds Vince in need of emergency kidney stone removal. By April, Vince is also talking about one final round of Mötley tour dates.

APRIL 17, 2013 A lush, orchestral version of Crüe ballad "Time for Change" is used in an uncharacteristically dramatic IKEA commercial.

APRIL 20-MAY 14, 2013 The band mount an intensive cross-Canada tour, hitting many smaller cities, followed by three legs of mostly casino shows in the US. Support for the Canadian campaign comes from Big Wreck.

What comes around, goes around. One helluva bill. Kevin Estrada Collection

MICK MARS:

There's something about when the four of us get onstage, it's like a weird thing that happens, it's like we become one person. Of course offstage it can get bad I guess, with disagreements and such, but once we hit the stage it's this powerhouse substance that absolutely stops anything that's going on. (*Beyond the Watch*, 2013)

Tommy, back where he belongs. © Kevin Estrada

SEPTEMBER 18-OCTOBER 6, 2013 Mötley Crüe stage a series of twelve shows in a Las Vegas "residency" situation, reprising their 2012 campaign, again at the Hard Rock Hotel. During this time, James Michael and DJ Ashba record guitars in Vegas for the next Sixx:A.M. album.

2014

JANUARY 26, 2014 Real estate's Coldwell Banker debut an ad featuring "Home Sweet Home" during the Grammys.

MICK MARS:

Alice is great. I'd met him a couple of times before at events and things but never really sat down and talked to him. And I got the opportunity to do that on this tour. We realized we had a lot of things in common. He'd go, "A lot of people come up to me and say, 'Are you Mick Mars?'" And I'd go, "You know, I get Alice Cooper a lot" (laughs). So we're sitting there laughing about this stuff. But he's brought a lot to the table on this tour. Growing up, listening to his music, I was going like, "I should be out there making this music." Because Alice is only a few years older than me. And so I was frustrated because I wanted to be out there doing that, too. I guess I was jealous.

Quite deserving of the legacy title, and he's playing on a Smashing Pumpkins album in 2014 as well! © Kevin Estrada

JANUARY 28, 2014 Mötley hold a press conference at LA's Hotel Roosevelt to announce *The Final Tour*, indicating that the band signed contracts to that effect (using the end of 2015 as firm cessation date) to amplify the finality of the situation, a retirement that also includes no new album at any point. Support for the American dates is Alice Cooper. The tour's subtitle of sorts is *All Bad Things Must Come to an End*.

FEBRUARY 19, 2014 Vince guests onstage in Nashville during a Justin Moore concert singing a number of Crüe classics, promoting a high-profile country music tribute album to the band. In a surprise move, Mick had recently relocated to Nashville, where he hopes to work with blues artists on his long-discussed solo debut.

Kevin Estrada Collection

Not to be taken away.
© Kevin Estrada

TOMMY LEE ON BEING MISUNDERSTOOD:

Yes. Yeah, I would say that. Because the information that people get is very blurred, so yeah, I do. And it's all in such little bits and pieces that has nothing to do with what I said. You know how communication works. It's like, by the time it goes from this person to that person, somebody has added their little version in there, and by the time it gets all the way around the room, the story has completely changed. That's just the way people are. Everyone adds their own little two cents to it.

All according to plan.
© Kevin Estrada

FEBRUARY 24, 2014 Tommy proposes to his girlfriend of four years, Sofia Toufa, who is both a choreographer and one of four dancers in the Mötley touring machine.

FEBRUARY 27, 2014 The Keep Memory Alive Center in Las Vegas mounts a benefit, with celebrity participants including Slash, Matt Sorum, Alice Cooper, Bill Murray, and Vince Neil.

MARCH 15, 2014 Nikki marries Courtney Bingham, the romance rendered quite public through a reality TV–type three-part special on *Entertainment Tonight*.

APRIL 25, 2014 Vince partners with two friends and associates in the Arena Football League's Jacksonville Sharks, but denies reports that he would like to see the team move to his hometown of Las Vegas.

APRIL 3, 2014 Nikki gets a new cohost for his radio show *Sixx Sense with Nikki Sixx*, in Jenn Marino; the two speak at the Worldwide Radio Summit luncheon on this date, in Hollywood.

JAMES MICHAEL, COWRITER AND PRODUCER OF THE SONG:

That was really fun. It was a tall mountain to have to climb, because we knew that this is probably the last thing that this band would ever do. So for me it was very important that it was a real collaborative effort, not only that it happen organically, but that the guys were excited about it. It's always a challenge at this stage of the band's career, because there's so many factors involved, the least of which is not being able to get the four guys together to work on stuff with such busy schedules. So I was really pleased with how that came about, because everyone was into it. I then realized what a responsibility it was to write something that was basically saying farewell, and to do it in a way that only Mötley can do. And so when we came up with the title, "All Bad Things Must End"—which is also the whole theme of the tour—it just started falling into place. And to me, no matter what happens, I'm always going to be able to look at that song and say, well, that was just a fantastic way to go out swinging.

MAY 15, 2014 Tommy Lee announces that he's finished his drum tracks on what is designed to be Mötley Crüe's farewell song, "All Bad Things Must End."

MICK MARS:

After thirty-five years playing the Mötley Crüe stuff, I can go into the studio and write a Motley Crue song in minutes. "All Bad Things," I wrote the initial music for that and took it over to James, and it became the goodbye song for Mötley. I had Mötley Crüe specifically in mind for the riff and everything else that I came up with. Which is different from the solo stuff I'm writing now, which is more an expression of my inner feelings. My new stuff is heavier, punchier, but I don't even know how to explain it, because I haven't heard anything like it. I've played it for some people that I know, and they're just flipping out. A lot of people want to put it on the radio, and I'm like, well, not yet.

Mick, July 22, 2014, Irvine, California. © Kevin Estrada

One more time for old times' sake. Let me kick your ass.
© Chris Casella

MICK MARS:

What happens with us after that, music-wise, is kind of vague, I guess. I'm not gonna paint myself in a corner and say, "Oh, yeah, there could be more music coming out," when I don't really know. I don't really have the answers. I know that the contract we signed says that in no way will any of us go out playing Mötley Crüe music as Mötley Crüe. And it's pretty binding and pretty heavy. So that's it. (*Guitar World*, 2014)

JUNE 8-14, 2014 Mötley conduct rehearsals in LA for their upcoming career-ending tour.

JULY 2, 2014 Mötley Crüe embark on *The Final Tour*, also known as the farewell tour, opening the open-ended campaign at Van Andel Arena in Grand Rapids, Michigan. A new version of Tommy's drum rollercoaster is unveiled, as is new song "All Bad Things Must End," which gets dropped after five shows. Dates through July, August, October, and November—the band take September off—represent the band's most thorough blanketing of US markets of their entire career.

NIKKI SIXX ON SIGNING ON THE DOTTED LINE:

We worked really hard on that document. We've had the idea for years. It just got more real. There are no loopholes and no grey areas. It's an agreement between us. It feels really good to have people, when they're interviewing us, going wow, this is no joke. I've thought about what it'll be like for the fans. I can see that final bow in Peoria, and they're going, "This is it." I know I'd feel emotional if one of my favorite bands was going out. (*Loudwire*, 2014)

MICK MARS:

I get Tweets from a lot of people who say it's sad to see you go, but you've given us this much, and you've helped me along with my life. And there are ones that say I wish you wouldn't go; please don't go. It's bittersweet, mixed feelings. But Mötley is a business, and the four of us will always be in a business together, probably for the rest of our lives, as Mötley Crüe. There probably won't be any records or singles or anything like that, but our corporation will still keep going. So it's not like we're going to be out of touch with each other. As for the guys, as an observer, I don't really think that they're going to feel the impact until the last show is done; that's my feeling on it. While we're touring, while we're doing this, it's business as usual. But when we play our last show, I think it's really going to hit home.

JULY 21, 2014 Once the numbers are in, the band's show at the Hollywood Bowl on this night turns out to be the overall most lucrative in terms of gross ticket sales, with $1.3 million raised.

JULY 25, 2014 Nikki and Courtney move into a 10,300 square foot mansion in Westlake, Nikki's most expensive home ever by about double.

AUGUST 5, 2014 Sixx:A.M. issue "Gotta Get It Right" as an advance single from their forthcoming third album, *Modern Vintage*, with the video emerging the following day.

AUGUST 7, 2014 Vince—and his one-of-a-kind Dodge Challenger—appears at a police fundraiser for needy families in Tinley Park, Illinois.

AUGUST 19, 2014 The high profile *Nashville Outlaws: A Tribute to Mötley Crüe* is issued courtesy of Big Machine Records, featuring the likes of Rascal Flatts, Big & Rich, Leann Rimes, Gretchen Wilson, and Justin Moore. The album debuts at #5 in *Billboard* and sells 31,000 copies in its first week.

VINCE NEIL:

When we play the songs, it's loud, fast, and heavy. These country artists, though, have stripped away all that stuff. When you take some of the heavy music out of it, the vocals come out, and all of a sudden you're listening to a beautiful song. So that's the fun part about when I first listened to this album. It was like, wow. I sing these lyrics, but I just didn't really listen to them before. (*Radio.com*, 2014)

AUGUST 20, 2014 It is reported that "Kickstart My Heart" is being used in an advertisement for the Dodge Charger; Dodge is a sponsor of the band's farewell tour.

AUGUST 23, 2014 Vince Neil and his partners in Rockstar Sports Group officially enter into an agreement to build an Arena Football League team in Las Vegas, to be called the Las Vegas Outlaws. In compliance with league rules, the company puts in motion a divestment of their minority ownership stake in the Jacksonville Sharks.

JAMES MICHAEL:

We have been in a luxurious position of being able to branch out a bit because that expectation of that very rigid active rock sound from the past has been kind of stripped away. And so, for instance, on a song like "Gotta Get It Right," I was able to really incorporate big, ambient, kind of '60s-style drums, along with a very different, less saturated guitar sound—but a rock sound nonetheless. So what that does is, if you listen to a song like "Gotta Get It Right," it's absolutely a rock song, but the listener gets a different flavor of rock. They're not listening to the same heavy, heavy saturated electric guitars. What I tried to do with *Modern Vintage* is make it sound aggressive, but use different instruments and arrangements to make it aggressive.

MICK MARS ON LIFE:

What do I think life is? You've probably heard this a million times but . . . People who say they never had a chance, never took the chance. How's that? (laughs). (*Beyond the Watch*, 2013)

Mick counting the days until he can finally get to that solo album.
© Chris Casella

AUGUST 26, 2014 Sixx:A.M. make their cover of the Cars' "Drive" available for streaming.

SEPTEMBER 3, 2014 Nikki Sixx goes through a double hernia operation, having played through Mötley's farewell dates with considerable pain.

JAMES MICHAEL ON NIKKI'S BASS PLAYING:

I think something that's going to blow people away about *Modern Vintage* is Nikki's bass playing. I mean, I just got goosebumps when I said that. Because what a lot of people don't know about Nikki, is that he's an incredibly soulful bass player. I remember, actually, back when we were making *Saints of Los Angeles*, we had done a take on one of the songs. It was just Nikki and me in the studio tracking bass. And I was like, "Okay, you just did a very Nikki Sixx take on this; now, can you do something that's a little more kinda R&B, that's just got a bit more soul to it?" And I'll be damned if he didn't . . . if I would've closed my eyes, I thought I was in the studio recording an Al Green record. Unbelievable. This guy has chops that you never hear in Mötley Crüe. And that speaks to his genius. He knows when and how to keep restrained. He doesn't use Mötley Crüe as an ability to go out and just always be dazzling people with amazing bass licks and stuff. He understands the importance of being that character in that setting. And I think Sixx:A.M. gives him an opportunity to go, you know what, I'm gonna go a little nuts here. And when he does, it's just a joy to listen to it as a music fan and it's a joy to record as a producer.

OCTOBER 7, 2014 Sixx:A.M. issue their third album, *Modern Vintage*. The band play their first full-length concert in five years, at the iHeart Theatre in Burbank, California.

JAMES MICHAEL:

Really, for the past three records now, we as a band have talked about all of our musical influences, and we always attempted to bring those influences in, whether they be kind of '70s rock or pop like 10cc or Bread or Babys, or bands we're all influenced by, like Queen and really some of the more kind of bold bands of that time. And so over the course of Sixx:A.M.'s history, we set out to incorporate some of those types of influences into the records. And then somewhere along the line, we would kind of start taking a new path—something inspired us, something sent us in a new direction, and we would follow the inspiration. And so by the end of the record, we see how the records turned out, and they really were kind of more of an exploration of something else. I think that the exciting thing about Sixx:A.M. for I think all of us is that, in a way, it is our escape from our day job. You know, for Nikki, what he's done with Mötley Crüe, obviously it's been an amazing career. But any career like that has parameters within which you work. So for me, writing and producing other bands, I'm dealing with those parameters that are just laid out first by the music industry. And Sixx:A.M. was this opportunity for all of us to just shed those parameters. Because we never had any expectations of anything happening with Sixx:A.M. So we have a band like Sixx:A.M. not having to abide by the rules of the industry. You've just got this beautiful blank canvas to be able to do anything with.

MICK MARS ON THE BAND'S LEGACY:

Speaking for myself, it's kind of like if I go back and hear "Rocket 88," a timeless song, the first rock 'n' roll song, it doesn't get old to me. I hear Robert Johnson, it doesn't get old to me. What I'm hoping will happen with Mötley, if they hear an old Mötley song, if it's redone by somebody, they'll go, "Wow, this is a really memorable song." If kids start a rock band in a garage and say, "Let's redo this 'Girls, Girls, Girls' song by Mötley Crüe," it stays theirs, like a timeless kind of a thing. (*The Village Voice*, 2014)

OCTOBER 10, 2014 Having taken September off, Mötley resume their farewell tour dates in Oklahoma City, Oklahoma.

OCTOBER 28, 2014 Mötley sell out Madison Square Garden, earning $1,082,041 in ticket sales, the second highest gross of the band's 2014 farewell dates.

NOVEMBER 1, 2014 The massive *Dodge Rocks Gas Monkey* car show in Dallas, Texas, features approximately a thousand Dodge car owners, as well as a concert by Mötley Crüe.

NOVEMBER 24, 2014 Sixx:A.M. debut the live performance video to their new single "Stars" on Fox News online. Tour dates commencing April 8, 2015 are announced, support to come from Apocalyptica, who share management with Mötley.

TOMMY LEE:

It breaks my heart to see some of the bands that I grew up on hobbling around on one foot. There's only one or two original members left. It's just sad. That's not how we envisioned it at all. It's to have some dignity and some respect for the game: "That was awesome. Thank you, guys. We're out." (*Drum*, 2014)

NOVEMBER 27, 2014 Mötley notches the #1 ranking on the weekly Hot Tours chart with $5.1 million in ticket sales, as 2014 dates come to a close with a show in Spokane, Washington.

MICK MARS:

The AS that I have is like, it can bother you if you let it. The doctors say, "You're going to end up in a wheelchair" and this and that. I call bull on that. So I'm out there, and sometimes it's not so bad. But I love my music, I love playing, I love touring, and that keeps me going. I'm not sitting here feeling sorry for myself.

Please Drive Safely

verizonwireless

MPHITHEATER

sch AUDIO   Klipsch AUDIO   Klipsch AUDIO

ALL BAD THINGS
MUST COME TO AN END

All bad things must come to an
end, and . . . please drive safely.
© Kevin Estrada

DECEMBER 9, 2014 Smashing Pumpkins issue their tenth album, *Monuments to an Elegy*. The drummer on all nine tracks is none other than Tommy Lee.

Talk about theatre of pain.
© Kevin Estrada

DECEMBER 30, 2014 Mötley Crüe end the year having booked a short Japanese tour in February of 2015, plus European festival dates into the summer. On April 21, 2015, the band announce additional US and Canadian dates for October and December 2015, with the band hitting "B cities" missed the first time around. True to character, the band is making sure that many additional smaller markets get to say their goodbyes to Mötley.

NIKKI SIXX:

When you really love an artist, what I think is the real legacy, is that when you take away their looks, take away their history, take away everything—whether it's Jimi Hendrix, Ray Charles, Led Zeppelin— you take away their entire lifestyle, and what is their real legacy? It's the music. In the end, that's it. When we're in band rehearsal, it's just the four of us in a dirty little rehearsal room with a half-eaten box of pizza just pounding through those songs. We put a lot of work into those songs. *They* are our legacy. (*Time.com*, 2014)

VINCE NEIL:

We started talking about it a few years ago. We don't want to be one of those bands with one guy left in it or somebody's brother, something like that. We wanted to go out with the four founding members of Mötley Crüe, and go out on top. You know, and just leave a legacy of a band called Mötley Crüe. (Press conference, 2014)

TOMMY LEE:
I don't know if I necessarily learned anything from all this. Hopefully, I've just left everybody with something—a memory? A smile? Hopefully I've given, and not taken. (*Drum*, 2014)

MICK MARS:
I'd be happy if people thought of us in the top 100 iconic bands that ever came along, like the Stones and Hendrix and Zeppelin, and those guys. That it be nice. If I could get in that category, then yeah, I'd be a happy man. (*Guitar World*, 2014)

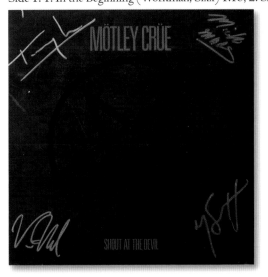

This discography is designed primarily as a handy checklist for one to quickly divine which songs derive from which albums (in their original form versus reissues—for significant additions, see entries in June of 1999), along with the odd extra crumpet one might be curious o'er, some of which is thrown into a notes section.

Just to keep things neat, I've overridden the convention of putting songs in double quote marks, except if referenced in the notes, where they are in sentences or phrases and thus could use some help. I've also provided timings (results vary across issues and sources, but not by any material amount). Side one/side two convention is maintained up until the end of the vinyl age, which for Mötley basically means *Dr. Feelgood*, given that the wholesale migration to the CD format happened in 1990 for the US and Canada. As mentioned, a notes section has been provided as a catch-all for any points I thought salient enough for mention. Band personnel is cited only at the outset and when there are changes.

Concerning live albums, compilations, videography . . . all I've done here is provide titles of key, "very" official releases along with month and year of issue. Again, the prime purpose of this discography is to highlight the original creativity, namely the organization of the songs as they first appeared in studio form. To reiterate, what I've documented is the information for the original albums, given that the reissue of Mötley material is a complicated space-taker of tangled webs.

STUDIO ALBUMS

Too Fast for Love
November 10, 1981; Producer: Mötley Crüe
Side 1: 1. Live Wire (Sixx) 3:16; 2. Public Enemy #1 (L. Grey, Sixx) 4:23; 3. Take Me to the Top (Sixx) 3:46; 4. Merry-Go-Round (Sixx) 3:27; Piece of Your Action (Sixx, Neil) 4:40
Side 2: 1. Starry Eyes (Sixx) 4:30; 2. Stick to Your Guns (Mars, Sixx) 4:20; 3. Come on and Dance (Sixx) 3:11; 4. Too Fast for Love (Sixx) 4:11; 5. On with the Show (Sixx, Neil) 4:04
Notes: Personnel is Vince Neil, vocals; Mick Mars, guitars; Nikki Sixx, bass; and Tommy Lee, drums. Elektra Records issue (August 20, 1982) contains the same tracks but in different order and with reduced timings, a remix by Roy Thomas Baker, and slightly altered cover art (different printings on Leathür also contain art differences).

Shout at the Devil
September 26, 1983; Producer: Tom Werman
Side 1: 1. In the Beginning (Workman, Sixx) 1:13; 2. Shout at the Devil (Sixx) 3:16; 3. Looks that Kill (Sixx) 4:07; Bastard (Sixx) 2:54; 5. God Bless the Children of the Beast (Mars) 1:33; 6. Helter Skelter (Lennon, McCartney) 3:09
Side 2: 1. Red Hot (Mars, Neil, Sixx) 3:21; 2. Too Young to Fall in Love (Sixx) 3:34; 3. Knock 'Em Dead, Kid (Neil, Sixx) 3:40; 4. Ten Seconds to Love (Neil, Sixx) 4:17; 5. Danger (Mars, Neil, Sixx) 3:51
Notes: Issued in gatefold sleeve with spot varnish. Tracks 1 and 5 on side one are (mostly) instrumental intros; track 6 on side one is a Beatles cover.

Kevin Estrada Collection

Theatre of Pain
June 21, 1985; Producer: Tom Werman
Side 1: 1. City Boy Blues (Sixx, Mars, Neil) 4:10; 2. Smokin' in the Boys Room (Koda, Lutz) 3:27; 3. Louder than Hell (Sixx) 2:32; 4. Keep Your Eye on the Money (Sixx) 4:40; 5. Home Sweet Home (Sixx, Neil, Lee) 3:59
Side 2: 1. Tonight (We Need a Lover) (Sixx, Neil) 3:37; 2. Use it or Lose it (Sixx, Mars, Neil, Lee) 2:39; 3. Save Our Souls (Sixx, Neil) 4:13; 4. Raise Your Hands to Rock (Sixx) 2:48; 5. Fight for Your Rights (Sixx, Mars) 3:50
Notes: Track 2 on side one is a Brownsville Station cover.

Yep, that's Vince's autograph.
Author's Collection

Girls, Girls, Girls
May 15, 1987; Producer: Tom Werman
Side 1: 1. Wild Side (Sixx, Lee, Neil) 4:40; 2. Girls, Girls, Girls (Sixx, Lee, Mars) 4:30; 3. Dancing on Glass (Sixx, Mars) 4:18; 4. Bad Boy Boogie (Sixx, Lee, Mars) 3:27; 5. Nona (Sixx) 1:27
Side 2: 1. Five Years Dead (Sixx) 3:50; 2. All in the Name of . . . (Sixx, Neil) 3:39; 3. Sumthin' for Nuthin' (Sixx) 4:41; 4. You're All I Need (Lee, Sixx) 4:43; 5. Jailhouse Rock (live) (Leiber, Stoller) 4:39
Notes: Track 5 on side 2 is a live rendition of a '50s standard made popular by Elvis Presley.

Signed by Vince and Nikki at a cool sit-down chat for *Greatest Hits*. Author's Collection

Dr. Feelgood
September 1, 1989; Producer: Bob Rock
Side 1: 1. T.N.T. (Terror 'n Tinseltown) (Sixx) 0:42; 2. Dr. Feelgood (Mars, Sixx) 4:50; 3. Slice of Your Pie (Sixx, Mars) 4:32; 4. Rattlesnake Shake (Mars, Sixx, Neil, Lee) 3:40; 5. Kickstart My Heart (Sixx) 4:48; 6. Without You (Sixx, Mars) 4:29

CD booklet for Mötley's last album widely issued on vinyl.

John Chronis Collection

Punk-styled cover, marred by a pointless quote from Nikki. Author's Collection

No umlauts. John's is yellow; mine's red. John Chronis Collection

Side 2: 1. Same Ol' Situation (S.O.S.) (Lee, Sixx, Mars) 4:12; 2. Sticky Sweet (Mars, Sixx) 3:52; 3. She Goes Down (Mars, Sixx) 4:37; 4. Don't Go Away Mad (Just Go Away) (Sixx, Mars) 4:40; 5. Time for Change (Sixx, McDaniel)

Notes: Track 1 on side 1 is a (mostly) instrumental intro. Recordings conducted in Vancouver included assorted session musicians, guest musicians, and backup singers.

Motley Crue
March 15, 1994; Producer: Bob Rock
1. Power to the People 5:12; 2. Uncle Jack 5:28; 3. Hooligan's Holiday 5:51; 4. Misunderstood 6:53; 5. Loveshine 2:36; 6. Poison Apples 3:40; 7. Hammered 5:15; 8. 'Til Death Do Us Part 6:03; 9. Welcome to the Numb 5:18; 10. Smoke the Sky 3:36; 11. Droppin' Like Flies 6:26; 12. Driftaway 4:00

Notes: John Corabi replaces Vince Neil on vocals. All music credited to the entire band and all lyrics to John Corabi and Nikki Sixx, except track 6, which is credited to the band plus producer Bob Rock. Also issued in conjunction was the five track "extras" EP, *Quaternary*, expanded to nine tracks for Japan.

Generation Swine
June 24, 1997; Producers: Scott Humphrey, Nikki Sixx, Tommy Lee
1. Find Myself (Sixx, Mars, Lee) 2:51; 2. Afraid (Sixx) 4:07; 3. Flush (Sixx, Lee, Corabi) 5:03; 4. Generation Swine (Sixx, Lee) 4:39; 5. Confessions (Lee, Mars) 4:20; 6. Beauty (Sixx, Lee, Humphrey) 3:47; 7. Glitter (Sixx, Humphrey, Adams) 5:00; 8. Anybody Out There (Lee, Sixx) 1:50; 9. Let Us Prey (Sixx, Corabi) 4:22; 10. Rocketship (Sixx) 2:05; 11. A Rat Like Me (Sixx) 4:13; 12. Shout at the Devil '97 (Sixx) 3:43; 13. Brandon (Lee) 3:25

Notes: Vince Neil replaces John Corabi on vocals.

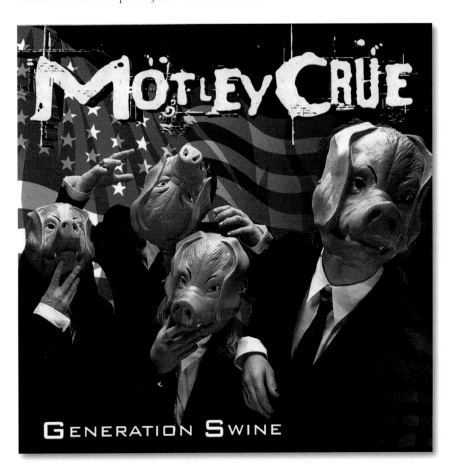

The label actually sent me one of those pig masks. Author's Collection

Simple images like this make the T-shirt designer's job easier. Or so the Def Leppard guys tell me. Author's Collection

New Tattoo

July 11, 2000; Producer: Mike Clink

1. Hell on High Heels (Mars, Neil, Sixx) 4:15; 2. Treat Me Like the Dog I Am (Michael, Sixx) 3:40; 3. New Tattoo (Mars, Michael, Sixx) 4:18; 4. Dragstrip Superstar (Michael, Sixx) 4:22; 5. 1st Band on the Moon (Sixx) 4:25; 6. She Needs Rock & Roll (Michael, Sixx) 3:59; 7. Punched in the Teeth by Love (Castillo, Mars, Neil, Sixx) 3:32; 8. Hollywood Ending (Michael, Sixx) 3:43; 9. Fake (Michael, Sixx) 3:44; 10. Porno Star (Sixx) 3:45; 11. White Punks on Dope (Evans, Spooner, Steen) 3:39

Notes: Randy Castillo replaces Tommy Lee on drums. Track 11 is a Tubes cover. The credited James Michael is Nikki's new songwriting partner, and lead singer in Sixx:A.M.

Saints of Los Angeles

June 24, 2008; Producers: James Michael, Nikki Sixx, DJ Ashba

1. L.A.M.F. (Sixx, Michael, Ashba, Frederiksen) 1:23; 2. Face Down in the Dirt (Sixx, Michael, Ashba, Frederiksen) 3:44; 3. What's It Gonna Take (Sixx, Michael, Ashba, Frederiksen) 3:45; 4. Down at the Whisky (Sixx, Michael, Ashba, Frederiksen) 3:50; 5. Saints of Los Angeles (Sixx, Michael, Ashba, Frederiksen) 3:40; 6. Mutherfucker of the Year (Sixx, Mars, Michael, Ashba, Frederiksen) 3:55; 7. The Animal in Me (Sixx, Mars, Michael, Ashba, Frederiksen) 4:16; 8. Welcome to the Machine (Sixx, Michael, Ashba, Frederiksen) 3:00; 9. Just Another Psycho (Sixx, Mars, Michael, Ashba, Frederiksen) 3:36; 10. Chicks = Trouble (Sixx, Mars, Michael, Ashba, Frederiksen) 3:13; 11. This Ain't a Love Song (Sixx, Mars, Lee, Michael, Frederiksen) 3:25; 12. White Trash Circus (Sixx, Mars, Michael, Ashba, Frederiksen) 2:51; 13. Goin' Out Swingin' (Sixx, Michael, Ashba, Frederiksen) 3:27

Notes: Track 1 is a (mostly) instrumental intro. The credited DJ Ashba is the guitarist in Sixx:A.M. The credited Marti Frederiksen is a well-renowned outside songwriter.

This design was on the booklet, which was hidden by a plain-white-with-text cardboard sleeve. Author's Collection

Author's Collection

LIVE ALBUMS

Live: Entertainment or Death (November 23, 1999)
Carnival of Sins Live (February 7, 2006)

SELECTED COMPILATIONS

Decade of Decadence (October 19, 1991)
Greatest Hits (November 14, 1998)
Supersonic and Demonic Relics (June 29, 1999)
The Best of Mötley Crüe: The Millennium Collection (July 10, 2003)
Red, White, & Crüe (February 1, 2005)
Music to Crash Your Car To: Vol. 1 (November 11, 2003)
Music to Crash Your Car To: Vol. 2 (June 29, 2004)

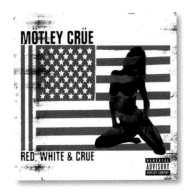

Tri-fold digipak. Author's Collection

There were two big boxes that included pretty much everything. This is *Volume 1*. Sweet. Author's Collection

SELECTED VIDEOGRAPHY

Uncensored (October 27, 1986)
Dr. Feelgood: The Videos (October 22, 1990)
Decade of Decadence '81–'91 (March 12, 1992)
Behind the Music: Mötley Crüe (April 27, 1999)
Lewd, Crüed, & Tattooed Live (July 17, 2001)
Greatest Video Hits (November 11, 2003)
Universal Masters DVD Collection (February 11, 2005)
Carnival of Sins Live (October 25, 2005)
Crüe Fest (March 24, 2009)

Mötley's first of three weird records. Kevin Estrada Collection

INTERVIEWS WITH THE AUTHOR

Quotes throughout the book that are not credited "in situ" are from the following interviews with the author.

Clarke, Gilby. January 26, 2006.
Corabi, John. 1998.
Corabi, John. October 1, 1999.
Cronin, Mark. March 15, 2010.
Greif, Eric. December 20, 2009.
Grey, Lizzie. December 21, 2009.
Fowley, Kim. 2009.
Frehley, Ace. September 17, 2014.
Hamilton, Vicky. January 19, 2009.
Haze, Leonard. August 19, 2014.
Kulick, Bruce. October 1, 1999.
Lawless, Blackie. May 15, 2002.
Lawless, Blackie. January 12, 2010.
Lee, Jake E. October 15, 2014.
Lee, Tommy. December 14, 1999.
Lee, Tommy. April 29, 2002.
Levine, Barry. February 19, 2010.
Mars, Mick. May 28, 2008.
Mars, Mick. April 21, 2015.
Michael, James. August 12, 2014.
Monroe, Michael. January 29, 2010.
Mustaine, Dave. August 15, 2000.
Neil, Vince. 1999.
Neil, Vince. August 15, 2000.
Neil, Vince. June 20, 2003.
Newsted, Jason. April 10, 2006.
Proffer, Spencer. January 7, 2010.
Scott, Andy. 2009.
Sixx, Nikki. 1999.
Sixx, Nikki. February 1, 2004.
Sixx, Nikki. May 28, 2008.
TiLo. December 14, 1999.
Werman, Tom. 2003.
Zutaut, Tom. March 10, 2010.

ADDITIONAL SOURCES

Quotes throughout the book that are credited "in situ," (i.e. at the close of the quote), are derived from the following sources.

About Entertainment. Mötley Crüe interview by Chad Bower. 2008.
Beyond the Watch. Interview: Mick Mars (Mötley Crüe) by Steve St. Jean. April 2, 2013.
Billboard. "Mötley Crüe on 'Sex' and Proving the Skeptics Wrong" by Gary Graff. August 28, 2012.
Brave Words & Bloody Knuckles. Motley Crue record review by Martin Popoff. Vol. 1, No. 2. May '94.

Brave Words & Bloody Knuckles. "Mötley Crüe: Here's Mud In Yer Eye!!!" by Tim Henderson. #18. June/July 1997.

Brave Words & Bloody Knuckles. "Mötley Crüe Want You!" by Martin Popoff and Aaron Small. #27. Year end issue 1998.

Brave Words & Bloody Knuckles. "Mötley Crüe: 'Someone always has to break the rules!'" by Aaron Small. #43. September 2000.

Brave Words & Bloody Knuckles. "Live and Raw" by Mitch Lafon. Issue #72. 2003.

Brave Words & Bloody Knuckles. "Brides of Destruction: Guaranteed to Kill Your Pastor!" by Aaron Small. #77. April, 2004.

Brave Words & Bloody Knuckles. "Nikki Sixx: 'How the hell am I still alive?'" by Aaron Small. #107. December, 2007.

Bravewords.com. "Mötley Crüe: Inside the Box!" by Aaron Small. January 3, 2004.

Bravewords.com. Saints of Los Angeles record review by Aaron Small. July 8, 2008.

Bravewords.com. Tattoos & Tequila record review by Aaron Small. June 22, 2010.

Bravewords.com. Tattoos & Tequila book review by Aaron Small. February 26, 2011.

Bravewords.com. "Mötley Crüe/Sixx:A.M. Bassist Nikki Sixx: *This Is Gonna Hurt* is 'premeditated assault'" by Aaron Small. March 21, 2011.

Circus. "Mötley Crüe—Are They out to Lunch?" by Richard Hogan. #289. March 31, 1984

Circus. "Face-to-face with Mötley Crüe" by Jeff Tamarkin. #291. May 31, 1984.

Circus. "Mötley Crüe's Three-Ring Circus" by Ben Liemer. #293. July 31, 1984.

Circus. "Mötley Crüe's Pursuit of the American Dream" by Ben Liemer. 294. August 31, 1984.

Circus. "Will the Real Vince Neil Please Stand Up?" by Ben Liemer. #297. November 30, 1984.

Circus. "Mötley Crüe: From the Gutter to the Glitter" by Paul Gallotta. #309. November 30, 1985.

Circus. "Inside Mötley Crüe's Trying Year" by Ben Liemer. #313. March 31, 1986.

Circus. "Mötley Crüe Achieves its #1 goal: A #1 LP" by Toby Goldstein. January 31, 1990.

Circus. "Crüe Mixes it up with Rock & Rose" by Maura McCormick. #381. November 30, 1991.

Circus. "Mötleys Cap Year, Decade with Crüe-tial LP" by Katherine Turman. #382. December 31, 1991.

Circus. "Why Was Vince Neil Fired?" By Corey Levitan. #387. May 31, 1992.

Classic Rock Revisited. "The Carnival of Sin Invades Sin City: An Interview with Mick Mars" by Jeb Wright. 2012.

Creem. "Mötley Crüe's Master Sleaze!" by Sylvie Simmons. January 1985.

Drum. "Tommy Lee: The Show Must Not Go On" by Andrew Lentz. August 2014.

Extreme. "Mötley Crüe" by Greg Campbell. Issue #30. Fall 2000.

Faces. "Mötley Crüe: Rampaging On!" by Lorena Alexander. December 1985.

Guitar One Presents Mötley Crüe. "Health Kick" by Richard Bienstock. October 20, 2009.

Guitar World. "Crüe Cut" by Richard Bienstock. Vol. 35, No. 6. June 2014. 2015

GuitarWorld.com. "Mick Mars Discusses Mötley Crüe's New Song, Final Tour, and Playing 'Memorable' Guitar Parts" by Richard Bienstock. May 2, 2014.

Hit Parader. "Mötley Crüe: Out for Blood" by Andy Secher. December 1983.

Hit Parader. "Mötley Crüe: The Wild Bunch" by Andy Secher. #239. August 1984.

Hit Parader. "Mötley Crüe: Band of Destiny" by Jodi Summers Dorland. #252. September 1985.

Kerrang!. Too Fast for Love record review by Dave Dickson. No. 29. November 18-December 2, 1982.

Kerrang!. "Crüe's Missile" by Xavier Russell. No. 30. December 2–15, 1982.

Kerrang!. "Halloween Special: Y&T, Mötley Crüe, Randy Hansen" by Xavier Russell. No. 30. December 2–15, 1982.

Kerrang!. Mötley Crüe/Faster Pussycat concert review by Steve Mascord. No. 289. May 12, 1990.

Late at Night. "Mötley Crüe: It's the Crüe that Matters" by Sir Thomas E. Goh. October 1994.

Late at Night. "Nikki Sixx: PT II" by Sir Thomas E. Goh. Vol. II, issue III. November 1994.

Live Wire. "Hard, New, 'n' Crüed" by Mike Smith. Volume 4. No. 5. April/May 1994.

Loudwire. "Mötley Crüe to Embark on Final Tour: Exclusive Q&A with Nikki Sixx + Vince Neil" by Chad Childers. January 29, 2014.

M.E.A.T. "Brotherhood from Hell!!!" by Drew Masters. Issue #14. July 1990.

M.E.A.T. "Defying the Laws of Longevity with Mötley Crüe" by Drew Masters. Issue #29. December 1991.

M.E.A.T. "Metal on the Rise: Vince Neil" by Drew Masters. Issue #42. May 1993.

M.E.A.T. "Mötley Crüe" by Drew Masters. Issue #48. March/April 1994.

Metal Edge. "Mötley Crüe – Swine: The Next Generation" by Paul Gargano. August 1997.

Metal Edge. "Methods of Mayhem: Tommy Lee: Life after Mötley" by Paul Gargano. Vol. 44, No. 5. October 1999.

Metal Hammer. "News Extra." Vol. 3, No. 3. February 29, 1988.

Metal Hammer. "Evil Entertainment" by Chris Ingham. #140. June 2005.

Metallion. "Pretty Boys Can Do What They Like . . ." by Lenny Stoute. No. 1, Vol. 1. Sept. 84.

Musician. "Big Deals: How Money Fever is Changing the Music Business" by Fred Goodman. No. 159. January 1992.

The New Heavy Metal Revue. *Too Fast For Love* record review by John Kornarens. Number Five. January 1982.

Powerline. "Nikki Sixx at his Best with Sixx:A.M. and Beyond" by Carol Anne Szel. January 20, 2012.

Radio.com. "Interview: Mötley Crüe's Vince Neil and Nikki Sixx Talk Country Tribute Album" by Kurt Wolff. August 20, 2014.

Revolver. "On with the Show" by Dan Epstein. No. 34. April 2005.

R.I.P. "All Bad Things Must Come to an End: Mötley Crüe Press Conference Emceed by Joey 'Vendetta' Scoleri." January 28, 2014.

Rock Scene. "Tommy Lee's Dream, Part 2" by Beth Nussbaum. #7. February 1986.

Rolling Stone. "Money for Nothing and the Chicks for Free: On the Road with Mötley Crüe" by David Handelman. #506. August 13, 1987.

Rolling Stone. "*Dr. Feelgood*: Mötley Crüe's Track by Track Guide to 1989 Classic" by Andy Greene. May 5, 2009.

Spin. "Beyond the Valley of the Ultra Glam Boys" by Dean Kuipers. Volume Five, Number Ten. January 1990.

Time.com. "Nikki Sixx Says Goodbye for Good: Inside the End of Mötley Crüe" by Melissa Locker. Feb. 5, 2014.

Toronto Sun, The. "The New Crüe" by John Sakamoto. Wednesday, March 16, 1994.

USA Today. "*The Dirt*: Confessions of the World's Most Notorious Rock Band: Nikki Sixx." Wednesday, May 23, 2001.

Village Voice, The. "Mick Mars of Mötley Crüe: 'We'll be Absolutely Done as a Band'" by Chaz Kangas. Feb. 5, 2014.

The author would also like to recognize the kind contributions of John Chronis, who provided a nice and tidy milk crate of research materials, with bookmarks.

I would also like to thank the legendary Kevin Estrada, for his image work well beyond the call of duty.

The contributions from photographer Rich Galbraith are dedicated to the memory of Niki Hamme, 9/12/66 to 7/2/14.

Finally, and indeed, most "Crüe-cially," I wish to acknowledge the immense Mötley scholarship and research of Australian expert Paul Miles, whose site Chronological Crüe served as a dependable corroboration and fact-check resource as this book came together.

IOTLEY CRI

In Concert • October 18th at Maple Leaf

IOTLEY CRUE

At approximately 7,900 (with over 7,000 appearing in his books), Martin Popoff has un-officially written more record reviews than anybody in the history of music writing across all genres. Additionally, Martin has penned forty-nine books on hard rock, heavy metal, classic rock and record collecting. He was editor in chief of the now retired *Brave Words & Bloody Knuckles*, Canada's foremost metal publication for fourteen years, and has also contributed to *Revolver, Guitar World, Goldmine, Record Collector*, bravewords.com, lollipop.com, and *hardradio. com*, with many record label band bios and liner notes to his credit as well. Additionally, Martin worked for two years as researcher on the award-wining documentary *Rush: Beyond the Lighted Stage* and on *Metal Evolution*, an eleven-episode documentary series for VH1 Classic, and is the writer of the original metal genre chart used in *Metal: A Headbanger's Journey* and throughout the *Metal Evolution* episodes. Currently Martin is consultant on Banger/VH1 Classic series *Rock Icons*.

Born April 28, 1963, in Castlegar, British Columbia, Canada, and raised in nearby Trail, Martin went on to complete an MBA, work for Xerox, and then co-own a graphic design and print brokering firm, before becoming a full-time rock critic in 1998. Martin currently resides in Toronto and can be reached through martinp@inforamp.net or www. martinpopoff.com. His website includes detailed descriptions and ordering information for the approximately thirty-five of his books that are currently in print.

MARTIN POPOFF'S COMPLETE BIBLIOGRAPHY

Kickstart My Heart: A Mötley Crüe Day-by-Day (2015)
Who Invented Heavy Metal? (2015)
Sail Away: Whitesnake's Fantastic Voyage (2015)
Live Magnetic Air: The Unlikely Saga of the Superlative Max Webster (2014)
The Big Book of Hair Metal (2014)
Steal Away the Night: An Ozzy Osbourne Day-by-Day (2014)
Sweating Bullets: The Deth and Rebirth of Megadeth (2014)
Smokin' Valves: A Headbanger's Guide to 900 NWOBHM Records (2014)
Metallica: The Complete Illustrated History (2013)
The Art of Metal (Editors Martin Popoff & Malcolm Dome, 2013)
2 Minutes to Midnight: An Iron Maiden Day-by-Day (2013)
Ye Olde Metal: 1979 (2013)
Scorpions: Top of the Bill (2013)
Rush: The Illustrated History (2013)
Epic Ted Nugent (2012)
Fade to Black: Hard Rock Cover Art of the Vinyl Age (2012)
It's Getting Dangerous: Thin Lizzy '81–'12 (2012)
We Will Be Strong: Thin Lizzy '76–'81 (2012)
Fighting My Way Back: Thin Lizzy '69–'76 (2011)
The Deep Purple Royal Family: Chain of Events '80–'11 (2011)
The Deep Purple Royal Family: Chain of Events Through '79 (2011)
Black Sabbath FAQ (2011)
The Collector's Guide to Heavy Metal: Volume 4: The '00s (2011; coauthored with David Perri)
Goldmine Standard Catalog of American Records 1948–1991, Seventh Edition (2010)
Goldmine Record Album Price Guide, Sixth Edition (2009)
Goldmine 45 RPM Price Guide, Seventh Edition (2009)
A Castle Full of Rascals: Deep Purple '83–'09 (2009)
Worlds Away: Voivod and the Art of Michel Langevin (2009)
Ye Olde Metal: 1978 (2009)
Gettin' Tighter: Deep Purple '68–'76 (2008)

All Access: The Art of the Backstage Pass (2008)
Ye Olde Metal: 1977 (2008)
Ye Olde Metal: 1976 (2008)
Judas Priest: Heavy Metal Painkillers (2007)
Ye Olde Metal: 1973 to 1975 (2007)
The Collector's Guide to Heavy Metal: Volume 3: The Nineties (2007)
Ye Olde Metal: 1968 to 1972 (2007)
Run for Cover: The Art of Derek Riggs (2006)
Black Sabbath: Doom Let Loose (2006)
Dio: Light Beyond the Black (2006)
The Collector's Guide to Heavy Metal: Volume 2: The Eighties (2005)
Rainbow: English Castle Magic (2005)
UFO: Shoot Out the Lights (2005)
The New Wave of British Heavy Metal Singles (2005)
Blue Öyster Cult: Secrets Revealed! (2004)
Contents Under Pressure: Thirty Years of Rush at Home & Away (2004)
The Top 500 Heavy Metal Albums of All Time (2004)
The Collector's Guide to Heavy Metal: Volume 1: The Seventies (2003)
The Top 500 Heavy Metal Songs of All Time (2003)
Southern Rock Review (2001)
Heavy Metal: Twentieth Century Rock and Roll (2000)
The Goldmine Price Guide to Heavy Metal Records (2000)
The Collector's Guide to Heavy Metal (1997)
Riff Kills Man! Twenty-Five Years of Recorded Hard Rock & Heavy Metal (1993)

See martinpopoff.com for complete details and ordering information.